Embroidery masterworks

classic patterns and techniques for contemporary application

from the textile collection
of the Art Institute of Chicago

VIRGINIA CHURCHILL BATH

Photographs by
Howard Kraywinkel
John Mahtesian
Richard Brittain

Henry Regnery Company
Chicago, Illinois

Acknowledgments

*For assistance in bringing this book to
completion, I wish to give special thanks to
Charles C. Cunningham, Director of the Art
Institute of Chicago, and to Russell G. Bath.
The cheerful and prompt assistance of the
Photography Department and of Mrs. Betty
Saxon, Reproduction Rights and Contracts,
the Art Institute of Chicago, is gratefully
acknowledged. Invaluable assistance was also
rendered by other members of the Art
Institute staff: John Maxon, Associate Director;
Jack Sewell, Curator of Oriental Art; Christa
Mayer, Curator of Textiles; Donald Jenkins,
Associate Curator of Oriental Art, and
Cynthia Cannon, Textile Department
Secretary. The generous Textile Committee,
actively serving the Art Institute at the time
this material was compiled, included Mrs. John
V. Farwell III, Mrs. Julian Armstrong, Jr.
(both of whom served as chairmen), Mrs.
Chauncey B. Borland, Mrs. Howell B. Erminger,
Mrs. Walter Byron Smith, Mrs. Theodore D.
Tieken, Mrs. Lawrence Armour, and Mrs.
Tiffany Blake. Many of the needleworks
discussed in this book are gifts from these
women. Special mention should be made of
the work Mildred Davison did during her
years as Curator of the Textile Department.
Her exhibitions provided the author with her
first opportunity to study great needlework.*

Gentle Reader, I would have you know that the Diversitie of Examples which you will find in the Schole-Howse for the Needle are only but patterns which serve but to helpe and inlarge your invention. But for the disposing of them into forme and order of Workes that I leave to your own skill and understanding. Whose ingenious and well practised wits will soe readily (I doubt not) compose them into such beautiful formes as will be able to give content, both to the worker and the wearers of them.

R. Shorleyker,
A schole-howse for the needle,
1624

Contents

Introduction, VI

Child's poncho-shirt, 1
stem stitch/Peru

Border of birds, 4
stem stitch/Peru

Last Supper, 8
threadcounted stitches/Germany

St. Mauritius, 15
silk and gold embroidery/Germany

Angel, 19
split stitch/Spain

Nativity, 25
silk and gold embroidery/Spain

Intertwined classic scrolls, 28
appliqué on velvet/Spain

Pillow cover, 33
blackwork/England

Man's cap, 38
ladder stitch in gold/England

Coif, 43
plaited braid stitch in gold/England

Beaded basket, 48
applied motifs/England

Framed looking glass, 53
stumpwork/England

Adam and Eve, 59
silk and metal embroidery/England

Noah's Ark, 65
long-armed cross stitch/Italy

Strapwork and leaf design, 69
long-armed cross stitch/Italy

Presentation bag, 73
raised work in purl/England

Multicolored panel, 76
wool embroidery/England

Monochrome panel, 82
wool embroidery/England

Pillow covers, 93
blue wool embroidery/England

Bed cover, 97
white embroidery/England

Color plates, 103-114

Bed cover, 115
multi-colored chain stitch/England

Panel for a sconce, 120
silk embroidery/England

Cope and chasuble, 124
gold embroidery and coral beading/Italy

Man's cap, 131
long and short stitch/France

Gentleman's coat sample, 135
satin stitch/France

Half boots, 140
chenille embroidery/England

Cap back, 144
white embroidery/France

Tablecloth, 148
embroidered patchwork/America

Bed valance, 152
darning stitch/Greece

Ship design, 156
reversible embroidery/Turkey

Towel ends, 162
double running stitch/Turkey

Sash, 166
double darning stitch/Turkey

Sleeve, 170
black wool embroidery/Spain

Cover, 175
Roumanian stitch/Russia

Border, 179
colored drawnwork/Russia

Mola[1], 184
reverse appliqué variation/Panama

Mola[2], 187
reverse appliqué/Panama

Materials & techniques, 192

Stitch directory, 204

Bibliography, 222

Index, 224

Introduction

A Seljuk carpet design
(detail), Turkey;
13th century.

Embroidery is on the rise again. In former times, it has soared to heights of amazing creativity, then plunged to the depths of banality. Now, after half a century of relative inactivity and little innovation, more and more people are taking up the needle, and proficiency in stitch making is greatly improving. Small skeins of rainbow hued wools are appearing in more shops, attesting to the popularity of needlepoint and embroidery in crewels. Artists are reevaluating embroidery as a means of expression, and many have been working with simple stitching in the manner of "action" painting, massing line, stem, or feather stitches or intermingling them in random fashion. Emphasis has been on things quickly or spontaneously made. But as people experiment with embroidery, they become more and more curious about the unfamiliar techniques that they see in museums or photographs. Once acclimated to the time involved in making embroideries, needleworkers become interested in trying more challenging processes.

The artist anxious to find ways to give his ideas form can profit from this book simply by learning more about technique. The so-called domestic embroiderer, who is not professionally trained in design, not only needs assistance in learning about methods but also needs help in finding designs of sufficient excellence to merit the time required to make them. One way to learn about embroidery design and technique is to examine carefully the successful work of another needleworker, perhaps even try to reproduce it. Few people have intimate or prolonged access to masterpieces of embroidery. The diagrams and descriptions of the pieces shown in this book have been presented in an attempt to give embroiderers an opportunity to study some of the Art Institute of Chicago's outstanding collected needleworks.

The patterns in these pages have, in a sense, received their pedigrees. They were taken from embroideries that have managed to pass the critical inspection of a museum curator and have been accepted by a textile committee accustomed to quality and disinterested in quantity. An effort has been made to include a variety of designs in different styles and with different types of embroidery, some simple enough to require no previous knowledge of needlework, some sufficiently complicated to vex the most experienced embroiderer. The selection includes both professionally

Trees (details from wall hangings) embroidered in wool chain and stem stitches on linen, eastern Mediterranean region; 4th-5th century.

and domestically made needleworks to develop the twofold idea of presenting a historical survey of techniques as well as providing workable patterns for embroiderers at all stages of proficiency. Some of the patterns to be embroidered include the complete design, some a portion of the original. Each is a direct copy rather than an adaptation. Rendered in the same scale and made with materials similar to those used in the original, an article like the original could be made. Some of the designs are types that assimilate happily with contemporary furnishings or costume. For many needleworkers' purposes, materials, colors, or stitches other than those of the prototype may suggest themselves.

In the Materials and Techniques section (M&T) at the back of the book, fabrics, threads, needles, types of thimbles, and pattern transferring procedures are discussed in detail. In the Stitch Directory, descriptions and easy-to-follow diagrams of over fifty stitches are given. Whenever the text instructs you to use a particular stitch (for example, a tent or stem stitch), refer to the Stitch Directory, which lists the stitches in alphabetical order.

Most of the embroidery patterns in this book have simple surface stitching, so that a mere description of the stitches used and their location on a particular piece are sufficient instruction for working the pattern. Others, however, have stitches more specifically arranged, and for these a grid, corresponding to the diagram, has been supplied. Diagrams of designs to be used for transferring have often been placed sideways on a page in order to provide you with a pattern on as large a scale as possible.

While the creative embroiderer eventually will be unwilling to spend all his time working on other people's designs, copying is, even for the experienced artist, a good way to probe into the secrets of a revered masterpiece. Although prejudice against copying has persisted for four generations, it is a relatively recent phenomenon. In the nineteenth century some rebellious young French painters forsook the pedagogy of the academy and took to the open countryside to have a close look at the atmosphere. Most of them had already put in long hours in front of casts of antiquities and dingy paintings before they dropped out of the

*A central Asian carpet
design (detail); 19th century.*

*Vase with tree
(detail), wool and
linen tapestry, Egypt;
5th or 6th century.*

academy, so it might be said that they already had their pockets full of valuables when one of them cried, "Burn the museums!" These painters (impressionists, post-impressionists, and neo-impressionists) although misunderstood and maligned, redirected the course of art. When the import of their contribution was finally understood, generations of example-following began, and nobody would admit to copying anything.

Left to themselves, most young artists will go through a period of painstaking copying. Imitation is a natural first step; what is copied, how it is copied, and what develops out of the copying are the important issues. The moral wrong occurs only if a copy is presented to others as the original idea of the copyist. It is regrettable that an exercise so potentially beneficial should so often be accompanied by feelings of guilt. Fortunately, perhaps, we recently have gone through a period when direct copies, used as a satire, have hung on museum walls.

A faithful copy is difficult to make. To do it, one must quell one's own personality in favor of another's—not an easy task. When you copy embroidery, the problem of materials also arises. Duplicating the ground fabric, the threads, the colors, or some other element of an original may prove impossible. A first compromise sets off a chain reaction. A series of adjustments leads to something quite different from the original. Thus the new begins to grow out of the old. Old engravings, pattern books, herbals, and other sources for needlework design rarely inspired exact copies. How far afield the imagination of one seventeenth-century embroiderer roved is clearly indicated by a comparison of an embroidered picture of Adam and Eve with the frontispiece of the Robert Barker Bible, 1602, from which it probably was adapted. (See pages 59-64.)

The textile arts, including embroidery, have a long history of excellence. It is only an accident that the earliest examples in this book have the simplest stitchery. By mid-fourteenth century most of the truly monumental embroideries in existence today had already been made. Embroidery thrives in a climate of wealth and leisure. By definition it is an art of embellishment and ornamentation. Yet even in this age of function-derived form,

embroidery is on the upswing, giving testimony, perhaps, to the abundance of this day.

The weaving and decoration of textiles are two of the oldest crafts. Ancient pots occasionally have surface textures that were made by pressing woven materials against them while the clay was still wet. Greek vase paintings and Egyptian murals show weavers working at their looms. The earliest existing embroideries contain not just simple running, stem, chain, and satin stitches, but also variations of herringbone, interlacing, and interlocking stitches. Moreover, every type of design, simple or complex, seems to be represented among these early pattern-woven or embroidered textiles. A Chinese bonnet and pair of mitts dated between 481 and 221 B.C. have patterns in the enduring overlapping lozenge or rhombus design that is now most frequently seen on rugs, but that also appeared in ancient articles from Russia, Egypt, Peru, and the Orient. Ancient Greek dresses have patterns of figures and stylized floral designs. A fourth- or fifth-century embroidered wall hanging, probably from the eastern Mediterranean area, has fruiting trees worked in wool on linen and

*Overlapping
lozenge motifs adapted
from details
in a pair
of Chinese mitts,
B.C. 481-221.*

looks very much like seventeenth-century English "crewel" (wool) embroidery. Stars, griffins, spotted deer, horsemen, and goddess figures appear on some of the oldest textiles; many date between the fourth and the third centuries B.C. These most interesting of the ancient needlework finds come from mounds excavated at Pazyryk, in the Altai Mountains near the border between Siberia and Mongolia. The contents of these burial chambers remained constantly frozen, never thawing during the short summers. In the tombs were found wool pile rugs, felt and leather patchworks, appliqués of considerable size, and many gold embroideries. The Altai region was gold-mining country, and the tombs originally contained much gold, a temptation to looters, who fortunately could carry away only what they could maneuver through narrow entry shafts. Large textiles remained in the chambers for later excavation. Among the most interesting of the embroideries found in this area are shoes with decorated soles (the ultimate in status?).

Animals are the subject of a great many early textiles, woven or embroidered. As in all the arts, symbolism plays an important role in textile design. In early times men expressed their admiration for the powers of animals and birds in their art. A man on horseback could travel farther, hunt longer, and fight better than a man on foot. A mounted man was to be admired. In Persia a symbolic meaning was attached to the hunting figure that battled the dragon (evil) and was lifted to enlightenment by the griffin (good). The eagle, lion, and elephant became symbols of royalty. Their images were woven into and embroidered onto many of the great textiles produced in medieval times. In the twelfth century Sicily was the center of a great Saracenic textile industry, which produced stately designs with geometric details of interlacing, palmettes, trees of life, and roundels, as well as the ever-present heraldic animals. Even though changes in embroidery design began to take place after the Pope named Roger II of Normandy "King of Sicily" in 1130, the Coronation Mantle of the Holy Roman Empire, made in Palermo in 1133, was designed in the long-favored attacking animal theme. Gradually griffins, eagles, and lions began to be joined in embroidery design by the pointed ogival arches and religious themes of the northern style.

A comparison can be made between the pearl and gold embroidered silk Coronation Mantle of the Holy Roman Empire, made in 1133, and the wool and linen Bayeux Tapestry (really an embroidery, not a tapestry), recounting the Battle of Hastings (1066) and the events leading up to

Eagle (detail from the supposed Coronation Mantle of Charlemagne embroidered in silk and gold couching on silk twill, Sicily or Spain; about 1200.

Emperor hunting lions (detail from a roundel) embroidered on a pattern-woven silk, Byzantine; 8th century.

Elephant (detail from a roundel) worked on a pattern-woven silk serge, Spain; 11th century.

A fantastic creature (detail) worked in felt appliqué, Pazyryk; 5th century B.C.

Goddess and rider (details from a wall hanging) worked in felt appliqué, Pazyryk; 5th-3rd century B.C.

A motif from a shoe sole (detail), embroidered in chain stitch.

Bayeux Tapestry (detail showing Harold on his way to Bosham) laidwork and wool chain, stem and split stitches on linen, Normandy or England; 1066-77.

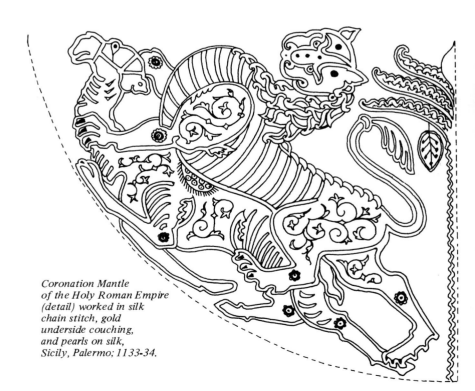

Coronation Mantle of the Holy Roman Empire (detail) worked in silk chain stitch, gold underside couching, and pearls on silk, Sicily, Palermo; 1133-34.

it. The lion and camel of the Coronation Mantle, seemingly derived from patterns for weaving, are schematic and decorative in design. The Bayeux Tapestry is emphatically naturalistic.

In the late thirteenth and early fourteenth centuries *opus anglicanum* came into full flower. This was English work painstakingly rendered in split and other stitches in silk and gold thread on layers of linen. Mantles and copes made in *opus anglicanum* were sent to many parts of the Christian world. The art deteriorated after the dissolution of the monasteries and the coming of the Black Plague, but until then England had no finer or more desirable offering. *Opus anglicanum* had its counterparts on the continent. Each European region exhibited the same national characteristics in its embroidery as it did in its painting. With painters making the drawings for embroidered works, painting and embroidery became so closely related that the term *needle painting* was appropriate. In contrast to the growing naturalism of English, Burgundian, Florentine, and other western European embroidery in silk and gold, the Eastern style, Byzantine, which was influenced by the flat, decorative art of Sassanid Persia as well as the naturalism of Hellenistic Alexandria, remained relatively unchanged through the years. Byzantine design is reflected in the embroidery of the Last Supper (see page 8).

It is against this background information that one must approach the designs in this book. They represent the new directions that embroidery followed as the years passed. The most splendid ecclesiastical embroideries were made between the twelfth and the sixteenth centuries. Domestic embroidery was never more vigorous than in the sixteenth and seventeenth centuries. In the eighteenth century needlework was at a peak of technical impressiveness and was exquisitely inventive, but its boldness of design was lessening. In the nineteenth century, when machine-made facsimiles of old handmade laces and embroidery became widely available, embroidery declined despite the valiant efforts of a few designer-craftsmen. For a long time embroidery has been a hobby. Now it may be time to restore it as an art.

Virgin and child (detail from orphrey in opus anglicanum*) embroidered in silk tent, split, and satin stitches and gold underside couching on a double layer of linen, England; 1330.*

Archangel Michael (detail from an altar frontal) embroidered in gobelin, split, satin, stem, and couching stitches on silk supported with linen, Italy or Sicily; late 12th or early 13th century.

Angel of the Annunciation (detail from a cope in opus anglicanum*) worked in silk split, satin, tent, and laid stitches and gold and silver underside couching on double layer linen, England; 1315-35.*

Angel of the Annunciation (detail from a band), woven design, probably Syrian; 8th century.

Child's poncho-shirt

stem stitch/Peru

color plate, page 103

The early textiles we have intact have been preserved through conditions of freezing or of constant dryness. This little Peruvian poncho-shirt, which comes from a Paracas Necropolis burial mound, is thought to date about A.D. 100. We are heir to hundreds of Peruvian weavings and embroideries because the people of the Paracas peninsula tilled the rain-touched regions and buried their dead in arid places. Mummy bundles preserved in various grave sites have yielded an extraordinary variety of textiles. The people who made them seem to have pursued the making of garments for the next life as their major industry. (See Junius Bird and Louisa Bellinger's *Paracas Fabrics and Nazca Needlework.*) Four hundred bundles of textiles were found in one Peruvian underground chamber; some bundles contained as many as fifty textiles, although not all of these were elaborately woven or decorated. Clothing apparently was made to fit the bundle, not the deceased who sat at the bottom of a conical heap of clothing and hats, knees tucked under chin, amid food, weapons, and ornaments.

Early Peruvian embroideries are uniquely successful in their integration of weaving and embroidery techniques. This poncho-shirt is a good example of close coordination between plain weave and stem stitch embroidery. On a simple loom a piece of cloth was woven in the shape of the garment to be made. (Cutting garments from larger pieces of cloth was not practiced until the idea was introduced by the Spaniards at the time of the Conquest in 1532.) Then, the design was embroidered on the fabric.

Today stem stitch is usually used as the most cursive of stitches; that is, if a freely moving line is wanted, stem stitch is apt to be the choice. But in this poncho-shirt, stem stitch is used in a manner that more closely resembles tapestry weave or the soumak technique of rug weaving than it does the usual variety of stem stitch embroidery. In soumak, weft threads twist around the warps as they progress the width of the warpage. In stem stitch, the needle moves from left to right, each stitch slightly lapping the previous one just above it. If stem stitch is worked into counted threads, the action amounts to twisting the embroidery thread around warps or wefts in orderly sequence, giving a result almost identical to

soumak. The essential difference is that in soumak the decoration is made simultaneously with the weaving of the ground, and in stem stitch the decoration is made after the fabric has been woven.

Many museum visitors who have seen this poncho-shirt assume that the designs on the garment are woven into it—an understandable mistake, since the surface appears to be perfectly flat everywhere. One expects embroidered motifs in isolated areas to appear in relief, however slight, against the background. Here there is no sign of relief. In this embroidery the black background behind the falling figures is worked entirely in stem stitch, although it looks very much like weaving. The technique is a combination of threadcounting and surface stitching.

The primary division in needlework is between those embroideries that are threadcounted and those that are surface stitched. For threadcounted embroideries, with the exception of a few unusual variations, the ground fabric must be plain, or tabby, weave with the warps and wefts clearly visible, because they must be counted as they are worked over, singly or in groups. In surface stitching the design is drawn on the fabric, which can be any firm weave, and the work progresses without attention to warps or wefts.

The stem stitches of the poncho-shirt are arranged in close rows, kept exactly horizontal and vertical where the pattern permits, and worked by counting four threads of the ground fabric forward and two threads backward. In threadcounted parts the stitches integrate with the weaving; however, where the freely drawn pattern requires, the stitches veer off into diagonals and curves of stitches of similar size, but they are not counted.

Probably the outline of the design for the poncho-shirt embroidery was first worked in the background color (black). Then motifs and background were embroidered, beginning with contours and working in concentric rows toward the center of the shape. Except for small pattern areas, the central space usually was worked in horizontal or vertical rows.

Tests made by Louisa Bellinger for the Textile Museum in Washington, D.C., showed that the thread used in Paracas needlework was dyed after spinning. This order of dyeing increased the cohesiveness of the fibers,

**CHILD'S
PONCHO-SHIRT**
*Peru, South Coast,
Paracas Necropolis
Culture; A.D. 100.
Overall measurement
22-5/8 in. x 19 in.*

giving them the hard, tightly twisted character that makes clearly defined stitches possible even when they are very small and worked close together. Also noteworthy is that in Paracas embroidery the threads are not knotted but spliced.

In the poncho-shirt the band bordering the neck and the discontinuous band around the edge (a not completely understood convention of these garments) show equally spaced falling figures in orange, olive green, and purple (the secondary triad of colors, interestingly enough; mixtures of the primaries—red, yellow, and blue). The purple figures around the edge are barely visible now. The figures in the border have touches of orange, green, and purple in the eyes, mouths, and fans. They measure approximately one and three-quarters by two and one-half inches. The rectangles are one and one-half by one and one-quarter inches. It should be noted that the positions of the falling figures reverse and alternate throughout the design. The overall measurement of the garment is twenty-two and five-eighths inches by nineteen inches.

Contemporary adaptation

In making a garment similar to this poncho-shirt it would be necessary to find a ground fabric of comparable texture. The weaving of the original is slightly loose and exceedingly supple. An ideal substitute would be woven with tightly twisted alpaca threads. Its color would be strong but not harsh. For embroidery, properly hand-dyed fabrics and yarns are much more satisfying than are most commercial products, but home dyeing is a time-consuming process and is disappointing if not well done. Therefore, many dedicated embroiderers are always on the lookout for good textiles and yarns, and they keep hoards for future work. Color remover, used for softening colors, is standard equipment.

For this Peruvian embroidery design, in which the same simple motif is used repeatedly, a pounced transfer made from the accompanying diagram is practical because the pricking can be used over and over. (See M&T.) White chalk should be used to pounce deeply colored fabrics; the transfer should be reinforced immediately with white tempera, keeping the lines as fine as possible. A pointed, sable, No. 00 brush is recommended for anyone who hasn't learned to work with the tip of a larger

The two large motifs are repeated on the border of the child's poncho-shirt; the two smaller motifs are repeated throughout the central part of the garment.

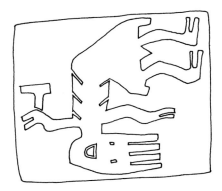

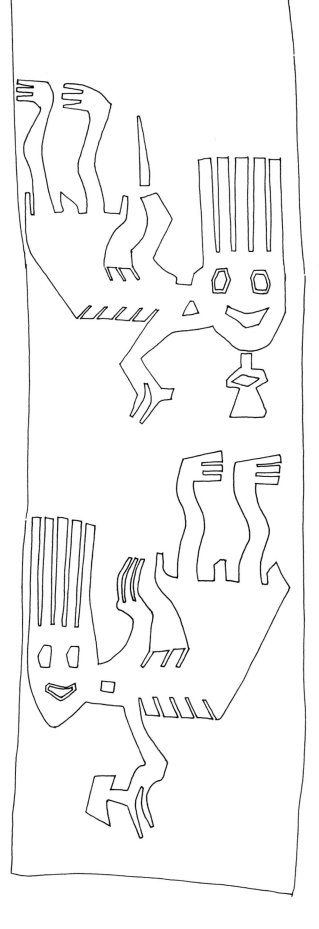

brush. If the embroidery pattern accompanying this piece is too large or too small, refer to the M&T section that discusses changes in pattern scale.

This needlework can be made in a hand hoop. Begin by embroidering the background. Following warps or wefts and using stem stitch (see Stitch Directory), count four threads forward for the stitch, and overlap two threads in making the next stitch. Around the contour of the figure work a row of stitches without counting. Embroider the figures in stem stitch, beginning with the outer contour. Keep the stitches threadcounted as much as possible; however, where there are curves follow them without attempting to count threads, but keep the stitches at a length comparable to the threadcounted stitches.

A poncho-shirt differs from a poncho only in that it is joined rather than open at the sides. The small spot and border motifs of this poncho-shirt could be used for other types of garments, such as blouses, skirts, or belts, as well as the original, and they also could be used to decorate carryalls or cushions.

The most familiar ancient Peruvian embroideries come from the Paracas peninsula. They were made in a variety of techniques: massed stem stitches, knit-like loopstitches, and chain or other stitches. The fragment of embroidery shown here was found in the Monte Grande area of the Rio Grande Valley. Its technique differs significantly from any of the well-known Paracas types in that the stitching intact on the seemingly unfinished fragment shows that its bird designs were to have colored fillings in running and cross stitch within stem stitch outlines. This free surface embroidery does not relate to the woven ground in the closely integrated fashion of other Peruvian embroidery, such as the poncho-shirt on page 2. It was worked in cotton on a plain, tabby-woven cotton ground fabric. The background is pale blue, the embroidered outlines are white, and the few remaining stitches of the filling designs are dark blue, pink, rose, purplish brown, and gold. A few strands of rose or brown have been plied (twisted) with a strand of white, a common practice in Peruvian weaving and needlework.

What the original function of this embroidery was to have been is impossible to decide. It has been called a sampler, but there are some indications that it might have been a border. An arrangement of three rows of birds, each measuring three and one-half by one and three-quarters inches, reversed and staggered in alternate rows, is bordered by single rows of smaller birds on each side. The narrow side band along one edge does not continue the length of the panel. Instead, larger motifs

Border of birds

again occur, as if the design were to turn a corner, suggesting that a neckline border or some other shaped opening was to be ornamented.

Smaller birds appear in profile, larger ones are seen in a combined top and side view. Motifs showing birds or fowl with prey are not unusual in Peruvian textiles. On Paracas borders, designs similar to the birds shown in profile here were worked in stem stitch either in strictly horizontal rows or in rows following the contours of the design. Color arrangements in Peruvian textiles vary from simple to complicated. Combinations of large and small bird motifs similar to the ones shown here can be found on pottery and in wood carvings. While in some designs the birds and animals portrayed became so highly stylized that they lost their identity and became part of an allover geometric pattern, here the birds are very recognizable, and the prey of each is depicted in detail. It is a point of interest that some of these birds, like the birds of European and Asian textiles, carry leafy twigs in their beaks. Botanical motifs, which seem to dominate most textile design, are uncommon in Peruvian weaving and embroidery before the coming of the Spanish.

The photograph of this fragment shows that it has been badly damaged. Fabrics of cotton have not survived as well as those made of alpaca, llama, or other fibers. Today the cotton portions of many Peruvian textiles crumble away at the touch. For the dyer, cotton also presented more problems than other fibers. A dye that worked well was indigo, the staple blue dye used everywhere because it is fast without mordanting (see page 149). However, cochineal—which produced, depending on the mordant used, either marvelous reds or black— did not work well on cottons. In Peru various natural colored cottons were grown, making it possible for the dyer to achieve several shades from a single dye pot. Natural cotton colors range from white to gray and brown. Peruvians used an extraordinary number of colors in their weaving and needlework, and most of their textiles retain their vividness today.

Contemporary adaptation

For this embroidery a slightly bulky, blue homespun cotton (plain weave) would produce an effect similar to the original. The design should be transferred to ground fabric using dressmakers' carbon or any other preferred transfer method that will provide a clear, narrow line. (See M&T.) The embroidery can be worked in a hand hoop; it is not necessary to mount it in an embroidery frame. Outlines should be worked in stem stitch, using cotton— unmercerized if possible—or linen threads. The number of strands needed to produce the desired effect will depend on the scale in which the design is worked. Not enough filling stitches remain in the fragment to give an indication of their distribution and pattern. If you want to add fillings, improvisation will be necessary.

Like most Peruvian embroideries, this one contains motifs that coordinate well with contemporary design. This neat panel design can be used for both garments and household accessories. It also would adapt nicely to materials and techniques other than the original. For example, worked in double running stitch on sheer fabric, the pattern could decorate a small curtain that would be presentable on both sides if back stitches were used instead of knots, and thread ends were neatly tucked out of sight. Worked in wool on wool, this border could decorate a handbag or cushion cover. The bird designs could be worked with areas of color, rather than line only, in massed stem stitches and handled in much the same fashion as the poncho-shirt on page 2. Enlarged, this design would make a fine wall hanging.

BORDER OF BIRDS
Peru, Rio Grande Valley,
Monte Grande Area;
A.D. 200-300. Fragment.

A detail of motifs taken from the lower half of the fragment.

Last Supper

threadcounted stitches/Germany

color plate, page 104

The square of embroidery shown on the accompanying page, depicting the Last Supper of Christ, was made in Lower Saxony in the early fourteenth century, at the same time that the rich silk and metal embroideries of England, known as *opus anglicanum,* were reaching their climax of perfection. Masterpieces of gold and silk needlework were beyond the means of many German parishes, and whitework of the type seen here was used instead. This little square was probably at one time part of an altar frontal. Two other pieces that seem to belong to the same set are known.

The problem of producing a technically painstaking and minutely detailed embroidery of large scale was solved by a number of ingenious arrangements. Cope and large altar frontal designs were assemblages of entwined circles, quatrefoils (a four-lobed shape familiar in Gothic design) or architectonic subdivisions, each containing its own individual, separately worked theme. With the total design subdivided in this fashion, it could be embroidered by several workers simultaneously. When finished, the parts were joined, and borders, arcading, or leafy boughs were worked over the joints.

Goldwork embroideries were carefully preserved, but whiteworks appear to have been valued less and to have been in more constant use. The technique of whitework, which juxtaposed densely opaque areas with openwork, as seen in the accompanying photo, was especially effective for screens and veils used to obscure choirs and altars. Gold embroideries of the day were architectural in their sculptural and enamel-like effects; whiteworks, conversely, were vulnerable to light in the same manner as pierced stone and stained glass.

This type of German whitework embroidery is called *opus teutonicum.* Not all writers agree with this definition of *opus teutonicum,* but the scholarship of Marie Schuette and Sigrid Muller-Christensen in *The Art of Embroidery* has been accepted here. *Opus teutonicum* was made of linen thread on a loosely woven linen ground. It often had accents of silk and

color. As with all white embroideries its distinctive features are its relief, shadow, and effects of transparency. Sometimes the entire background of an embroidery of this type was made mesh-like by embroidering Italian cross stitch or overcasting. At first whiteworks appear technically similar; on second glance they display considerable individuality and much more freedom in the working methods than a casual look at the face side would suggest.

In this square of the Last Supper, work was begun with the contour drawing, which was rendered in outline stitch (the counterpart of stem stitch, the overlapping of successive stitches occurs below the previous stitch rather than above it) in medium brown linen thread. Within the shapes of the figures, a variety of textured, darned fillings were used. In most areas as much thread was deposited on the back as on the front of the work, so that a dense, heavy embroidery was built up in the gauzy linen. In a few areas the play of opacity against translucency was carried further by the use of two-sided Italian cross stitch, which opened the ground fabric in a meshy effect, possibly for iconographic purposes—that is, to give "light" to the halos and holy vessels. The only other stitch used in this work, aside from darned filling, was a freely worked filling of oblique, encroaching stitches. The back of the piece shows that these were inserted as closely placed rows of stem stitch. Areas of hair and shoes were worked this way.

An interesting fact can be noted about the pattern stitches that were darned in. Of the four types that Mrs. Archibald Christie mentions in *Samplers and Stitches,* the two flat, weaving-like varieties are present, but those that allow a random play of light on the surface do not appear. The types used are "pattern darning," which involves geometric designs made with running stitches threadcounted into the warp or weft of the ground fabric, and "double darning," in which double running stitches are arranged in sequence for a pattern. The types avoided are "damask darning," in which the threadcounted running stitches follow the warps in some parts of the design and the wefts in others so that the various areas catch the light differently, and "irregular darning," in which the stitches follow the contours of the drawing rather than the warp or weft. Thus the embroidery here, as in the poncho-shirt on page 2, closely integrates with the weaving,

LAST SUPPER
Germany, Lower Saxony; early 14th century, 15 in. x 14½ in.

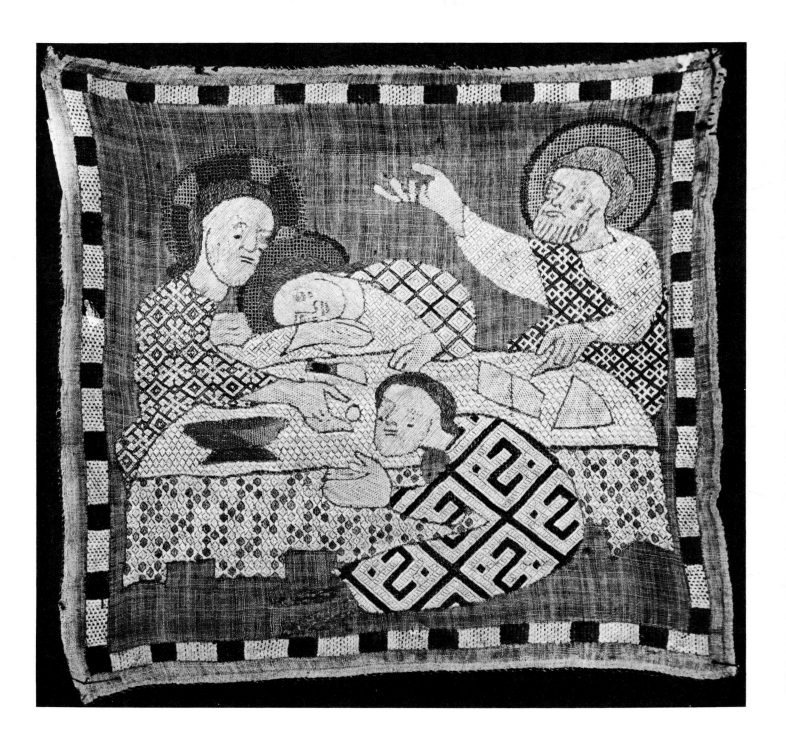

This numbered diagram indicates which sections of the design are to be worked in one of the accompanying embroidery patterns. The numbered patterns correspond to the numbers on the diagram.

avoiding accidental or relief effects. But a look at the back of this piece shows that in some instances the more complex designs, which seem to be darned, were in fact worked in a more expedient method akin to satin or flat stitch.

Once the contour drawing was transferred to the linen (the drawing probably had been supplied by an itinerant designer) and the outlines worked in brown linen thread, the fillings could be made. The accompanying diagram of the Last Supper has numbered areas that correspond with the following numbered patterns. Refer to these patterns when working specific areas of the embroidery.

Pattern 1. These rectangles were worked in double darning stitch and were arranged brick fashion.

Pattern 1a. Alternate rectangles of the border were worked in a simple over-one-under-one double running stitch.

Pattern 2. These areas were worked in double darning stitch arranged twill fashion as shown in the diagram for this pattern. The twill no longer shows clearly on the face of the embroidery, but it is prominent on the back.

Pattern 3. Both colors of this design were worked in satin stitch. (The gray area represents a different color of thread.) The geometric design elements were completed as separate units rather than as a part of the whole; the pattern was not counted out and each row of the entire area was not worked completely from side to side. The back of the work shows crossings of threads

Pattern 1

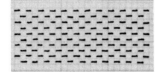

Pattern 1a

Pattern 2

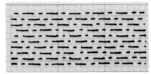

Pattern 3

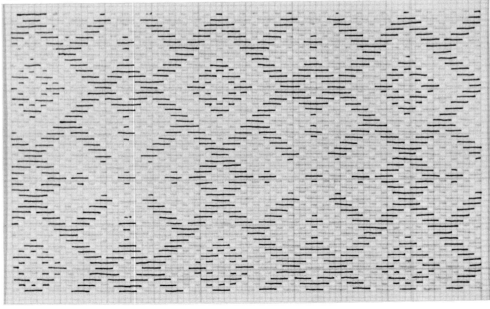

Pattern 4

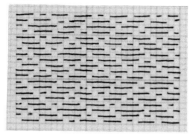

Pattern 5

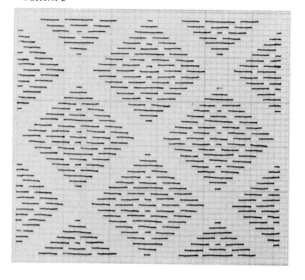

Pattern 6

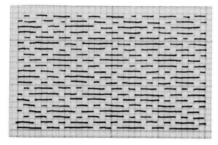

Pattern 7

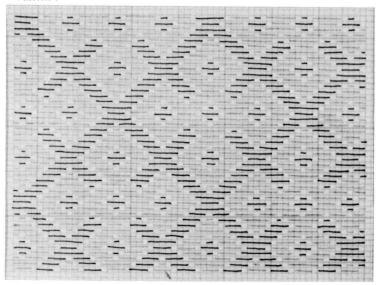

and skips from row to row. The mosaic-like motifs of the white part of the design were worked like Hungarian stitch. The colored parts of the design were worked in satin stitch.

Pattern 4. For this basket weave pattern double darning was used.

Pattern 5. White, diamond-shaped elements were worked separately in double darning. Colored bands were worked "up and down" in silk so that the silk on the back is minimal.

Pattern 6. Squares and diagonal bands were worked separately in satin stitch.

Pattern 7. Both colors of this pattern were worked in satin stitch.

Pattern 8. This design was worked in rows across the whole area in double darning stitch.

Pattern 9. Both colors were worked in satin stitch.

Pattern 10. The white elements were worked in satin stitch; the brown (dark) open-work bands and S-shapes were worked with Italian cross stitch.

All the patterns were worked with stitches running vertically, with the exception of the faces and hands, some of which are vertical, some horizontal. The table objects on the left side of the embroidery are done in horizontal stitches, those on the right are done in vertical stitches.

The same restraint and selectivity that characterize the design and textures in this embroidery are evident in the arrangement of colors. Although predominantly white, the square is enlivened with color areas that are interesting in the originality of their placement. Some colors—the pale gold particularly—seem to have been reserved for symbolic use. The scheme can be determined by looking at the color plate on page 104. Originally most of the colors seem to have been of medium value. Most of the colored threads were silk rather than linen.

Contemporary adaptation

To reproduce this needlework as it originally appeared, a piece of open, plain weave linen with evenly spun threads must be found. A piece of handwoven linen would be ideal, and if a loom is available it would not be unduly difficult to weave a piece of cloth, since

Pattern 8   *Pattern 9*

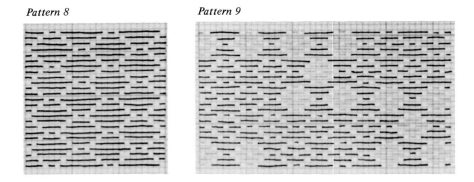

Pattern 10

Only this portion
of the pattern needs
to be transferred
to make the embroidery.
To enlarge this design
see the M&T section
at the back of the book.

the overall size of the square is only fifteen by fourteen and one-half inches. If handwoven material cannot be acquired, linens appropriate for work of this type can be found in shops that sell fine quality drapery fabrics. Fabrics with nubs or thick-and-thin threads should be avoided. Standard evenweave and hardanger linens, intended for counted and drawnwork embroidery, are too opaque to give this design the desired effect. Theatrical gauze is too flimsy and also should be avoided.

The diagram on page 13 should be transferred to the linen as delicately as possible. A trial transfer onto a scrap of fabric will determine whether dressmakers' carbon, sugar solution, or transfer pencil will make the most satisfactory transfer. (Refer to the M&T section at the back of the book for a complete description of these transfer methods.) The embroidery can be done in either a hand hoop or a frame. If worked in a hoop, the size of the hoop should be large enough to accommodate in their entirety those areas that must be worked in rows from side to side, thereby eliminating the need for constant shifting of the fabric. The embroidery should begin with the halos, which are worked in two-sided Italian cross stitch. Then the outline stitch contours can be added. Next the various fillings should be worked. The border, if used, should be drawn freehand directly onto the fabric, not transferred, so that the threads of the ground weave can be followed accurately. The position of the border can be marked out with threads, rather than pencil, ink, or tempera, if preferred. In the original the square is hemmed and has a red silk thread couched along its border.

The procedure of this Last Supper embroidery can be used with other compositions. It could be adapted for use with St. Mauritius, page 16; the angel or the nativity scene in the altar from Burgo de Osma, page 22; Adam and Eve, page 60; or with any flat, simple design of specific pictorial nature. It could also be used with purely decorative designs: pillow covers, page 34; purse, page 74; French cap back, page 145; Skyros bed valance, page 153; or Russian border, page 180.

The designs for the pattern darning used in this embroidery can be translated for use in needlepoint. Single filling patterns would work well for cushions, chair seats, handbags, eyeglass cases, wastebasket and box covers, and other needlepoint-covered objects for which a small allover pattern is desired. Enlarged, these designs also could be adapted for larger needlepoint and hooked or knotted rugs. Whether the designs are rendered in darning or needlepoint they also are appropriate for use in contemporary abstract and nonobjective compositions.

St. Mauritius

silk and gold embroidery/Germany

In the legends of Christianity St. George ranks as the favorite among the knights of Christ. Second to him in Italian art is St. Sebastian; the Greeks give this second place honor to St. Demetrius. In French and German art St. Mauritius (St. Maurice) has special importance. Mauritius, sometimes shown as a black man because he came from Africa, was the leader of the Theban legion of the Roman army at the time of Diocletian. The size of this legion and the details of the story vary. In fact, although several towns (including St. Moritz in Grisons) and the abbey of St. Maurice at Agaunum have been named for St. Mauritius, some authorities believe the legend about this saint is entirely fictitious.

It is said that Maximinianus Herculeaus, gathering an army to march into Gaul, called up the Christian Theban legion. The year of this event is variously given as A.D. 286 and 303. To reach Gaul, the Alps had to be crossed. When this hazardous part of the campaign had been accomplished, the troops, including the Theban legion, halted to celebrate. (In one account it is said that part of them camped on the banks of the Rhine, while the rest stopped at Lake Geneva.) The Theban legion, all Christians, refused to join the pagan festivities and moved to Agaunum. Angered, Maximinianus informed his troops that the purpose of the campaign was to annihilate the Christians who lived in the conquered land. Mauritius refused to fight against his brothers and replied, "O, Caesar! we are thy soldiers, but we are also the soldiers of Jesus Christ." Twice the legion was decimated for its refusal; then it was completely destroyed. The massacre met no resistance; St. Mauritius' legion met death rejoicing.

Gregory of Tours (c. 539-593) relates that part of the army camped on the Rhine at Cologne, led by St. Gereon, met the same fate as the legion led by St. Mauritius.

St. Mauritius, although not an extremely familiar subject in art, has been interpreted by painters and printmakers of all persuasions, from the great Italian mannerist, Pontormo, to the Swiss folk artist, C. F. Brun. El Greco's painting. *The Martyrdom of St. Mauritius' Legion,* is an outstanding version of the story. Mathis Grünewald's *Saints Erasmus and Maurice* shows the saint as a black man. Usually St. Mauritius wears fifteenth-century armour and carries either a lance and banner or a banner and palm. It is the view of the massacre of St. Mauritius that seems to have intrigued most artists who have dealt with the subject. The gentle little figure shown here barely suggests the legend of the courageous martyr.

This fragment was probably part of an orphrey. Orphries are bands of embroidery, sometimes cruciform (in the shape of a cross), on ecclesiastical vestments. These bands usually contain the richest decoration on the garment and are adorned with much gold embroidery. The term *orphrey* relates to this metalwork. Gold threads appear in some of the earliest embroideries. The Phrygians called their work auriphrygium, from which the term *orphrey* was coined in the middle ages.

The figure of St. Mauritius shown here was appliquéd onto a band that except for a detail of landscape in silk threads was embroidered entirely in gold. When working with gold threads it is essential that the ground fabric be firmly mounted in a frame. The gold threads are very delicate and must be carefully handled so as not to injure them. The type of metal thread used in this embroidery consisted of a fiber core around which a very thin strip of metal was wound. This type of thread is called passing.

The design for St. Mauritius was transferred or drawn directly onto heavy linen. Originally the ground was completely covered with embroidery, and the coarse linen did not show through. The figure of St. Mauritius was embroidered separately and then appliquéd on the ground. The grassy hillock at the bottom of the piece was embroidered on the background band.

Work on the main band of the orphrey began with the couching of the background. The basket weave pattern that the couching stitches were to follow for the background was marked clearly and accurately on the linen ground (this pattern is shown in the accompanying diagram). The metal threads of the background are now darkened with age and worn, but originally they were probably gold. The couching thread was red silk floss, and the stitches were tiny, even, and rather tightly pulled. (Precision is important in couching of this type.) In the background pairs of metal threads, worked back and forth horizontally,

ST. MAURITIUS
Germany; 15th century.
Overall measurement is
12 in. x 6-1/8 in.,
figure from head to toe
measures 9½ in.

This diagram of St. Mauritius is just slightly smaller than the original.

If you decide to do the basket weave couched background behind St. Mauritius, like the one done in the original, follow this pattern for the couching stitches.

were caught in place by little red stitches made to correspond to the geometric diagram drawn on the ground linen.

When the background was finished the green hillock was embroidered. This is badly worn in the original, as you can see, but it is apparent that it was laid work. To make the hillock, shades of green silk floss, darker shades at the top of the mound, were arranged horizontally across the space to be embroidered. Next, long green threads, laid diagonally—thus the name, laid work—in two directions and at right angles to one another produced a checkerboard grid on top of the original horizontal threads. Finally the threads of this loose gridwork were secured to the ground by means of tiny stitches over each crossing. Tufts of grass were made with twisted silver threads couched over the green silk embroidery. The metal threads were put through the ground textile with an awl or stiletto especially made for gold embroidery. These tools were used to make openings through which the fragile thread could be pulled without harming it.

After the ground work was finished the border of the panel was made. Four heavy cords were sewn along the edge, and metal threads were couched in pairs at right angles to these cords, making a pattern. The first five rows of couched stitches were secured tightly at both edges and between the second and third cords. Then in the next five rows of couching the pattern was changed by securing the stitches at the beginning and end of the row and between the first and second and the third and fourth cords. (If you look closely at the photograph of St. Mauritius you will see clearly the alternating pattern.) Five rows of the second pattern were worked; then five rows of the first pattern repeated, creating a brick-like design around the border. To keep the sculptural form of the cord, the metal thread was pulled down to the ground fabric. Two silver threads, twisted to make a cord, were couched over the edges of the border to hide the turnings of the thread.

When the background of the piece was completed it was ready for application of the figure, which was embroidered separately and then applied. On the hands and face of the figure the original silk embroidery has worn away so that the texture of the ground fabric is now showing. Originally the face and hands were worked in split stitch or in long and short stitch. They had a rather pale but natural tonality. The mantle was worked in long and short stitch in chartreuse shaded to blue-green; it has a maroon and rust lining. The banner and shield are blue and were worked in the same manner as the hillock. The hat and hosiery of the figure are ivory silk and were worked in long and short stitch. The shoes were probably black or brown; black dyes were injurious to fibers, and in many textiles these colors have disappeared with their fibers while adjacent fibers with other lighter colors remain intact. The armor, halo, and lance and the crosses on the shield and banner are silver. The threads in these sections are paired and closely couched; the stitches are alternated brick fashion in each row. The figure was outlined with two twisted metal threads, couched into position around the figure. A similar twisted thread covers the edges of the figure where it has been sewn to the background.

Contemporary adaptation

All the original materials and methods used in making this vestment orphrey can be duplicated today. Since the finished work entirely covers the ground fabric any transfer method can be used. Directions for mounting the ground fabric in a frame are given in the M&T section at the back of the book. The figure measures approximately four and one-half by ten inches.

This figure and the threadcounted Last Supper embroidery on page 9 are similar in their simplicity and in their combination of natural and geometric elements. Each could be worked with the technique used for the other. Being illustrative ecclesiastical subjects, St. Mauritius and the Last Supper probably would be best used as wall hangings or treated as framed pictures. However, the gold techniques used for the background and border might well be used in designs suitable for clothing and furnishings.

Angel

split stitch/Spain

The angel on page 22 and the Nativity on page 26 are both Spanish embroideries from the Burgo de Osma altar set. Scenes from the life of Christ appear on the dossal (back panel) and antependium (altar frontal) of this embroidery masterwork. The coat of arms in enframing medallions around the outer edge of the upper portion of the work identify the set as the property of Don Pedro de Montoya, Bishop of Osma, for whom it was originally made. Inscriptions on the frontal read: "Remember, O man, that Jesus suffered these pains for you," and "The Lord indeed is risen and appeared to Simon." Although the drawing of these needleworks is medieval and provincial, in their naturalism they reveal traces of Flemish Gothicism, which by the time they were made in 1468 had been comfortably assimilated into the national idiom.

In the fifteenth century Flemish painters were experimenting with oil paint. It was employed originally for decorations to be used out-of-doors, because oil is waterproof and its transparency made possible jewel-like effects. Gradually oil was clarified and thinned to a color and consistency that made it a desirable medium for general use in painting. Because of its fluidity, intricacies of detail were achieved more easily with oil than they were with fresco or egg tempera. The newly developing medium, coming as it did at the same time as the rise of humanistic sentiment, made it possible to produce an art that demonstrated love for the natural world in all its detail. Although the view of the Nativity seen here most likely was embroidered somewhere in the vicinity of Burgo de Osma in the northern part of Spain, it reflects this new humanistic vision. These figures are not classically ideal and beautiful; their individual faces were made carefully to show the state of mind of each. The Christ Child, in the left panel of the top portion of the altar frontal, truly appears to be a newborn infant.

In Flemish painting of the fifteenth century an architectural frame was an integral part of the artwork. The same is true of the altar embroideries from Burgo de Osma. The framing, however, is not gesso (similar to plaster) and gilding on wood but is a sculptural embroidery of spiral pillars and interlaced ornaments. The embroidered spiral pillars cover the joinings of several individually made flat, silk and metal embroidered pictures, which when finished were assembled to make the whole. Even today after so many centuries the ensemble effect of this embroidery remains dazzling. A variety of threads—silk floss, tightly twisted and plied silk, and metal—were worked into a base of linen, completely covering it. Spangles made from circles of flattened wire, jewels, beads, and pearls also were used. The stitching used in this work is complex: split, chain, knot, and a variety of satin stitches, couching, and laid work. Light-capturing metal threads enlivened and enriched the surface.

The use of gold backgrounds in painting and embroidery were widely popular. In medieval times it was a perfect solution for the problem of how to situate figures that didn't really belong in an earthly, or natural, setting. A gold background gave saintly creatures a realm of evanescent light to abide in, and it was suitably princely in its lavishness. But with the rise of humanistic thought, gold backgrounds gave way to settings that showed perspective and landscape.

The way that embroiderers translated the painters' and goldsmiths' use of gold into their own medium is intriguing. In the Western world designers tended to use gold threads in two basic ways. First, if the gold thread was used in backgrounds or for drapery it was laid on in straight rows, usually horizontal and couched in a geometric pattern. (In Byzantine embroidery this was the principal manner in which gold threads were used.)

Second, if the embroiderer wanted to emphasize the shimmer of gold he padded his work with some sort of cord or wadding, or he worked a raised effect over a padding of extra stitches. In other words, he made needlework in relief so that the light would have a chance to play over the irregular surface of his work. In oriental embroideries, by contrast, the surface was usually kept flat, but a play of light was

This detail
of the altar frontal
shows the sculptural effect
achieved by the gold
couched passing threads,
which were worked
over cording (visible
in worn spots).

RETABLE AND
ALTAR FRONTAL
*Spain, Burgo de Osma;
about 1468.*

ANGEL
*Detail located
in the extreme left arch
of the antependium
(lower half of the work)
of the Burgo de Osma
altar frontal,
3½ in. high.*

*This diagram of the angel
is more than twice as large
as the original.*

induced by working the threads in undulating curves. In the Osma altar embroideries gold threads have been used in typical Western ways.

The embroidery diagram for the tiny angel, located above the extreme left arch of the antependium (lower half of the work), is approximately twice as large as the original, which measures three and one-half inches in height. The angel is one from a series of angels, each of which carries an instrument of the Passion. Three types of gold embroidery were required for the angel. The headband, the feather motifs on the wings, and the staff that holds the sponge (from the Passion) were produced by couching gold threads in pairs, a common technique already seen in the embroidery of St. Mauritius (pages 15-18). The braid-like edging of the angel's robe was made by plaiting pairs of gold threads and sewing them in place. The crown of thorns in the angel's hand (from the Passion) was constructed by wrapping two cords with gold threads and twisting the two together.

The small angel was embroidered separately and sewn into place, as were several intricate parts of the work. In this set of embroideries it is interesting to note that some of the secondary parts are of finer quality than some of the central figures. All parts of this embroidery not worked in metal threads were worked in silk floss in split stitch. The robe was shaded from palest blue to deep cobalt; the midshades are now somewhat faded. The face has pale flesh tones with bright red lips, and the hair is flaxen. The gold sponge was worked in knot stitch. A black couched outline surrounds the figure. Actually the threads are silver, but they have tarnished over the years.

Contemporary adaptation

The size of the small angel makes it possible to consider doing the needlework in a hand hoop (see M&T), even though gold thread is to be used, because the whole design could be encompassed in the hoop, and the embroidery would not have to be moved as work progressed.

To render this embroidery in the original scale the diagram would have to be reduced to three and one-half inches in height. The drawing could be transferred to linen using dressmakers' carbon, transfer pencil, or sugar solution. The silk parts of the embroidery should be worked first. When silk floss, which has virtually no twist, is used, it is impossible to tell the difference between split and chain stitches if they are very tiny and the back of the work cannot be seen. The tiny loop of the chain stitch becomes invisible when the stitches are infinitesimal, and its slightly bulging outline is obscured in the massing of rows of stitches. Both split and chain stitches characteristically make a very straight line. The modern embroiderer, who probably won't achieve stitches so tiny as those of the original, could use either. Chain stitch goes faster, but split stitch is smoother. Long and short stitching is the usual way of speeding up split stitch.

Gold passing threads (gold strip wound around a fiber core) should be handled and added to the embroidery just as they were in the original. (See the detailed description on the preceding pages.) If desired, a background of couched passing can be worked before the final black outline covers the edges of the figure. The figure and background could be done separately or on the same piece of linen.

Although this is an angel for the Easter season, the little figure could be changed slightly for use at Christmastime. For the crown of thorns and sponge you could substitute some other objects appropriate to the season. The enlarged design, as it appears in the diagram or raised to larger scale, could be used for embroidery in crewels, using chain stitch, long and short stitch, or a combination of the two. A banner design using this angel as the central motif or as a part of a more complex design would make a lasting and beautiful needlework.

Nativity

silk and gold embroidery/Spain

color plate, page 105

A second example from the altar embroideries of Burgo de Osma (see page 20) involves a scheme of needlework more complicated than that for the angel. In this work gold threads have been couched flat or worked over cords and secured with gold or contrasting shades of silk stitches arranged in geometric patterns. Elaborate foundations were prepared for the golden architectural details. A heavy, rope-like core was covered with linen and wound with cords of varying thicknesses. These cords were sewn into place. Then they were covered with gold threads couched into place with back stitches pulled tightly against the wrapping cords. The work proceeded back and forth from side to side in horizontal rows.

If you take a closer look at the background in the photograph of the Nativity scene you will see that the area is divided simply into geometric shapes. Its air of complication does not result from a complex design but, rather, from the richness of the embroidered textures. You will notice that the highly decorative pattern of simply checked laid work directly behind the central figures does not interfere with the focal center of the composition. The design behind the central figures appears again, alternating with a design of paired couched threads, in the area of the rafters. Long and short stitch was used for the shingles and the watering trough at the right. The more aggressive tile-like pattern in the lower portion of the picture is worked in long and short stitch and outlined with couched passing threads. Note that the tile section, like similar sections with geometric

patterns in the Last Supper (page 9) and in St. Mauritius (page 16), are not modeled in any way, nor do they show perspective. Notice, however, that all the figures, including the smallest angel and the animals, are delicately modeled in chain or split stitch.

The figures for the Nativity scene were embroidered directly onto the ground, not worked separately. Halos were worked in couching with corded edges, and the "jewels" in the halos were made with satin stitch over heavy padding. Many real jewels that once appeared on the work are now gone. The exact nature of the gems and stitching used to create the radiance around the Christ Child is no longer discernible. Medallions on the madonna's mantle were couched in gold thread and edged with cord. The faces and hands of the figures were worked in silk floss in split stitch. The Christ Child's and the angels' hair were done with silk in knot stitch. The draped garments were worked in very fine chain or split stitch and have borders made by twisting and braiding gold threads. The overall size of the picture is approximately fourteen by fifteen inches.

Contemporary adaptation

This design should be transferred carefully with dressmakers' carbon, transfer pencil, or sugar solution to a heavy linen ground. A linen with a firm weave will make your work more accurate. Mount the transferred pattern on a frame in such a way that it will not have to be moved. (See M&T.) The silk parts—figures, animals, and background—of the embroidery should be worked first, beginning with the background areas. The photographs will be helpful in determining how the garments and faces are to be shaded. The direction of lines of stitches follows the form and contributes to the modeled effect.

Because gold thread wears easily, areas and outlines done in gold should be worked last. Medallions, jewels, and any other raised effect that could catch working threads should be embroidered at the very end. The finished work could be mounted as a picture or a wall hanging.

NATIVITY
*Detail located
on the left side
of the retable (upper half)
of the Burgo de Osma altar
(see page 20).
Overall measurement is
14 in. x 15 in.*

*This diagram
of the central portion
of the Nativity is
smaller than
the original.
For a more elaborate effect,
the diagram can be easily
enlarged.
(See M&T.)*

Intertwined classic scrolls

appliqué on velvet/Spain

In this altar frontal from the cathedral at Seo de Urgel, Lerida Province, Spain, scenes from the life of Christ have been depicted. This velvet frontal, produced in the sixteenth century, is adorned with ten roundels embroidered in silk floss and gold thread. The circles, which look very much like painting, have a shaded type of gold embroidery called *or nué*. Just as gold relief embroidery was an attempt to reproduce the art of the goldsmith in needlework, *or nué* was an attempt to translate into thread the effect of transparent enamelwork in which gold foil was laid under the glassy enamel color to enhance its brillance. The embroiderer, whose objective was the same as that of the artist working with enamels, added liveliness to his silken colors by allowing a little gold thread to show between the stitches. In German the word for this technique is *Lasurstickerei,* which means "glaze embroidery." Glaze is a term used as frequently in discussing painting as in discussing enamel procedures. The two are connected in that, in the early stages of painting, glazing was an effort to produce in the painting jewel-like effects that would simulate the enamels and real jewels that so often adorned the works of the goldsmith. Later, transparent oil glazes were used to give painting the rich depth of color so characteristic of enamelwork. In all the arts of the sixteenth century what was sought was an effect of princely brilliance.

It is doubtful that anyone would have the patience or time to make *or nué* embroidery today, but the method is of interest because of the beautiful result it produced, and because it was probably the most technically demanding embroidery technique ever practiced. *Or nué* is easy to identify because in most pieces the silk threads have worn away or decayed, at least in part, and gold threads, lying in rows, are exposed.

To begin *or nué,* gold threads were laid horizontally across a stretched linen foundation and sewn in place. Then they were overcast or closely couched with silk floss in varying shades, in most places completely covering the gold threads. Wherever a glimmer of gold was wanted, the couching threads were worked slightly apart from one another, allowing the gold threads beneath to show. The Seo de Urgel altar frontal contains three large and seven smaller medallions worked entirely or in part in *or nué.* All the medallions have accents of gold purl (a twisted wire ornament), gems, and gold cord along drapery edges and at focal points, and all contain figures with faces and hands worked in silk in split stitch, even though the substantial parts of the work were rendered in *or nué.*

The medallions, arranged on dark red silk velvet, are framed with leafy scrolls and banderoles in the classical manner of the Renaissance. These motifs, some worked separately and later attached to the frontal, are couched gold, silver, and colored silk threads. The accompanying diagram was taken from the pilaster-like panel that appears at both sides of the work. The portion that has been diagrammed measures slightly over twelve inches long in the original. Most of the embroidery is gold, but here and there touches of contrasting color appear.

Contemporary adaptation

To recreate the segment of this embroidery that has been diagrammed, the design should first be transferred to sturdy linen. The design will cover the linen completely, so any quick, relatively smudge-free transfer method will suffice. Dressmakers' carbon, transfer pencil, or sugar solution would make a satisfactory transfer. The linen must be securely mounted in a frame. (See M&T.) It is not necessary that tendrils and other curlicues be marked on the linen transfer if you intend to appliqué the finished embroidery onto velvet or some other background. The tendrils are so fine that they would be distorted when you cut out your appliqué, and you can easily stitch them onto the velvet to complete the work.

Begin working on the design transferred to linen by making the padding. In the original the padding was made of long stitches of linen thread. These stitches were worked up and down the length of leafy scrolls and flowers so as to be at right angles to the couched gold threads that were worked horizontally to cover them. The rule to follow in making the padding should be: let the largest, thickest parts of the design have the most padding; let narrow stems have very little padding. The padding threads in the original are yellow where gold threads cover them. The gold passing threads used for this type of embroidery are so wiry that inevitably the padding accidentally peeks through. For this reason padding should always be approximately the same color as the thread that is to cover it.

When you have finished the padding and before you begin working with gold threads, work the silk floss accents. These accents in the original were worked in long and short stitch in shades of pale blue and yellow-green, and they were limited to the small circular buds and scalelike shapes behind the flower at the bottom of the design. The centers of the flowers at the bottom and top of the design and the first curling outer leaf above the lower flower were couched in silver and have an edging of light blue cord. Remember that although these were the colors of the original you may use your own color choices wherever desired. On parts of this altar frontal not included in the diagram the ratio of colored silk and silver to gold is greater than it is in this segment, which is almost entirely gold.

When the accents have been completed, passing threads can be couched into position on the rest of the design. Passing threads were worked in pairs in the original, according to the tradition. The pairs were laid across the shape, caught into position with couching stitches, and turned sharply at the edge of the shape to be in place for the next row. Each pair of threads lies snugly close to the previous pair. The couching stitches are arranged in a neat, brick-like pattern, each stitch placed midway between the stitches of the row above until the shape has been completely covered.

When the couching has been finished, the embroidery can be cut out of the linen. A velvet ground fabric can be stretched in the frame and the embroidery basted on it in the correct position. Then the basted embroidery can be sewn into place with small overcasting stitches. The edges of the embroidered linen should not be turned under because they will create an unattractive bulge around the outside of the work. After the embroidery has been sewn to the velvet or other ground fabric, the edge should be concealed under finishing cording. In the original needlework cords were made by twisting two strands of passing. These were couched into place over the edges of the appliqué and allowed to extend past them at certain places to spiral into tendrils and curlicues. The ends of cords are drawn to the back of the work by opening a hole in the velvet ground with an awl or large tapestry needle. The cords can then be secured in position with a few stitches; no knot is needed.

If the velvet used for the ground fabric does not have sufficient body to support the embroidery in a satisfactory way, it can be backed with linen and the two layers used as one in the appliqué process.

While this design adorns an ecclesiastical needlework it is of a type that was used as much for secular purposes as in the service of the church, and it would be appropriate for any setting where classical design is at home. The design could be changed in scale and worked in other materials, but if you want to keep something of the character of the original you should limit yourself to a few colors. The design would be appropriate for door or wall panels, a decorative cushion, or, if worked without padding and gold, chair seats and backs. The design also could be embroidered in wool or other fibers with long and short, couching, or laid stitches used to cover larger areas, and chain, stem, outline, or couching stitches used for edges and spirals. Double or triple rows of outline or stem stitch can be used when a single row is too weak. This design also is appropriate for cloth appliqué. After the design is cut from a fabric of one color, the appliqué can be placed on a ground of a different color and the details and contours accented with couched cording. Using

the same color for both appliqué and ground but varying the textures will give a more subtle result than you would achieve with contrasting colors. The use of soft leathers for ground or appliqué might be considered.

As it stands, the intertwined classic scrolls design could be used to decorate a handbag, but revised to band or circle shape it could trim a hat. Split down the center, this design could be used for trimming a neckline or a slit in a skirt.

ALTAR FRONTAL
Spain, Lerida Province,
Seo de Urgel;
late 16 century
92½ in. x 42 in.

**INTERTWINED
CLASSIC SCROLLS**
*Details located on the left and
right sides of the Seo de Urgel altar frontal.
The panel is approximately 12 in. long.*

*This diagram
of the intertwined classic
scrolls can be used
effectively
in the size shown or
enlarged for a wall hanging.*

Pillow covers

blackwork/England

In England the Reformation saw the decline of great ecclesiastical needlework and the rise of domestic embroidery. Medieval preoccupation with the mysteries of the next world gave way to an enthusiasm for the creature comforts of this one, and with the dissolution of the monasteries more than a few church textiles were cut up to make household furnishings. This exchange of secular and ecclesiastical roles is not unique. Many an emperor's mantle was given to a church; there it was fitted with orphries, and it was recut for use as a cope. More recently the gay skirts of the ladies of the island of Crete have been remade into altar frontals.

Black embroidery enjoyed a heyday of popularity in Elizabethan times. Although Catherine of Aragon was thought to have introduced blackwork into England when she came from Spain in 1501 to marry Henry VII's second son, Arthur; more careful inspection of royal inventories now has shown that a kind of black embroidery similar to that for which Spain was famous was already being made in England when Catherine arrived.

Embroidery was an important accessory in both furnishing and clothing; sometimes the same patterns were used for both. The design of this late sixteenth-century pillow cover, one of a pair, can be found on sleeves now exhibited in the Royal Scottish Museum in Edinburgh. The design, very much like those published at the beginning of the seventeenth century in the pattern book of Thomas Trevelyon, is an example of the earliest version of blackwork, of which several types emerged as time went on. The earliest style combined heavy gold scrolls with stylized flowers that had lacy, threadcounted fillings. The design was used on wall hangings, coifs, nightcaps, jackets, and "pillow beres," or covers. This type of rather regularly spaced scroll-and-flower design is distinctly English and persisted well into the Stuart period—perhaps, it has been suggested, because James encouraged his wife Anne to make do with Elizabeth's old dresses.

In time there emerged a second blackwork style that showed greater naturalism in the drawing. In a final phase this naturalism was augmented by the use of embroidery stitches that would enhance the chiaroscuro—shaded or modeled—effect. "Speckling"—small running or back stitches spaced so as to create a shaded effect—and the use of surface stitching that accentuated curves and perspective replaced the old flat threadcounted stitches of earlier types. Excellent steel needles from Germany or Spain could be had; they were greatly treasured and carefully kept because of their scarcity. No doubt they gave impetus to the zeal for embroidery that required miniscule stitches.

A typical collection of English floral motifs was chosen for this cover, including the Tudor rose, daffodil, and carnation. Also on the cover is the pomegranate, ancient symbol of fertility and immortality. Mohammed taught that the pomegranate would rid the soul of evil. It was used as a wedding motif when Arthur married Catherine, but when Henry VIII, who married her after his brother's death, divorced her, it became a political device. Mary, Catherine's daughter, used the pomegranate as a symbol in memory of her mother. None of the English symbolic uses for flowers and fruit, Ronald King recalls in *The Connoisseur's Complete Period Guides,* recommends the pomegranate as a happy domestic decoration. But there is a reassuring window in a Suffolk church that shows it along with the inscription: "Quod Deus junxit homo non separet," popularly translated as, "Whom God has joined together, let no man put asunder."

This pillow cover was intended for decorative use in a bed-chamber, possibly only for special occasions. Pillow covers remained in fashion until bed hangings done in polychrome embroidery in crewels (woolen yarns) became popular, replacing the more delicate blackwork. In the pillow cover shown here the ground fabric is a fine, plain-woven linen. The embroidery is a combination of heavy gold needlework in braid-like and buttonholed stitches and delicate threadcounted fillings in geometric designs. Fillings and outlines were made in black silk. This embroidery is entirely black (the fillings and outlines were made in black silk) except for the metal passing threads used for the gold embroidery. The size of the area shown in the photograph is approximately thirteen by fifteen inches.

PILLOW COVER
England; late 16th century,
the area shown here measures
13 in. x 15 in.
the entire pillow measures
28½ in. x 19 in.

The geometric filling stitches of the petals and leaves were worked first, because once the goldwork was in place it would have added stiffness and relief to the ground, and the embroidery process would have been more difficult. These black geometric filling patterns were made by counting the threads of the ground fabric and making small running stitches over one or more threads of the ground to form the designs. Some of the most interesting of these threadcounted designs are diagrammed here. The patterns that have larger repeats were used, in general, for the larger shapes. Small patterns were used for small, broken, or more complicated shapes. A single motif may contain more than one filling pattern. If you examine the petals of the rose you will see that three filling patterns appear on the five petals.

Five different stitches were used in making the gold portions of the embroidery. Their position on the original piece can be determined by examining the coded diagram on page 36. In general, Ceylon stitch was used to build up long, narrow shapes. Buttonholed couching was used for borders and small shapes. Small circles were filled with woven wheels. The diagram shows that fancy couching was used in a few places, such as in leaves. This odd handling of couching was done with gold threads couched with black silk; the couching stitches slant alternately left and right with some space left between the couched rows. A couched line was used for the veins of some of the leaves, which were defined with two strands of gold thread twisted and couched into place with black silk.

Contemporary adaptation

As this design was worked originally on the blackwork pillow cover it was taken from, it was an exacting embroidery to make; the tiny threadcounted fillings must have been somewhat taxing to the eyes. However, the elegance of this

*For transferring purposes,
this is all of the design
you will need. In comparing
this section
of the pillow cover
with the photograph, notice
that even though
the pomegranate is not
complete in the original,
the diagram gives
the entire repeat.*

The numbers appearing in certain sections of this diagram correspond to the numbered embroidery patterns on page 37. When you begin to work an area of the embroidery, locate the numbered pattern that corresponds with the section to be embroidered and work the area in that pattern.

Ceylon

Detached buttonhole

Fancy couching

Couching

Woven wheels

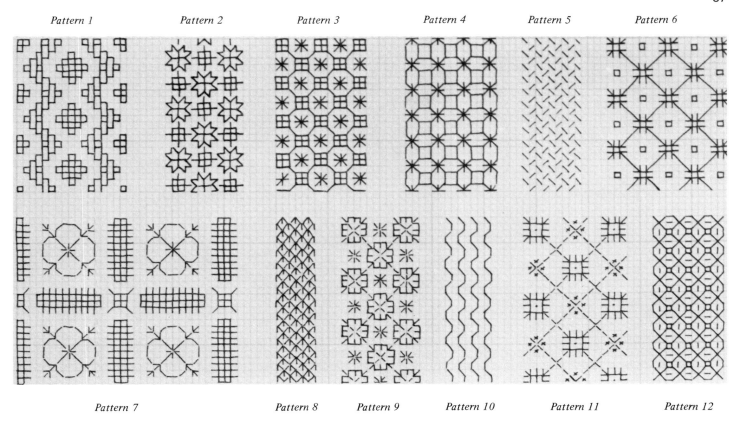

Pattern 7 *Pattern 8* *Pattern 9* *Pattern 10* *Pattern 11* *Pattern 12*

The accompanying legend indicates which stitches are to be used in the shaded areas of the diagram.

needlework tempts one to seek a less demanding alternative that will preserve as much as possible the integrity of this type of embroidery.

Because even a simplified version of the threadcounted black filling patterns used in this kind of needlework will be fairly intricate, even-weave linen, which permits threadcounting with relative ease, is recommended, although its texture is considerably coarser than that of the original ground. (See M&T.) You should try out the various filling designs on the fabric you have chosen so that you can determine what the scale of the design will be on the material you propose to use. If the design cannot be repeated at least four times in the area where you want to use it, you probably should choose another filling pattern with a smaller repeat.

To begin work on the needlework panel transfer the simpler of the two diagrams shown here to the ground you have selected. The shaded diagram is intended to be used only as a code to tell you which stitches should be used for the gold embroidery. Dressmakers' carbon or sugar solution should be satisfactory for the transfer, which should be made delicately and carefully. The threadcounted geometric fillings should be embroidered first in black silk floss. Mercerized cotton can be substituted for silk, but if silk can

be acquired it makes a much richer embroidery. The fillings should be worked in running and double running stitches. The gold embroidery can be duplicated without undue difficulty. Use the coded diagram to find the location of the various stitches. Directions for stitches can be found in the Stitch Directory at the back of the book.

This English blackwork design is typical of many similar ones that were used for both furnishing and costume, and it remains appropriate for both. For ease in working, the design can be enlarged slightly without losing its look of authenticity. This design, omitting the threadcounted fillings, could be adapted for use in woolen embroidery. An unusual variation might be made by enlarging the design and using appliqué of black-printed fabrics in place of the threadcounted fillings, then embroidering the outlines and gold-embroidered areas of the original in more casual-looking threads. Most of the stitches used in the original gold embroidery can be rendered attractively in substantial woolen or linen threads.

Man's cap

ladder stitch in gold/England

From about 1580 until 1650 the nightcap was a popular fashion for men in England. With its heavily decorated incrustations it was obviously not intended to be worn while sleeping; for night wear a plain kitted cap called a biggin was worn. Nightcaps were intended for indoor wear during social hours at home. They were worn by men of all ranks and ages. That older professional men and people of rank wore them is evidenced by their appearance in numerous portraits of such individuals, but nightcaps seem to have been the choice of younger men as well. In 1629 an Oxford student paid 17s. 6d. for one, a high price; and an effigy of a six-year-old shows that he, too, is wearing a nightcap.

The nightcaps of the period, from the time of Elizabeth I until shortly after the death of Charles I, have great similarity to one another, and in their embroidery they do not differ greatly from women's coifs, the female equivalent of the nightcap. The example here is distinguished by the extreme simplicity of its motifs and the richness of its raised embroidery. Most men's nightcaps seem to have been blackwork. Many had the same type of coiling stem and flower design seen on the pillow cover on page 34, except that on the caps the scale of the design was smaller.

An entire cap was cut from a single piece of cloth and had four petal-shaped sections that were joined to mold the crown. The band was not made separately but was embroidered on the reverse side of the piece in such a way that when it was turned up the design was positioned correctly to correspond with the top part of the cap. The example shown here was made of fine but substantial linen of plain weave and was embroidered in silk and metal passing threads (metal strip over fiber core). The linen ground fabric, with the design marked on it, was mounted in an embroidery frame, and the padding for each petal on the outside of the cap was cut and sewn into place before the piece was embroidered. Over the padding the petals were embroidered in gold thread in buttonholed couching, and the heavy coiling stems were worked in ladder stitch in gold thread and outlined in stem stitch in black silk floss. Petal outlines and short stems were also made in stem stitch with black silk floss. Small gold spangles speckle the background of the design. Each spangle was sewn on with

MAN'S CAP
England; late 16th century,
measures 7½ in.
from turned-up band to peak
and has a 22-in. headband.

two stitches of yellow silk floss; each stitch started at the center hole of the spangle and ended at the outer edge in such a way that a straight line was made across the spangle. The band was edged with gold bobbin lace and decorated with dangling spangles. From turned-up band to peak this cap measures seven and one half inches; it has a twenty-two-inch headband.

Contemporary adaptation

This pattern could be embroidered using only the design of the coiling stems marked on the ground, but in working them a double line is needed as a guide to keep the width of the stems even. The petal motif is essentially the same all over the work, and a suitable padding for the petals could be cut from gold-colored felt. Make sure that the size and shape of the padding for each petal is approximately the same. The padding and spangles and the black outlines and short stems could be placed by eye once the drawing for the gold embroidery has been made. Short stems, coils, and padding should be finished before the gold embroidery is made. The spangles should be put on last. A nice alternative to the gold bobbin lace edging used on the original would be an edging crocheted in gold thread.

To make a hat pattern in the correct size, measure the circumference of the head that is to wear it, and also measure across the top of the head from one side to the other, beginning and ending the measurement at the points where the lower edge of the headband should be. On layout or tracing paper draw a line one-quarter inch longer than the measured circumference of the head. Draw another line parallel to this lower line at a distance that measures half the length of the overhead measurement plus one inch. Connect the upper and lower lines at each end to make a rectangle. Then, either by measuring and marking (the preferable method) or by cutting and folding, divide the longer dimension of the rectangle into eighths. Measure two and one-half or three inches up from the lower edge of the rectangle and make a dotted line parallel to the lower line. This dotted line will be used as a guide in making the petal shapes at the top of the pattern. If the pattern has been folded into eighths all the petals can be cut at the same time with one snip of the scissors, but if a more precise pattern is wanted an appropriate curve should be drawn (see the accompanying diagram) and used to cut each petal separately. To make the petals use either a tracing of the curve laid under the pattern or a template cut to shape.

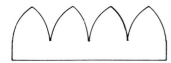
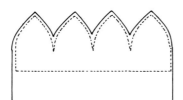

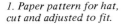

1. Paper pattern for hat, cut and adjusted to fit.

2. The paper pattern (dotted-line shape) has been laid over the ground and the fabric has been cut, allowing for a seam all around the shape and an extra allowance for the brim of the hat (the extra fabric along the straight side of the pattern).

3. On the original cap the embroidery for the band was positioned as it is shown here, and the brim embroidery was worked on the reverse side of the ground fabric. The brim was then turned up so that the embroidery was in position, and the brim was sewn into place.

4. There is another way that the brim can be made so that it can be embroidered without having to turn the ground fabric. Note the positioning of the brim embroidery in this diagram as compared to the diagram for the original. In making the brim, the ground is turned up once and is then turned back on itself; the edges are sewn under the brim.

At this point the pattern should be cut out, taped together, and tried on for size. It may be necessary to adjust the pattern two or three times before you achieve a satisfactory shape. In taping the pattern the edges should be carefully butted, and no seam allowances should be made because these will be added later. When the fit is correct, carefully cut the tape apart and trace the pattern onto a sheet of wrapping or other heavy paper. Draw a line parallel to and five inches below the bottom line, which represents the headband. This five-inch-deep area will serve as the brim and brim lining. Then draw a five-eighths-inch seam allowance around the entire pattern.

The pattern you have made can be traced with basting stitches onto the fabric from which

the cap is to be made (see M&T, velvet transfer), but it should not be permanently drawn on the fabric with lead pencil or ink, and the pattern should not be cut out. Much embroidery tends to draw up the ground fabric. Mounting the work in a frame will minimize this shrinkage, but you can guard against the possibility of making a cap that is too small by not permanently marking or cutting the pattern until the embroidery is complete. If you find that the fabric has drawn up you can compensate by slightly extending the motifs to enlarge the embroidery. Carefully inspect the photograph of this cap and notice that the embroidery design does not closely follow the shape of the cut pattern. Most of the caps and coifs of the period have this characteristic, which indicates that the needlework was completed before the pattern

5. There are two ways of constructing the cap, depending on whether the embroidery for the brim has been worked on the reverse of the ground (A) or on the same side as the embroidery for the crown (B). In both of the diagrammed versions (A and B) a indicates the unembroidered area at the base of the crown, b is the brim band, c is the facing, and d is the hem allowance. Wherever the embroidery for the cap is on the reverse side of the ground it has been drawn with dotted lines. Both versions, A and B, look essentially the same when they are completed; but in version B the brim face is turned up as a hem on the inside of the cap, while in version A the brim band is turned up as a hem on the outside of the cap. In version B the hem should be slightly wider and

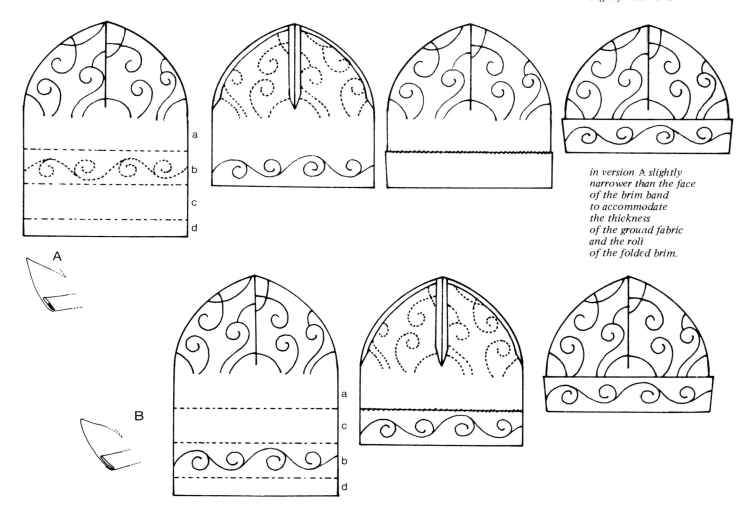

in version A slightly narrower than the face of the brim band to accommodate the thickness of the ground fabric and the roll of the folded brim.

*This diagram
for the cap petals is
slightly larger
than the original, so
you may need to reduce or
enlarge it to fit the size
of cap you are making.
(See M&T for changing scale.)
Each petal of the cap
is embroidered
following this same design.
As the original
photograph shows,
this pattern does not
connect over the entire cap.
After the cap
is sewn together, the seams
are covered
with gold ladder stitch.*

for the cap was cut from it. By making the embroidery somewhat larger than you expect will be necessary you can avoid some fitting problems. Notice that the cut-off edges of the embroidery design as it was used in the original are neatly finished with wide rows of ladder stitch worked over the joined sections of the crown.

Old nightcaps generally were worked on linen that was the same on both sides. The embroidery for the crown was made on one side, and the embroidery for the headband was made on the other; thus it was necessary to remount the piece in the frame when the fabric was turned to embroider the headband. It also is possible—and necessary if the cap is made of fabric that is not the same on both sides—to alter the manner of turning the headband so that all the needlework is done on one side of the fabric. In this variation you fold the brim and then work it back on itself, turning the bottom edge under the brim. Therefore, you must allow twice as much depth for the brim, and the embroidery must be worked on the bottom half of the area you have allowed for the brim.

The embroidery diagram for this nightcap should be transferred with carbon or sugar solution onto sturdy linen or other substantial material and then mounted in an embroidery frame. As has been suggested, it may not be necessary to transfer the entire design, but you should notice that each petal has a narrow stem joining it at a certain angle to the scroll nearest it. Each petal has three little spirals at the top and is finished with a spangle. The petal stem, spirals, and spangles can be put in without a transferred guide, but in making the scrolls a carefully transferred double line will be helpful.

After the design has been transferred and the fabric mounted in a frame, the stitching can be made by following the description of the original embroidery, using buttonholed couching for the petals, ladder stitch for the coils, and stem stitch for the outlines and stems (see Stitch Directory). The completed embroidery can then be cut out according to the cap pattern you have made, the seams joined and concealed under ladder stitch embroidery, and the brim turned and hemmed. A fancy edging of bobbin lace, crochet, or braid festooned with spangles can be used to finish the brim edge.

If you made this cap after the original, you could use it for evening wear. It would be an attractive complement to a black velvet theater suit or the richly textured costume look, which today has reached such heights in fashion. It could also be used in the daytime if made of wool for winter or linen for summer. This cap could be made with simpler stitches, perhaps rows of chain stitch or a braid-like stitch such as Cretan or Van Dyke. Ladder stitch, the braid-like stitch of the original scrolls, works best if the threads are stiff. All sorts of variations for the design are possible; felt or suede applique could be combined with chain stitch and tiny punched-out circles of felt or suede in place of the spangles. Satin stitch in wool or silk in a bicolor arrangement could be used with Cretan or Roumanian stitched scrolls.

This design need not be used only for a cap. It is essentially an allover pattern and, as such, is suitable for all sorts of furnishing and costume projects.

Coif

plaited braid stitch in gold/England

color plate, page 106

All but the most impoverished women of the Elizabethan era engaged in the making of needlework garments and home decorations, and it was not until the time of Charles I and the beginning of the Civil War that this busy pursuit diminished. Coifs were a favorite article for domestic embroidery. They were worn when entertaining at home or receiving in bed. They are the equivalent in women's costume to the men's nightcaps. Coifs were made from a single piece of fabric. The shape was peaked at the forehead and was curved at the sides to set away from the face at the temples and to round forward over the ears. A drawstring was held in a casing along the lower edge. Some coifs were edged with lace or braid around the face. Some had a matching triangular piece, attached or separate, that tied under the chin and was worn over the forehead with the point to the back. By the 1640s a coif was often an all-white, lace-trimmed affair, carefully fitted to the head and without drawstrings.

The coif had come into fashion in the first half of the sixteenth century, when it was frequently worn under a peaked hood (said to be gabled or pedimented). It was also worn under a fur hat that had ear flaps. Although all sorts of women's indoor and outdoor headgear existed, it was not considered necessary that women have their heads covered. In fact, they often went bareheaded.

The coif shown on these pages is a late sixteenth-century model intended for indoor wear. The usual motif of coifs is floral, with the designs compartmented in scrolling stems or a diamond-shaped framework. The embroidery stitches varied, although the buttonholed couching, seen in this example, was popular. Other techniques used for coifs were cutwork embroidery, in which patterns were cut out of the ground fabric as part of the decoration, and openwork embroideries, in which lacy effects were created by taking threads out of the ground fabric or by opening holes by pushing threads out of their normal alignment. Another type of coif showed flowers that had quite natural shading effects. This shading was usually accomplished by "speckling"—that is, by making tiny running or back stitches at varying distances from one another, thereby creating with the variation a lighter or darker "gray" effect in the flowers.

The floral motifs used in the embroidery of coifs often were copied from herbal or pattern books. In the sixteenth and seventeenth centuries pattern books came mainly from France and Italy, but they were also published in Germany and England. Pattern books were never so widely used in England as they were on the continent. The exception was Shorleyker's *Schole-howse for the needle,* published in 1624. Among the herbals used in England was *Catalogus plantarum* (Catalog of Plants), published in 1542 by Konrad von Gesner, a German-Swiss naturalist.

In the sixteenth century the flower garden was a new development. Prior to that time gardening was limited to edibles, although some flowering plants, such as borage, were used commonly in salads. During Elizabeth's reign botanical gardens were established, and although English gardens were nothing like the Parisian gardens, in which rare varieties of flowers were raised with the particular interest of the embroidery designer in mind (see page 124), they did arouse curiosity about the characteristics of given species. Pansies and strawberries, easily recognizable flowers when embroidered but smaller than present-day varieties, appear in the design of the coif shown here.

The coif has a repeated pattern of coils in plaited braid stitch worked with metal thread. Plaited braid stitch is ineffective in softer material and shows to best advantage in wiry metal thread. Gold embroidery threads came from many places. Old records of supply purchases frequently indicate the origin of this precious material. From medieval times Cyprian gold had been exported from the Levant. Damask gold—the name originating from the ancient silk-producing city of Damascus but also indicating a principal technique in which the material was used—was another variety of metal embroidery thread. Gold threads were made in Italy, Spain, the Rhineland, and England. Although used extravagantly, the worth of gold thread was not underestimated. Unfortunately, many embroideries were destroyed to retrieve the gold, and embroideries that had no precious metal threads stood a better chance of survival.

In the coif shown here, gold passing thread was used for chain stitch accents, and bullion

COIF
*England; late 16th or
early 17th century,
20 in. x 9 in.*

This diagram shows
the entire repeat, which
is placed
across the 9-in. width
of the coif. In
transferring this pattern,
repeat it as often
as necessary
to cover entirely the
shape you are making.
(See M&T
for changing scale.)

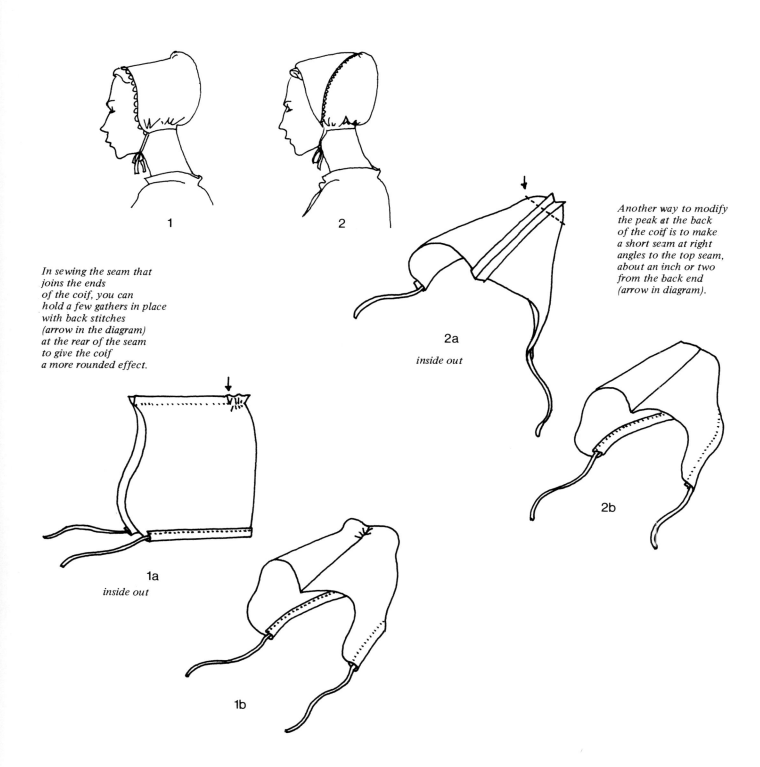

In sewing the seam that joins the ends of the coif, you can hold a few gathers in place with back stitches (arrow in the diagram) at the rear of the seam to give the coif a more rounded effect.

Another way to modify the peak at the back of the coif is to make a short seam at right angles to the top seam, about an inch or two from the back end (arrow in diagram).

1

2

2a

inside out

1a

inside out

1b

2b

knots represented stamens. (Investigation shows that in other needleworks braid-like "stitches" were sometimes worked independently of the ground and applied later.) The remainder of the embroidery (everything except the coils and knots) was worked in silk buttonholed couching. No attempt was made to create effects of shading in flowers or fruits, either with color or by the direction of the stitch. All stitches were couched in straight parallel rows. The colors are clear and bright (see the color plate for this piece on page 106), but the red was softened by threading the needle with one strand of taupe thread and one of red silk floss. This coif, like many similar to it, measures twenty by nine inches.

Contemporary adaptation

This design can be transferred to linen with dressmakers' carbon, transfer pencil, or sugar solution. (See M&T.) The silk portion of the embroidery can be worked in a hand hoop, but the gold work can be made only if the ground fabric is mounted securely in an embroidery frame. Work should begin with the colored silk embroidery. Use the colors of the original (see the color plate) or invent your own color scheme. Because embroidery tends to draw up the ground fabric, the overall shape should not be cut or permanently marked before the needlework is completed. Making the gold plaited braid stitch coils should be the last step in the procedure. Plaited braid stitch is beautiful, but it requires a very stiff thread, and some practice is needed before you will be able to keep all the loops of the braid the same size. Ladder stitch is sometimes found in old embroideries of this type. It is a good substitute if plaited braid cannot be worked in a satisfactory way with the thread you have on hand. Broad coils can also be made by combining stitches. If you are using a thread other than gold, Van Dyke stitch with a row of chain stitch at each side looks quite rich. Cretan, herringbone, and Roumanian stitches, possible substitutes, are simpler than Van Dyke with rows of chain stitch.

The woman's coif was a remarkably comfortable, attractive, and becoming cap for a woman, and was especially well suited to the coiled hair arrangements fashionable during the sixteenth century. The triangle worn over the coif has been very popular with today's girls and young women. For any woman who does not object to looking completely feminine the coif itself would be just as suitable. It is also an exquisite shape for little girls.

The shape of the coif, as you can see in the photograph, is basically rectangular. The short ends of the rectangle are cut in a gentle S-curve. The outward-pointing ends of this curve are brought together. They form a point that is worn in the middle of the forehead. In making the seam that joins these ends you can pull in a few gathers at the back of the hat and secure them at that end of the seam by making a few back stitches. These gathers will serve to round the crown so that it will not be as pointed as it would be without them. Another way to modify the peak at the back is to make a short seam at right angles to the top seam about an inch or two from the back end. The lower edge of the cap is hemmed to make a casing for a drawstring to be tied under the chin, or a facing can be added to the lower edge if the top fabric is bulky. In either case, the finished cap should measure nine inches by twenty inches.

The allover pattern of fruits and flowers on this coif could be used for numerous other costume and furnishing projects, either in the scale shown, enlarged, or possibly even reduced. The design could be rendered in blackwork, woolen (crewel), or colored silk embroidery. Enlarged, this pattern would serve for cushion covers, upholstery, or bedcovers.

Beaded basket

applied motifs/England

color plate, page 107

Beading was one of the popular needlework diversions of the seventeenth century. It was used to decorate boxes, mirror frames, bags, and numerous small articles, but it was at its prettiest and most fanciful in wire baskets of the type shown here. These baskets are thought to have been used for displaying layettes and possibly were made as gifts for the new mother. Made from the same patterns used for boxes and jewel caskets worked in raised embroidery, or stumpwork, beaded baskets were even less functional than were their embroidered counterparts, but they were admirably ornamental.

In time the vigorous design of beading of the type seen here gave way to a more delicate variety. In the eighteenth century greater refinement of design became possible as glass production improved and beads "as small as a grain of sand" (sablé) were made.

The basket shown here is not unusual in shape; several baskets in other museum collections have the same shape and placement of lobed handles that this one has. The bottom of this basket measures ten and one-half by thirteen inches. The flaring sides are four inches high, and the top measures eleven by fifteen inches. The basket stands on a flaring pedestal, one and one-half inches high, that measures eleven by fifteen inches at the base. The basket was constructed of heavy, rigid wire, with joints made by bending one wire around the other. These bulky joints are covered with sprigs of flowers and leaves or little rosettes (notice the corners of the basket). The long sides of the basket are divided into five sections, the short sides into three sections, and the bottom into twelve sections. A latticework of green beaded wire fills the spaces. Each division of the sides and bottom has an applied motif: strolling figures, ladies and gentlemen on horseback, flowers or birds. In the center of the bottom of the basket there are figures of a man and woman. They are surrounded by a lion, leopard, stag, musicians, a fountain, and a swan in a pond—all familiar motifs in the needlework of the day. These motifs were constructed of beads sewn onto a molded cardboard base with heavy linen thread. The finished motifs were painted gold on the back and then were sewn or wired into place on the frame.

The beaded basket was prepared by wrapping the wire frame with beads strung onto fine wire. Beads of each color were threaded onto the wire in quantities large enough to wind around the heavier wire of the basket frame three times. The color sequence is unusual and beautiful, and while it can be seen in the color plate on page 107, the sequence is listed here for the convenience of anyone who may want to duplicate it.

1. translucent white
2. transparent brown
3. transparent amber
4. transparent crystal
5. transparent dark green
6. transparent lighter green
7. translucent white
8. opaque medium blue
9. opaque lighter blue
10. translucent medium green
11. translucent lighter green
12. translucent pale green
13. translucent white
14. translucent rust
15. translucent crystal
16. translucent medium yellow
17. translucent lighter yellow
18. translucent lime
19. translucent white
20. transparent dark blue
21. translucent medium blue
22. transparent crystal
    repeat

BEADED BASKET
England; 1645,
bottom measures
10½ in. x 13 in.,
sides are 4 in. high,
and top measures
11 in. x 15 in.

After the wire frame was neatly wrapped, latticework was made to fill the open spaces of the basket. Doubled wires were hung onto the frame at regular intervals, each length about twice as long as the height of the space to be filled. Enough beads were strung onto each of these wires to cover it for the length necessary to reach a wire of the adjacent pair; each wire moved diagonally toward the other until they met. When two wires met they were threaded through a slightly larger bead, then each was bent diagonally back to a point directly under the point from which it started, and the process was repeated. Wires at the outer edges of the areas were wrapped around the frame. (See accompanying diagram.)

Flower sprays and rosettes positioned at joints were made by threading beads on wires and bending the wires into petal shapes. Several petal shapes then were gathered together onto a stem of wire that had a bead "flower center" twisted onto it. Leaves were made with beads sewn on cloth and were wired onto the frame at appropriate places. Berries were made over a little padded cushion, which was made by gathering the two longer sides of a small rectangular

strip of fabric and securing them tightly with needle and thread, stuffing the little case with wadding, and then sewing the short ends together to form a ball. Beading then could be worked over this form in buttonhole stitch, one bead strung into each stitch.

Contemporary adaptation

Duplication of this basket would require a wire frame especially made for the project. To make such a frame is not impossible, and a needleworker then would be able to produce a very good replica of one of the more whimsical artistic efforts of the seventeenth century. With the measurements previously given and the accompanying photograph as a guide, a craftsman could construct a copy of this basket's framework. However, beaded motifs could also be applied to a more easily attainable framework, such as a reed basket. Occasionally a kit in a crafts shop contains an open type of metal or plastic picture frame that would serve nicely as a base for your beadwork. A revamped wire dish drainer with some of the wires sawn out also would make a suitable frame. An even simpler solution would be to construct a frame from wire circles of the type intended for wreath-making.

Probably most needleworkers will be more interested in using these small figures for projects other than the making of a basket. The little motifs can be used for any of the projects for which such designs were originally used; beading can decorate a frame, a box, and a handbag among other things. These beaded motifs also would make charming Christmas tree ornaments.

To make the small motifs shown on the basket, begin by picking out some detailed area of one design and, with the beads collected for

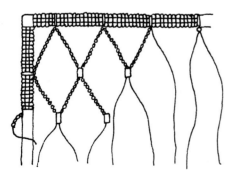

This diagram shows how the frame was wrapped with beads and how the lattice structure for the basket was constructed.

*Although not all
of the motifs on the basket
have been shown
in this diagram,
the more interesting ones
are presented. The dotted
lines represent the way
in which the beads were
worked in any one section
of a figure.
(See M&T for changing scale.)*

the project, work by eye to duplicate the design. Because the size of the beads will determine the size of the finished motif, transferring the design to cloth is pointless. The beads should be sewn with back stitches onto a piece of cloth. The fabric can be held in tension in a hand hoop if it seems probable that the entire motif will fit onto the portion of cloth that will be held firmly within the hoop. If the motif is too large to be contained within the hoop, then the ground fabric should be mounted in a frame. (See M&T.)

Some of the motifs have been diagrammed to give you some idea of how the beads have been arranged. Solid lines indicate areas that have different colors; dotted lines indicate rows of beads of like color and show the direction of the row. Consult the color plate on page 107 for the original color schemes, or invent your own. In the original the eyes, noses, mouths, and other small accents were put in with embroidery stitches. Finished motifs should be cut out of the ground fabric. Leave a sufficiently large margin all around the work for a hem. Hemmed motifs should be tacked with small stitches to a piece of bristol board or other good, white, heavy paper, and the paper trimmed to

conform to the edges of the design. Then the entire construction should be wrapped in a damp towel, put in a plastic bag, if desired, and left to moisten for several hours. The slightly damp, but not wet, motif can then be shaped so that it is slightly convex; then it should be allowed to dry thoroughly. If necessary, the paper can be retrimmed after the motif has dried, and the back can be painted. The motif is now ready for application to a larger construction. If it is to be used as a Christmas tree ornament, it can be paired with another motif made in the same design, but reversed, and the two then can be sewn together to make a presentable three-dimensional ornament.

The designs shown here are as well suited to embroidery as to beading. They can be used for woolen or cotton embroidery or felt appliqué. Two motifs, one the reverse of the other, could be padded and joined to make a small toy for an infant.

Framed looking glass

stumpwork/England

Mirrors with embroidered frames were made as early as Elizabeth I's time. They were the domestic needlewoman's version of the elaborately framed looking glasses that in professional hands were rendered in marquetry, silver repoussé, enamel, or tortoise shell. For use with embroidery a favored choice was tortoise shell, whether genuine or a japanned and lacquered imitation. Shops of the time sold designs on white satin intended to be embroidered as pictures, looking glass frames, coverings for work boxes, and other small articles. Mirror frames of various shapes were made. The shape of the one shown on page 54 is not unusual; others almost identical to it exist. The modification of its contour design along the lower edge is a clear clue to its use as a standing mirror for a dressing table.

The embroidery surrounding this beveled oval mirror was worked on white silk with a satin weave in silk floss; other threads were used to enrich the texture and heighten effects of "realism." Individual motifs for embroideries like this one were selected from pattern books and spotted, or positioned appropriately, to make a pleasing composition. One of the favorite sources for animal designs was *Historia animalium* (History of Animals), four volumes published by Konrad von Gesner between 1551 and 1558. Almost without exception the embroiderers planned *horror vacui* arrangements (compositions with motifs that left no vacant spaces but, rather, evenly filled the entire available area).

This looking glass embroidery includes some areas rendered in what is now popularly called stumpwork. The stump, or stamp, referred to is the molded form over which some parts of the embroidery, which are raised in various ways, is worked. Mary, Queen of Scots, who busied the time of her imprisonment with needlework, indicates in a letter that she made stumpwork; at least once she anxiously awaited "moulds to come from France." The idea of making relief embroideries was not new and may have been introduced into England from Italy or Spain. English ecclesiastical embroidery made after the great period of *opus anglicanum* (thirteenth and fourteenth centuries) has raised gold effects along with silk embroidery, but the term "stumpwork" is never attached to them. In the *Catalogue of English Domestic Embroidery,* John L. Nevinson points out that Lady Marion Alford's reference to "embroidery on the stamp" in her *Needlework as Art* (published in 1886) is the earliest use of a comparable term. It has been assumed that Queen Mary's "moulds" and other carved wooden bases for the raised embroidery gave stumpwork its name.

The playful spirit of the raised and padded embroideries made in the seventeenth century makes it difficult to correlate them with sophisticated professional church embroidery that shows sculptural effects. Some writers believe that the type of raised embroidery used for this looking glass was the work of young girls, and that objects made in the technique were the virtuoso performances of children. The toy-like quality of the work would tend to substantiate this view, but in fact some of these needleworks were the efforts of many years' endeavor. A stumpwork casket—a workbox or storage box with several compartments—in the collection of the Art Institute of Chicago has a known history. Its maker, Rebecca Stonier Plaisted, worked on it for twenty years. Its top compartment is fitted out like the ballroom of a doll house, but it was not the work of a child.

Some of the motifs of stumpwork embroidery of this time are symbolic. The unicorn was the device of James I. Charles I and his Henrietta Marie appear in countless embroideries, many of them made after his execution. The caterpillar

LOOKING GLASS
*England; 17th century,
overall measurement
16½ in. x 20 in.*

↑

*Some of the leaves
on this embroidered frame
are made in pairs—
for example, those
in the trees on the right
and left at the top
of the frame.
One leaf of the pair is made
in long and short stitch
on the ground fabric
(the leaf has long and short
strokes in the diagram).
The second leaf is worked
in detached buttonhole
stitch and is not attached
to the ground (as you can
see in the photograph)
toward the tip.
The unattached leaf adds
to the relief effect
of the frame. An
attaching row of buttonhole
stitches may be made
at the central rib
of the top leaf, or only
a few stitches may be
used to join the two leaves
at a common point
on a stem (note the arrow
in the diagram).*

and the butterfly are Charles's symbols. The oak tree and acorn are emblems of Charles II, and this mirror frame shows him with Catherine of Braganza, his Portuguese wife. Both of these royal couples always appear in stumpwork embroidery wearing the costumes of their day, although in many of the compositions they appear as actors in a biblical play.

It is interesting to observe that the leopard and stag on this mirror frame are exactly the same in design as those on the beaded basket shown on page 51. The designs probably come from the same source. The little animals were individually embroidered in tent stitch on linen and afterward applied to the satin ground of the mirror frame. Separately made motifs of this kind were called slips. Occasionally an uncut piece of fabric embroidered with a group of unused slips is mistaken for a sampler. It was necessary to make the animals that appear on this mirror as slips, because the tent stitch used to embroider them must be threadcounted and cannot be worked on satin. In addition, the slips could not be worked directly on the satin because a little padding was to be put under the slips as they were applied to the satin in order to give them a raised effect.

The overall measurement of this frame is sixteen and one-half by twenty inches. The satin ground was probably backed with linen for stability, since the work would have to be mounted into an embroidery frame. When the work was finished, it was stretched on a shaped wooden mirror frame; the edges of the frame were then covered with rose-colored velvet ribbon. A braid outline covered the edge next to the mirror.

The color schemes and stitches for the motifs are as follows.

Charles II. Rose trousers were worked in buttonhole stitch. They button with seed pearls and have salmon-colored ruffles made in detached buttonhole stitch. The mantle is shaded from pink to maroon. Its lining, worked in darned silk pile to look like ermine, is cream and black. The collar is ivory, worked in detached buttonhole stitch. The boots are shades

*Most of the motifs
on the stumpwork frame are
presented in this diagram.
If you want to change
the scale of any of these
motifs, check the M&T
section at the back
of the book
for the proper procedure.*

of brown. The scepter is gold purl. The hillock is silk pile in shades of green. The faces of both figures are satin tinted with watercolor and are slightly padded. The features were worked in small straight stitches and couching. The hands are wire wrapped with silk thread. Both crowns are appliquéd in rose-colored silk with designs in yellow silk cord.

Catherine. This figure was worked in satin and long and short stitches. The dress is pale rose, yellow, and green on white. Couched outlines surround the flower motifs of the dress design: red around pinks, yellows and dark greens around the leaves. The queen's curls were made of stretched, blonde-tinted purl that now has dulled. Her collar is buttonhole stitch with a looped edge to represent lace. The underskirt showing at the center of her dress is shaded blue with a trim of cream-colored cording. The brown rabbit next to Catherine was worked separately in fine petit point (tent stitch). The outlines of the rabbit are red couched in tan.

Trees and houses. In the upper right and left trees, the fruits are shaded rose to yellow and worked in buttonhole stitch. The leaves are shaded in blue, rose, and white, or in white, yellow, and green. The tree trunks are red and gold. Each leaf was worked twice, once on the ground fabric in long and short stitch and again directly over the first leaf in detached buttonhole stitch; the attaching few stitches are at the base of the leaf. The upper leaves curl, revealing the ones beneath. (See accompanying sketch on page 55.) Outlines around the fruits and trunks of the trees were made with a tightly twisted silk thread in red or gold and were couched into place. The grassy hillocks were couched in frisé, a thread much used in the seventeenth century to represent grass and foliage.

The top center tree was worked in the same way as the others. The shaded clouds near the tree are blue, and were worked in long and short stitch. The houses, whose windows are made of small pieces of mica, were embroidered in long and short stitch. The shrubbery is tiny loops of purl, painted pink, yellow, and green. A tiny man and woman appear in the doorways of the houses.

Lion and stag. These two animals were done separately on fine linen in brown and black silk in tent stitch. They were applied to the ground over padding, and their raw edges are concealed under red silk cord couched in tan. Birds and insects surrounding the lion and stag were worked in yellow, blue, and rose silk in long and short stitch; the blue outlines were done in outline and stem stitch. The striped leaves on the birds' trees are combinations of rose and white, dark and light green, yellow and browns, and three blues.

Grotto. In the grotto at the bottom of the frame, the waves are shaded blue in silk cord. The "land" is frisé in green; the grotto is purl in browns and dark reds. The padded fish in the water, difficult to see in the photograph but clearly visible in the diagram, was worked in dulled silver in double buttonhole stitch in tightly twisted thread and was outlined in blue. The larger flower sprays shaded in blue to green to yellow were made by overcasting a thick thread with finer silk. The large flowers above the leopard and stag were made in shades of blue and rose in purl. The butterfly is yellow, brown, white, and rose, and the snail is yellow, brown, and white.

Contemporary adaptation

As originally worked, most domestic needleworks of the seventeenth century were pastiches put together from this source and that, so it is not illogical to reassemble the motifs according to preference. For instance, Charles and Catherine might be left out of this composition and two riders from the beaded basket (page 49) substituted to make a less political arrangement.

Embroidery of the type shown here is essentially collage. Materials no longer available need not necessarily be imitated in making a substitution. Bullion stitch or French knots can stand in for frisé and purl.

To make an embroidery-framed mirror like this one you need a mirror with a frame that has sufficient flat front area to accommodate some needlework. A composition to decorate the frame should be worked out, using small motifs from the looking glass shown on page 54 or from other similar embroideries in the book. The usual seventeenth-century English composition was entirely filled with a variety of people, animals, birds, and fragments of landscape. When you have decided on the arrangement, transfers can be made. Sugar solution is suggested for the transfers. (See M&T.) The white satin ground fabric should be stretched over linen in an embroidery frame. Since you must stretch the fabric around the mirror frame later, allow an amount of overage in measuring for the satin.

Embroidery should be worked according to the description of the original, but substitutions may be made where needed or desired. When the needlework has been finished, the looking glass frame can be covered. Attach a layer or two of white flannel or felt to the frame with wheat paste and trim it to size. The satin with its linen underlayer is then stretched over the frame and tacked or stapled along the sides. The way that the edge next to the mirror is finished will depend on the construction of the frame. In the one shown the satin was clipped and covered with braid. The raw edges of satin along the sides of the frame were covered with rose-colored velvet ribbon. For a modern version of the mirror frame, braid or ribbon can be sewn, glued, or tacked into place. Some braids are dense enough to allow tacks or staples to be hidden under the threads. Glue should be avoided as much as possible in mounting needleworks; removal of the glued fabric will be difficult if you want to remount your work, and glue will ruin the portion of the fabric to which it is applied. Sewing is the best method of joining, but wheat paste can be used when sewing is impractical.

Adam and Eve

silk and metal embroidery/England

One of the effects of the Reformation in England was the strengthening of adherence to the second commandment, which forbids worship of devotional images. In needlework, Christ, the Virgin, and the saints were avoided, and subjects from the Old Testament replaced them. Moreover, Thomas Digges had introduced in England the writings of Copernicus, which were completed in 1543 and dealt with the position and movements of earth, other planets, and the moon in relation to the sun. The Copernican theory initiated a new scientific outlook that made it necessary to find a place for God within the order of the cosmic system. New understanding of universal order increased men's confidence in their own power even as it forced them, as Arnold Hauser writes in *The Social History of Art* (Volume 2), to consider themselves as "tiny, insignificant factor[s] in the new disenchanted world." Ethical concepts, the senses, the elements, and the seasons now became popular subject matter.

Inspiration for embroidery could be found in many sources. There were pattern books, of course, but bestiaries, herbals, zoological texts, and Bibles were more popular sources. Schedel's *Chronicle of the World* has among its woodcuts a version of Adam and Eve that was much used, but the needlework picture shown on page 61 certainly was based on the frontispiece of the Robert Barker Bible (1602), as a number of still-existing embroideries evidently were. This version of Adam and Eve makes an interesting comparison with an embroidered bible cover made by Ann Cornwalys Legh, now in the Pierpont Morgan Library. Each of the two needleworks is a free adaptation of the Barker Bible frontispiece, but the silk threads of the embroideries have not been forced to imitate the characteristics of the print medium used for the frontispiece. Each embroidery has raised work in some areas, a reminder that stumpwork embroidery, a kind of cloth bas relief (low relief)

sculpture made over padding and molds, continued in vogue through the reign of William and Mary (see page 61). Both the Chicago Art Institute's Adam and Eve and the bible cover from the Morgan Library have low relief passages, and curiously they both have other similarities not shared with the woodcut. But a comparison between the Art Institute's picture and the bible illustration offers convincing proof that the frontispiece was the prototype for the embroidery. Elephants, cattle, horses, lions, leopards, reindeer, bears, hares, and camels have exactly the same poses in both works, and other similarities can also be found. It is noteworthy, too, that the Barker Bible illustration corresponds in several respects to a Venetian version of Adam and Eve published in 1492 in *Bergomensis, supplementum chronicarum.*

The Adam and Eve needlework shown on page 61 was worked on satin-woven silk in split stitch; silk floss was used for most of the figures. (Split stitch made a reappearance in the seventeenth century, after having gone out of use

TEMPTATION
*A drawing
based on the left side
of a woodcut in*
Bergomensis,
supplementum chronicarum,
Venice; 1492.

GARDEN OF EDEN
Frontispiece,
Bishop's Bible, printed
by Robert Barker,
London; 1583.
(Courtesy:
Pierpont Morgan Library)

ADAM AND EVE
Panel, England;
17th century, 8¾ in. x 13½ in.

GARDEN OF EDEN
Bible cover, embroidered
by Anne Cornwalys Legh,
England; 17th century.
(Courtesy:
Pierpont Morgan Library)

*This diagram shows the
entire Adam and Eve panel.
Methods for changing scale
are discussed
in the M&T section
at the back of the book.*

A detail in the center section of the Adam and Eve panel makes a fine embroidery all by itself.

when *opus anglicanum* declined.) Areas worked in metal thread were couched. The snail at the left under the tree was couched gold passing; some of the fish were couched silver, and spangles were used for scales. The sea monster in the right corner is silver, the serpent is gold and silver worked over padding with some threads of a crinkled type called frisé, which are no longer readily available. Adam and Eve were outlined in silk, as were most of the animals, but elephants, cattle, and monkeys were outlined with silver. The tree trunk was made of shaded green frisé. Fruit and leaves are shaded satin stitch. The hillock at Adam's foot was made by couching cord over padding; the shaded green hillock at Eve's foot is darned silk pile—a technique, sometimes referred to as plush stitch, that has gone out of use. The trunk of the tree at the extreme right is shaded silk frise in yellow-green to virdian (bluish green) and has an outline of twisted gold cord. The sun, raised in high relief, is gold thread with a silver cord outline. The cloud is silk in satin stitch shaded yellow to white with a gold cord edge. The moon is couched silver with a silver cord outline, and the stars are silver purl. The rays of the moon are couched gold plate (gold metal strip), with turned edges concealed under a couched gold cord outline. The panel measures eight and three-quarters by thirteen and one-half inches. The general impression of the color is that it is slightly pastel, but natural shades have been used. The stitching is tiny, and the "drawing" with the needle is very fine. Minute vertical stitches that appear in the background are the work of a conservator. These running stitches help to preserve very brittle satin.

Contemporary adaptation

A fine silk embroidery like this one requires a carefully made transfer. Sugar solution or dressmakers' carbon is suggested. (See M&T.) The work should be mounted in a frame with a supporting linen lining to make the delicate silk ground substantial enough for work. Bullion or French knot stitches can be substituted for frisé. Velvety surfaces can be made by knotting threads into the work and clipping them on the front, leaving little pile-like ends. At the time this embroidery was made, much pile embroidery had the appearance of but was not chenille. Bullion stitch can be used to substitute for purl if purl is difficult to obtain.

This design could be enlarged for work in techniques other than the original. It could be worked in crewels (woolen yarn) in the same stitches as those on the original silk version. It also could be worked in linen as a whitework embroidery, using overcasting or Italian cross stitch in the background, a few pattern darned or satin stitch fillings, and some accents of pale color.

Noah's Ark

long-armed cross stitch/Italy

Monochromatic embroideries like the Noah's Ark shown on page 66 are as typical of Italian embroidery as coiling stem-and-flower designs are typical of English needlework. In this Italian border the designs are said to be "in reserve." This means that while the subject matter may be outlined it is not filled with embroidery, and that the background (negative area) is entirely covered with embroidery stitches. Thus the color of the ground fabric becomes the color of the principal motifs (positive areas). In Italian work of this type the ground is invariably fine textured, plain-, or tabby-, woven linen.

Embroideries of the type shown here, the earliest dating from the sixteenth century, were usually made as long bands or borders, and some of them were used as valances. This Noah's Ark is a portion of a border that shows scenes from the Old Testament. The embroidery was worked in green silk floss. In work of this type color was always monochromatic; red, blue, green, brown, or yellow. (Modern pieces done in this technique are sometimes made in a combination of orange and black.) The same design used for this border in the collection of the Art Institute of Chicago was also used for a red one at the Hermitage in Leningrad. The backgrounds of both were embroidered in long-armed cross stitch, which is sometimes called long-legged cross stitch. The technique is a combination of surface stitching and threadcounted embroidery. The outline for this design was freely drawn and worked in back stitch, but the stitches of the background were carefully threadcounted. Long-armed cross stitch differs from plain or Italian cross stitch, both of which are sometimes used for this type of work, in that the overall effect simulates a braided ribbing rather than ranks of small squares or meshes as plain and Italian cross do. Long-armed cross stitch is substantial but economical, because only a minimal amount of thread appears on the back of the work. In this piece a powdering of cross stitches adds a decorative note to the motifs.

It is likely that the original version of this Noah's Ark, like the English embroidery of Adam and Eve seen in the previous example, was made from a woodcut illustration in a bible of that time. Many of the Italian borders of this type deal with Old Testament themes or the Labors of the Months, traditional subjects that suggest book illustrations more strongly than pattern book motifs. However, the compositions also contain tree and flower elements more like those in other textiles than like the foliage in woodcuts.

These Italian borders in which white appears against a dark background strongly suggest the heavy blooms and curling leaves that were being worked in needle lace at the same time. It would be a simple matter to translate the basic design of this embroidery to the lacemaking technique. The fact is that needlework of the type shown was usually only a part of the decoration of a larger assemblage that included lace. (But it should be borne in mind that the laces were usually of a geometric type, reticella or filet.) A great many of the techniques developed for linen embroidery, of which this is only one, were intended for use in conjunction with linen lace, and it is interesting to note how, by various means, they make graceful the transition from densely white linen to boldly open-patterned lace. The type of embroidery seen here is now called Assisi work.

In the course of a nineteenth-century revival of earlier embroideries, the women of Assisi worked on designs copied from needleworks made in their town centuries before and preserved in churches or convents or owned by noble or aristocratic families. The replicas the women made were worked in the traditional colors on linen woven to resemble the fabric of antique prototypes. Frequently, the determinant in distinguishing between older and newer work is the nature of the drawing; in the later embroideries, which were abridged from drawings made from older work, the drawing is much abstracted, sometimes deteriorated.

Italians rarely made all-white embroidery, which was popular in other countries. Marie Schuette in *The Art of Embroidery* (Marie Schuette and Sigrid Muller-Christensen) suggests

NOAH'S ARK
Fragment, Italy;
late 16th
or early 17th century,
16½ in. x 8¾ in.

an explanation: "To the Italian, in the intense light of his climate, work in color comes more naturally than pure white linen embroidery, which reflects back the full glare of the day."

The Noah's Ark seen on these pages measures sixteen and one-half inches by eight and three-quarters inches. It was worked in the traditional fashion: a contour drawing was transferred to linen, and back stitches were made to follow the contour. These stitches were not thread-counted. Then a filling of long-armed cross stitch was worked, the stitches carried horizontally throughout. These stitches were threadcounted. A few decorative cross stitches were added in the white "reserved" areas.

Contemporary adaptation

This embroidery must be worked on a plain-, or tabby-, woven linen that has smooth warp and weft threads of even weight and size. Even-weave, the special linen intended for thread-counted embroideries, would be an ideal choice. A transfer could be made with dressmakers' carbon or sugar solution. (See M&T.) The work can be done in a hand hoop, because it is not necessary to contain the entire pattern within the hoop. While cotton thread could be used, silk floss is recommended. Its sheen and texture produce an incomparably soft embroidery. The

Although you need not transfer the small crosses that appear within motifs, the rest of this diagram should be transferred to a linen that is easily threadcounted. For changing the scale of this design, see the M&T section at the back of the book.

stitches should be worked according to the description of the original.

The illustrative nature of the design limits its use. "Pictures," of course, should not be sat on or draped, so this composition should be used as a wall hanging or framed picture. For a contemporary version, to hang in a window to block an unsightly view, the design could be used as an applique. For a window or as a wall hanging a leno or other open weave background fabric should be lined with a translucent material, possibly organdy, for stability and added opacity. The animals, figures, and flowers could be put on as applique, using white felt or fabric-supported plastic. Embroidery details could be added with linen thread in the same color as the background in chain, stem, back, or couching stitches; the choice would depend on which works best with the applique fabric chosen. Although it would not be necessary to hem or cover the edges of animal, figure, and floral shapes if felt or plastic were used, for the best effect the shapes should be very carefully sewn into position with tiny stitches.

The original technique of this needlework could be used for other compositions in the book. Last Supper (page 9), Adam and Eve (page 61), and the Skyros bed valance (page 153) are but a few.

Strapwork and leaf design

long-armed cross stitch/Italy

Compared to the clearly defined composition of the Noah's Ark (page 66), this Italian altar frontal border appears complex and enigmatic. The design is red-on-white here and white-on-red there. There are no outlines, and the repeats mesh so subtly with one another that the pattern seems continuous. This design is of particular interest because apparently it does not stem from nor imitate any of the graphic or other textile arts but is purely and simply an ingenious use of the peculiarities of threadcounted embroidery.

Vast numbers of white and monochrome-on-white needleworks have been made. (The Last Supper, page 9, was an early version made for ecclesiastical use.) In the sixteenth century, improved linen manufacture gave impetus to the making of white and monochromatic embroideries. Linen undergarments were worn initially in the fifteenth century. At first they were decorated with silk and metal embroidery, but by the end of the century washable white needlework had become standard. No doubt the development of whitework was helped along by such events as the passage of the sumptuary law in Venice in 1535, by which colored silk decoration on household items and clothing were forbidden.

As openwork effects practiced in various types of white embroidery were explored and became more intricate, the groundwork for needle lace was laid. The timetable for the development of white embroidery can be imagined if you know that by 1600 Venice alone had published 100 manuals for lacemaking.

The interlaced strap and leaf design of the altar frontal shown here closely resembles a design published in Venice in 1558 by Mathio Pagan in *La gloria et l'honore dei ponti Tagliati.* Knot patterns had long been a staple of the Islamic-originated weaving designs of Spain and Sicily. In the mid-fifteenth century Islamic metalworkers had settled in Venice and were producing damascened ware that had interlacing patterns. Leonardo da Vinci was interested in designs of this type, and his versions found their way into the hands of Albrecht Dürer, who reproduced some of them in wood engraving. Interestingly, Dürer's engraved pages, like this altar frontal, have corner devices of scrolling leaves.

The pattern shown on these pages combines geometric and curvilinear design. Its composition is compartmentalized with strapwork and leafy branches in lozenges that intrude on one another. The overlapping lozenge arrangement has been a basic design configuration from the earliest times. This design is seen in embroidery, tapestry weaving, and carpets, where, repeated in even the smallest elements in broken form, it looks like small combs or hooks (see Introduction, page VI).

Tucked among the strapwork and foliage of this design are sun and moon motifs that give only the faintest hint of the Italians' love of surprising juxtapositions and grotesqueries. Droll figures, hybrids of humans and animals, were a favored subject for monochrome borders like this one.

This embroidery was worked predominantly in long-armed cross stitch, as was the Noah's Ark preceding this needlework, but the method of procedure differed. Whereas the Noah's Ark was begun with a drawing on linen, this piece was worked from a diagram that showed stitches to be made and spaces to be left as threads were counted. To begin, the threads of the ground were counted to find the center of the cloth, and this point was marked with a line of running stitches in contrasting thread. Then the design could be worked right and left of the center, the long-armed cross stitches sometimes worked in vertical and sometimes in horizontal rows, so that there would be variation in the manner in which the soft silk floss caught the light.

In counting the stitches in the process of making the accompanying diagram, it was discovered that despite the apparent precision of the work quite a few disparities of count could

STRAPWORK
AND LEAF DESIGN
*Detail of altar frontal,
Italy; 17th century.*

This diagram shows
a portion of the repeat
that appears on the top
part of the altar frontal
(not shown
in the photograph).
In the top portion
of the altar frontal
the small face
is upside down, whereas
in the bottom portion
it is right side up.

*This diagram
shows the face repeats
that appear throughout
the design.*

be found. This difference is mentioned to encourage those who may want to try to duplicate the design but fear an irretrievable disaster in trying to count out such a maze of pattern.

In the accompanying diagram a little more than a fourth of the design repeat is shown. The repeat can be clearly understood if you think of the motif as showing a large diamond with the face of the sun as the center of the pattern. As arranged on the original altar frontal border, the design is two repeats high. Where these two repeats come together triangular devices join, forming a diamond. The face of the moon appears in the diamond shape formed by the joining of two repeats.

For ease in counting stitches the diagrams have been drawn with small squares to represent each stitch. The work within a given area seems to have begun with the longest central row of stitches, whether it ran horizontally or vertically. The direction of subsequent rows of stitches within given elements may change, depending on the shape. In addition to long-armed cross stitches, line and stroke stitches were used. These stitches, used with satin or various cross stitches, are sometimes referred to as Holbein work, after the artist by the same name whose portraits often show sitters wearing garments trimmed with dark embroidery made with these simple stitches.

Contemporary adaptation

It would be wise to choose evenweave linen for this embroidery. (See M&T.) It is impossible to estimate the size of the repeat without calculating the relation between the size of a single stitch in the cloth you intend to use. Work should begin in the center and should proceed outward, working equally in four directions. Working in this way, symmetry will be easily maintained.

Duplicating this embroidery may be somewhat monotonous but not very difficult. Portions of the design could be used effectively on a cloth handbag or as a border for linens or clothing. One repeat, worked in silk or wool on needlepoint canvas in any of the various crossed stitches, would make a handsome cushion cover. The restraint and formality of the design make it appropriate for many settings in which other types of needlework may be too casual.

Presentation bag

raised work in purl/England

During the time of the Stuarts in England (seventeenth century) embroidery moved rapidly toward a climax of flamboyant exuberance. Needlework was a preoccupation of every household. All manner of articles were made by skilled and unskilled needlewomen, sometimes with the aid of a professional or semiprofessional designer. Among these articles were presentation bags that held gifts such as money or small objects. The use of a bag made especially for giving or receiving gifts originated with the medieval alms bags, which were intended for gifts of food, not money. Crusading knights filled their empty scrips (shepherd's bags) by begging for food. Later, tokens of gratitude to the church were offered in bags made especially for the purpose. In England private gifts or payments, as well as New Year's gifts to the queen (mandatory from noblemen and bishops), were presented this way; therefore, many presentation bags exchanged hands among the aristocracy. (Many existing presentation bags show little sign of wear and were apparently stored away after their original use.)

Other bags were designed for utilitarian service, such as carrying needs while hunting or traveling. Garments of the day had no pockets, so small bags, sometimes with matching pincushions, were a welcome convenience even to stay-at-homes.

Bags were made in various shapes, but most were of simple two-piece construction. Every sort of design and technique was used to decorate them. Like other embroidered works, presentation bags tended to have designs that followed national trends. Some Italian bags were made with classical restraint; German and Spanish bags had heavy and ornate designs; English bags were often made in some version of the coiling stem design, using minute tent or other thread-counted stitches.

The bag shown on page 74 is a not so easily identified English example of the seventeenth century. If the Calthorpe purse (Victoria and Albert Museum) with its 1250 tent stitches per square inch is the epitome of English virtuosity in making needlework bags, and the national characteristic of English bags is taken to be their technical excellence, no one would have any idea that this little bag came from England. Its simplicity of design and technique, practiced everywhere on the continent as well as in England, appears to be a domestic version of a kind of raised goldwork embroidery that was made professionally for court and church.

This bag measures four by four and one-quarter inches. It is made of purple silk satin backed by heavy linen and lined with a greenish yellow damask-woven silk. Its silk drawstrings are yellow. Yellow silk floss was used to pad and raise parts of the embroidery and to couch the metal threads—an indication that originally some of the metal threads, all of which now have the appearance of old silver, may have been gold. The outlines of the design were made by using two strands of metal thread that were twisted to make a cord. The raised portions of the embroidery were made with purl, a type of metal material much used in gold embroidery. Purl is made by twisting a gold or silver wire around a core, then removing the core to leave the wire a hollow spiral or "spring." The twisted wire is then cut to a desired length, a needle and thread are slipped through its hollow center, and the little piece sewn into position on the needlework like a bead. The wire from which purl is made may be crimped, polished, or otherwise textured so that the purl is sometimes brilliantly "checked" or sometimes satiny smooth and dull. Checked and satiny smooth dull purl were the two types used for the bag shown here. Time has diminished the contrast between the two textures, but when new the difference must have been striking.

This bag was worked in an embroidery frame, beginning with the preparation of areas that were to have raised effects. These areas were embroidered with one or more layers of long and short stitch; the top layer of padding was always worked lengthwise. The padding stitches were made in yellow silk floss so that they would be inconspicuous anywhere they might happen to show under the covering layer of purl. Next, the pieces of purl were cut and

sewn into place crosswise on the shapes. To finish the edges, twisted passing threads were couched into place. The seams and upper edge of the little bag were finished with plaited braid stitch worked with two fine strands of passing. These threads are so fine that the completed braid is only one-eighth inch wide. The design as diagrammed on page 75 is larger than the original piece.

Contemporary adaptation
This gold relief embroidery should be worked in a frame. The design may be transferred to the velvet after the fabric has been stretched.

PRESENTATION BAG
England; 17th century, 4 in. x 4¼ in. (almost exactly the size shown in the photograph).

*The diagram
for the presentation bag
can be enlarged
for a more ambitious
project. The procedure
for enlarging may be found
in the M&T section
at the back of the book.*

By stretching the fabric before you transfer the design you will avoid any distortion of the symmetrical design that may occur during the stretching process. For transfers onto velvet special care must be exercised. Sugar solution can be used if the painted tracing is delicately made and steamed, rather than pressed, onto the fabric. Another method, more reliable and particularly well suited for embroidery to be worked directly onto velvet, involves basting a tracing in position on the velvet and then working the design in running stitches through both paper and velvet. When the design is finished, the paper is torn away, leaving the design in running stitches on the velvet.

A linen underlayer will give added firmness to the velvet and will help the material to wear better. The needlework can proceed according to the description of the original.

It may strike you that the design of this bag taken by itself, without the texture of the materials used to make it, closely resembles the peasant designs of central and eastern Europe. This design would be quite appropriate as a pattern for embroidery in crewels, using padded satin stitch for petals and leaves, and stem, chain, or couching stitches for lines and edges. For a different effect the design could be worked without padding in concentric rows of chain and stem stitch, varying colors of the rows and using either a subdued color scheme or a brilliant one. As a linen embroidery the design might be monochromatic, with contours of stem or chain stitch and fillings of satin stitch and tightly pulled Italian cross stitches. Specific directions for these stitches can be found in the Stitch Directory at the back of the book.

This embroidery design lends itself to many projects. Enlarged and split down the center it could trim the front of a shirt. It would also make a simple but elegant motif for chair cushions or pillow covers.

In England a vogue for bedcurtains embroidered in large-scale patterns in woolen threads called crewels, or cruells, began some time in the second half of the seventeenth century, although the exact date is uncertain. Today embroidery of this type is popularly called crewel work—a term that can lead to both historical and technical confusion, for the purchase of crewels did not necessarily mean that embroidery of the sort shown on page 78 was to be made with them. Crewels were used for tent stitch (petit point) embroidery as well as for other types of needlework in the Tudor and early Stuart periods, long before bedhangings embroidered in crewels began to be made.

In the late seventeenth century an audience with a king was apt to be scheduled in his bedchamber, a stately room with a magnificent canopied bed as the central appointment. Ladies also held receptions in their sleeping quarters. In fine houses floral marquetry, shell inlay, lacquer work, and various kinds of silver work accompanied luxurious tapestries and damasks. The Restoration period required a style that would break with the past and convey, in Pepys's words, "a merry mood." Charles II had spent the period of his exile on the continent, and on his return the style of England became that of the traveled man; a desire for a heterogeneous assortment of memorabilia from many places in the world replaced the taste for more common, characteristically heavy, homogeneous forms of earlier times.

The most elegant beds were hung with tapestry, damask, or other pattern-woven textiles, and although some embroidered bedhangings were designed in imitation of these expensive fabrics only a few remain today. In many more bedhangings the earlier coiling stem design (seen in the man's cap, page 38, and the woman's coif, page 44) continued but simply was enlarged in scale. Quite a few crewel-embroidered bedhangings relate to the designs of painted cottons—*pintadoes and palampores*—that from the beginning of the seventeenth century had been imported by the East India Company for use as quilts or bedhangings. The eccentric botanical designs of these textiles were in some measure the result of

Multicolored panel

embroidered in crewels/England

color plate, page 107

the Indian artists' misinterpretation of the English prototypes sent to them for copy. The English sent to India designs for copy that were rendered in the illusionistic third dimension, a concept not understood by the Indian painter. His reworking of the design tended to flatten and abstract the original. Rather than displeasing English customers these translations were found charming. In the panel shown here, probably from a set of bedcurtains, curious clam-like blooms and flower-filled lanceolet leaves set in undulating rhythms remind one of the painted cloths from the Indian Coromandel coast.

This embroidery also seems to correlate in some obscure way with the bizarre silks of the eighteenth century. Called bizarre because of their fantastic designs, their origin is in doubt, but they first appeared in port cities of England and Holland and in Venice. Their layout is exactly like the layout of this crewel embroidered panel; each has a very long lengthwise repeat and two repeats to fill a loom width. The patterns are vaguely flower-like, asymmetric, graceful, and ambiguous in the relation of background to motif. Very often they have a Chinese or Indian flavor. In the late seventeenth century one of the most distinctive features of many types of textiles for both furnishing and clothing was their assimilated exoticism.

As much as its strange shapes and exotic color suggest Indian chintzes, this panel is curiously Western in its repeated pattern. Despite the presence of a hillock border, the design is composed of a branching pattern that is repeated with a regularity as accurate as were patterns of printed and woven designs. The repeat panel is eighteen inches wide and thirty-nine inches long. The regularity and discipline of the work give a high degree of professionalism.

Bedcurtains were made from loom-width panels, eighteen to twenty inches wide. The foot of the bed and the portion of the sides toward the foot required two curtains made of five breadths of cloth each. At the head of the bed were two curtains made up of two and a half or three breadths each. Base panels and valances also were embroidered, but the tester and bedcover were seldom embroidered with crewels (see John L. Nevinson, *A Catalogue of English Domestic Embroidery*).

In the bedcurtain panel shown here the colors of the worsted are strong and unusually combined. The color plate on page 107 shows that the thick central stems are shaded within chevron-like segments from yellow to rust to brown. The rib in the center of the stem has chevrons of green-red-green, with narrow stripes of the ground fabric in reserve between the ribs. The long leaves with star-shaped flowers have two color schemes: white flowers with red on green, and pink flowers with yellow on deep rose. The dark green leaf with five-petaled blooms and cloverleaf-shaped leaves has yellow to green flowers with rose French knot centers and pink to rose shaded leaves. The outline of the leaf is rose in slanted satin stitch. The other leaves have flowers or fruits that are pink to rose with leaves of yellow to indigo. The backgrounds are brown, and the edges of the leaves are yellow. The pineapple-like blooms are shaded red or yellow to orange with green leaves. The rest of the leaves are shaded from light green or yellow to indigo or dark green; the larger leaves have central veins in brown. The curling, lobed leaf is handled in this way but has a broad central rib decorated with orange-veined yellow leaflets on a brown ground. One twisting lobe of the leaf is red.

This embroidery was accomplished with few stitches. Satin stitch in a brick, or block, arrangement was used for the center of the clam-shell-like blossoms along the main stalk. Block shading was used for the large stems. Long and short stitch was used for the leaves, with lines in stem stitch and accents in running stitches and French knots.

Contemporary adaptation

This bedcurtain panel was embroidered on the usual ground for this kind of needlework—a linen and cotton twill. A somewhat similar twill can be purchased for embroidery today. Its dense weave makes possible accurately placed stitches. The design, diagrammed in three parts with an overlap for tracing convenience, can be transferred for use in the scale shown here or enlarged.

To begin, first make a drawing in the required scale. Transfer the drawing to the cloth you have chosen, using sugar solution or dressmakers' carbon. (See M&T.) This embroidery can be

MULTICOLORED PANEL
*England; 17th century,
35½ in. x 42 in.*

worked in a hand hoop. Using crewels (woolen yarn), follow the stitch description of the original, and refer to page 107 for the color. It might be wise to bear in mind that many seventeenth-century bedhangings made with crewels finally were discarded, not because of devastation by moths, but because the woolen embroidery was too heavy for the twill ground fabric, which eventually weakens and tears. On many seventeenth-century bedcurtains the needlework itself is in fine condition; the ground alone is tattered. Putting the embroidery on a new ground is an arduous, time-consuming task that diminishes the beauty of the embroidery stitching. With the lesson learned from decayed old needleworks, you should coordinate thread and ground fabric to achieve a safe as well as an eye-appealing combination.

This design can be used for upholstery, cushions, wallhangings, or other needleworks that require a heavy, large-scale embroidery.

The three diagrams on the following pages are a continuation of the same repeat. Trace each one on the same large sheet of paper, overlapping them at the points indicated by the dotted lines on either side of the diagrams. By placing the diagrams in the order of their appearance you will have one complete repeat. If you want to embroider a panel that has more than one repeat, make another tracing of the first diagram and connect it to the end of the third pattern; then make another tracing of the second pattern and connect it to the first. Continue in this manner until you have as many repeats as you need. Notice that the dotted lines on the first pattern indicate precisely where the diagram is to be placed in relation to the third pattern.

Monochrome panel

embroidered in crewels/England

Bedcurtains made in monochromatic embroidery in crewels were as popular as their polychrome counterparts (see page 78). Among the one-color embroideries was a variety that had undulating branches and gigantic leaves, some as long as eighteen inches. The leaves in these embroideries are veined with flowers and other designs, and they suggest an Eastern inspiration as well as another influence. It is generally accepted that embroidery was copied both freely and closely from other textile forms. Many large embroidered hangings, usually in needlepoint, virtually duplicate the designs of tapestry. That threadcounted embroidery on canvas is still sometimes erroneously called tapestry underscores the point. Tapestries were an obvious source of design for needlepoint. A famous example of embroidery made in the spirit of tapestry, though not necessarily copied from one, is a set of six panels that show classical columns and arcading entwined with flowers and large leaves. This set was found in a house in Hatton Garden, London, and is now in the Victoria and Albert Museum. In technique these embroideries are a combination of threadcounted and surface needlework. They were used as wall panels in the same manner in which tapestry was used.

In the second half of the sixteenth century in France and Flanders some tapestries were woven in designs predominantly composed of great curling, green leaves. The tapestries had little additional subject matter except for some architectural details or some birds or animals. Dominantly green, these tapestries are called verdure tapestries. Since they had no narrative subject matter, the number of tapestries in an original set of verdures cannot be estimated, but in *Tapestries of Europe and Colonial Peru in the Collection of the Museum of Fine Arts in Boston* Adolph Cavallo notes that sets of seven to fifteen and also a set of bed furnishings are known. The similarity between the enormous twisting leaves of the verdure tapestries and the large leaf designs of some seventeenth-century English embroidered bedcurtain designs is undeniable.

Although the verdure tapestries are predominantly green and the bedcurtains are often blue, it is likely that when it was new much of the bedcurtain embroidery was also green. Green was a popular color because strong contrasts were much admired at the time, and green was dramatic in juxtaposition with the warm wood furniture tones of the day. Green was, however, an elusive color and long defied attempts to find a recipe for a one-application dye. The color was achieved by dyeing indigo over yellow or, more often, yellow over indigo. (Double dyeing did not present such a serious problem in coloring threads and yarns, but it precluded the use of green in mechanical printing procedures. Chemists engaged in spirited competition to find a satisfactory green dye for textiles, but not until 1810, long after the search was begun, did a chemist from Oberkampf, the famed French textile printing establishment at Jouy, finally succeed in making a single-application green.) That the greens in the late seventeenth-century embroidered bedcurtains are now often blue is related to the problem of dyeing greens. Indigo—the original fast dye and the only color that was lasting without the use of a mordant in the dye process—remains, while yellows have faded and washed away, leaving green foilage blue. It seems fair to assume that in the beginning the bedcurtains discussed here had the same blue and green color scheme apparent in the Flemish *verdure* tapestries.

The curtain panel shown measures seventy-four by sixty-four inches and has worsted embroidery on the usual cotton and linen twill ground. Numerous stitches were combined: satin, chain, Bohkara couching, buttonhole,

MONOCHROME PANEL
England; 17th century,
74 in. x 64 in.

outline, stem, coral, rococo, fishbone, running, plain and patterned couching, speckling, link powdering, and various lacy fillings made with detached buttonhole, basket, Roumanian, rope, and French knot. In this pattern the large leaves are connected by a vertical but irregular treatment of bending stalks, which serves to join the motifs.

Contemporary adaptation

The great number of stitches used in this embroidery precludes any written description that would adequately cover their use. The stitches of some of the leaves, photographed as details, are listed with the photographs. These listings will give you an idea of how stitches are grouped and arranged. The best way to approach the making of a similar embroidery is to study the technique until the principles behind the design and selection of stitches as well as their combination have been grasped. Then it will not be necessary to depend on copying; you can merely apply similar principles when the exact detail of the original seems unclear.

In this composition large leaves are rather evenly distributed over the area. The leaves are arranged in a regularly repeated format, but the filling designs of the leaves do not repeat exactly and are varied occasionally. A characteristic of crewel embroidered leaves is that they are often "charged," or filled with small motifs. That the charging does not always follow a precise pattern of repetition is one of the reasons that needlework design is so often more intriguing than textile patterns produced by mechanical means.

You will notice that in many places the contour of a leaf is made with a line of chain stitch and an adjacent line of stem stitch. Some edges are buttonhole stitch, worked so that little "teeth" point outward. Zigzagged rows of stem stitch worked close together make a herringbone filling.

To lay out a large embroidery like this one the following method is suggested. Cut templates from cardboard for individual leaf contours, and lay out a design, tracing the templates on wrapping paper. For a quick impression you can use chalk or charcoal markers. Errors can be rubbed out and shapes redrawn until a satisfactory overall composition has been made. Stems can be drawn freehand on the sketch. Next, lay out the ground fabric. If the piece of fabric is large, the work can be spread out on the floor, and piles of books or other

weights can be used to keep it flat and in position. If widths of fabric have to be joined, they should be basted at this stage and the basting removed after the design has been drawn on the ground fabric. If you embroider one width at a time the fabric will be less unwieldy as the work progresses. The stitchery can be completed on each width of fabric, except where it approaches the seams. At the end of the work the seams can be permanently joined and worked over with embroidery.

In preparing the ground fabric, outlines can be traced in pencil using the templates. Following the wrapping-paper sketch, draw in the stems freehand. If you are afraid of making mistakes, tailor's chalk can be used to begin the drawing. It will dust away easily if lines go awry. Final chalk lines should be reenforced with pencil or paint. Do not use a pencil that will leave an easily smudged mark. Work your embroidery over penciled lines as soon as possible to lessen the possibility of accidentally smearing parts of the drawing. If the "charging" of the leaf to be worked is studied carefully, in most cases it will be necessary to transfer only an indication of the dark tips on leaf lobes and serrations as well as the positions of central stems plus a few key lines of venation. Everything else can be copied by eye, improvising wherever wear has destroyed the embroidery of the original. If designs are to be repeated, any part of the design to be transferred from a traced sketch can be pounced (see M&T). A pricking can be used over and over. If the leaf fillings are not to be repeated, a sugar solution or dressmakers' carbon transfer will be more expedient. It would probably be best to work a large embroidery such as this one in an embroidery frame, but it also would be possible to work it in a hand hoop.

Small versions of this design would be fine for chair seats or more ambitious upholstery projects. Winged chairs, often covered with worsted embroidery, were an innovation of the time of William and Mary and were called, appropriately, Sleepynge chairs. Embroiderers of contemporary designs may find the stitch combinations and abstract fillings of these freely worked surface embroideries a spur to ideas for their own work.

To work the embroidery for the monochrome panel, you will need to transfer only as much of the pattern as is shown here. Diagrams for the individual leaves are on the following pages. If you want to enlarge this pattern, refer to the M&T section at the back of the book for the proper procedure.

*This leaf
measures 10 in. x 11 in.
Beginning at the outer
contour, the border
of this curled leaf
was made by combining
rows of chain, outlines,
Roumanian, and speckling
stitches, in that order.
The speckled areas contain
some French knots.
The body
of the caterpillar is
Roumanian stitch; the
scrolls of the interior
are satin stitch;
delicate line patterns
are back and line stitches.*

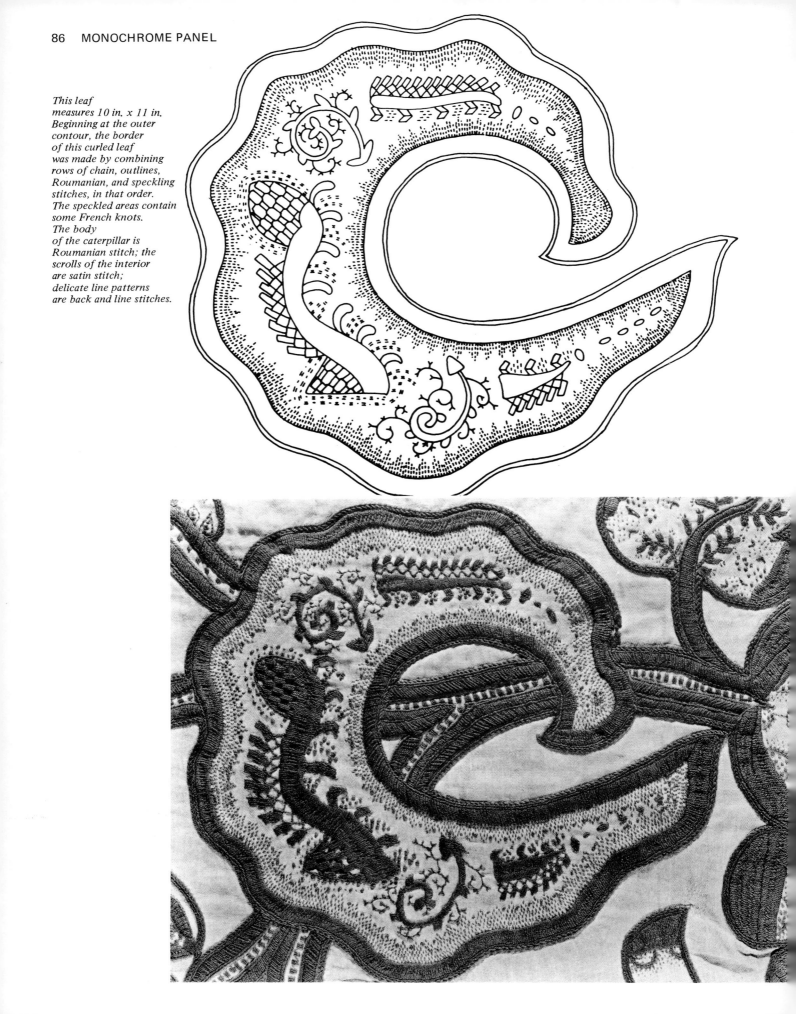

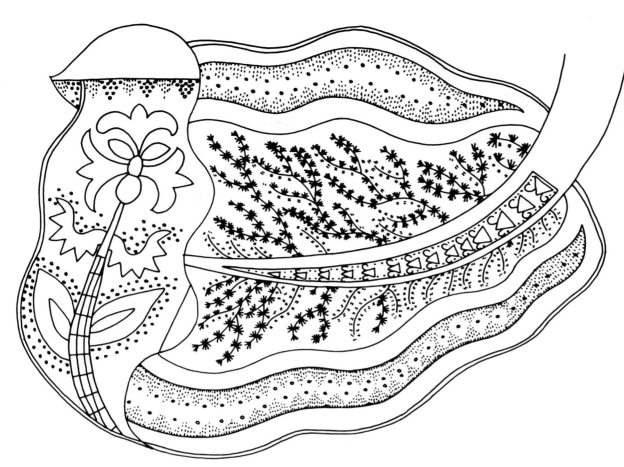

This leaf measures
8½ in. x 11½ in.
Beginning at the outer
edge, the border
of this leaf was made
with chain, overcasting,
and satin stitches.
Speckling
with French knots
was made
along the inner edge
of the border. The
large floral motif
on the curling end
of the leaf was made
with Roumanian stitch,
basket stitch in the stem,
and some details
of French knots, line
stitches, and overcasting.
Intricate stems
in outline stitch are
decorated with sprigs
of line stitches and rows
of French knots.
The triangles
in the central stem
are Roumanian stitch.

This leaf measures
8 in. x 13 in. If you
measure the photograph
and diagram, you will
have some idea
of the actual size
of the original.
Beginning at the outer
edge, the narrow borders
of this leaf were made
with one row of chain
stitch beside one row
of outline stitch. The
broad borders were made
by adding Roumanian
stitch, line stitches,
and French knots
to the narrow border.
Lacy fillings within some
petal-like shapes
were made with detached
buttonhole stitch;
consecutive rows
of stitches were worked
in pairs between each two
stitches of the row above.
A border of scallops
around these petal-like
shapes was made
with line stitches
and double running
stitches. Other
petal-like shapes were
bordered with alternating
running stitches and
French knots. These
shapes were filled
with rows of basket stitch.
Triangles in the center
stem are Roumanian stitch.
Veins were made
in coral stitch outlined
with running stitch.
Stars were made with
straight line stitches
tied in the center
with short stitch,
as is done in couching.

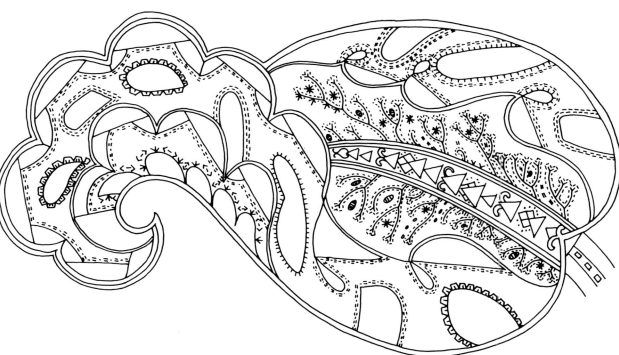

This leaf
measures 10 in. x 10½ in.
Measure the photograph
and diagram
to get some idea of
the actual size
of the original.
The outer border is chain
stitch with outline stitch
and overcasting. The
inner outline of the leaf
is coral stitch.
The scrolls inside the
leaf begin
with coral stitch
and have bands of satin or
Roumanian stitch
along the inside.
On the outside are two
rows of outline or one row
of chain and one row
of outline stitch.
Spines along the edges
of these heavy scrolls
are line stitches.
Long, narrow, spiraling
shapes near the contours
are basket stitch.
Delicate veins
between the heavy scrolls
were made
with coral stitch,
with cross, line, running,
and French knot stitches
powdered around the edges.

*This leaf
measures 9 in. x 10½ in.
The narrow border
of the leaf was made
with chain stitch and one
or two rows of outline
stitch. Lobed leaf
scallops are filled
with Roumanian stitch.
The stem is slanted satin
stitch with a center rib
decorated with motifs
that consist of three
adjacent line stitches
spaced at intervals
along the length
of the stem. The flowers
that fill the leaf
are double running and
speckling stitches, and
their stems are
overcast stitch.
Lacy effects along the
edges of the scallops were
created with
speckling, powderings
of French knots, and
a few line stitches.
One lacy filling
in a petal-like shape
along the edge of the leaf
was made by tying
together bundles of line
stitches with a tight
crosswise stitch.*

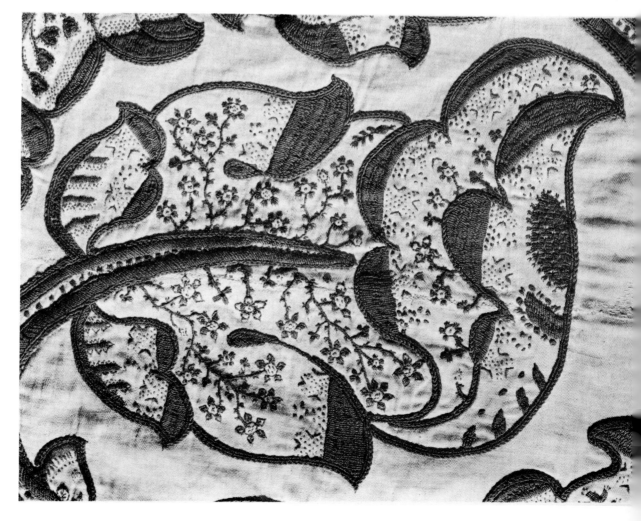

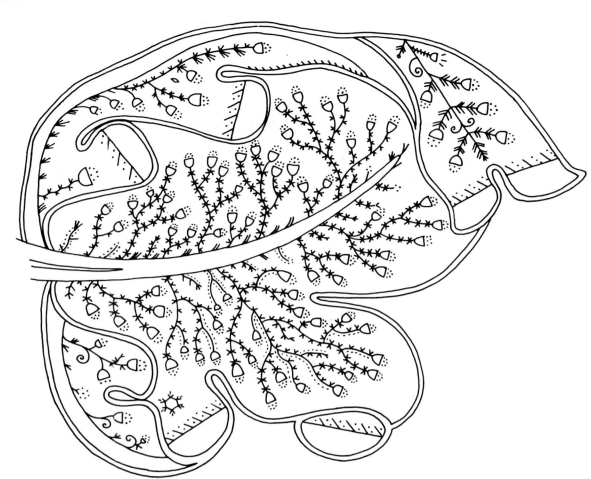

This leaf
measures 11 in. x 11¼ in.
Compare this measurement
with the photograph
and diagram
to get some idea
of the actual
size of the original.
Most of the borders
of this leaf are chain
stitch alone or
combined with Roumanian
couching, Roumanian
stitch, and overcasting or
stem stitch.
Flowers are satin stitch
with French knots.
Stems are stem stitch
with leaflets made
in line stitch. Running
stitches were used
to outline some
of the stems. Running
stitches and tied line
stitches were used
to decorate
the leaf lobes.

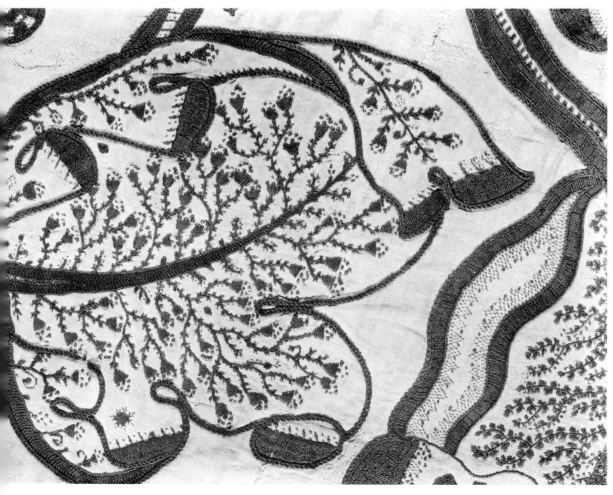

*This leaf
measures 10 in. x 9½ in.
The borders are chain and
stem stitch
for the most part;
some have Roumanian
stitch or Roumanian
couching and speckling
in addition.
The flowers are Roumanian
stitch with overcast
stems and outer borders
of running stitches.
The central stem
of the leaf is slanted
satin stitch and
overcasting.*

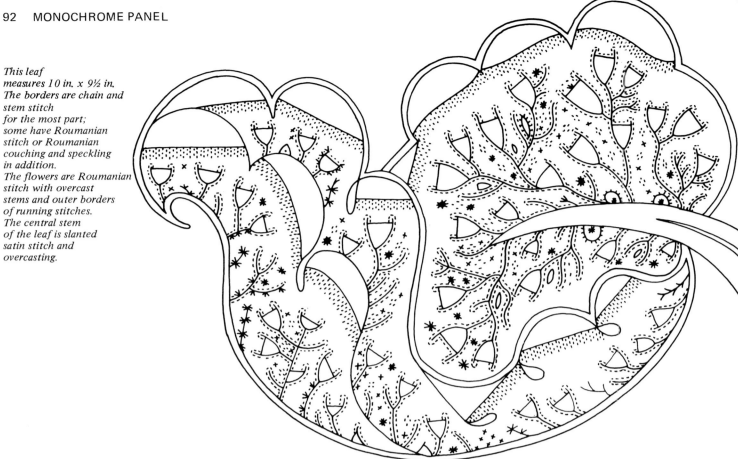

Pillow cover

embroidered in blue crewels/England

From 1688 until 1702 the king of England was Dutch, and life of the time reflected foreign contacts everywhere. At court, influences came from Rotterdam and Amsterdam or from France. Daniel Marot, the fine French Huguenot architect and decorator who had fled to Holland shortly before revocation of the Edict of Nantes in 1685, followed one of his patrons, William III, to England. Thereafter, Marot's Dutch-French style influenced English decoration. Many other Huguenot craftsmen came directly to England in their flight from persecution, and with their coming the weaving industries, including tapestry-making, flourished. Astonishing quantities of lace and embroidery were produced during this time, and Queen Mary herself loved to make needlework. The period saw a climax in the making of domestic embroidery. So preoccupied with their needlework were the ladies that Addison rebuked them for being so dedicated to the needle that they never learned to read or write.

In the time of William and Mary, England became a stable parliamentary monarchy, the Bank of England was formed, and freedom of press and worship were allowed. Gentlefolk of the period lived comfortably, with a degree of privacy previously unknown. There was much recent wealth, social mobility, and enthusiasm for establishing great houses, many of them in the country where a garden could spread. Most domestic embroidery of the day reflects a love of leisure and comfort.

One of a set of matching pillow covers from this period, each nineteen by twenty-one inches, is shown here. These pillow covers are unusual in their spontaneous drawing and richness of texture, which was achieved simply by speckling and a variety of easily made stitches. (Speckling is a term used to describe an area in which running or back stitches are dotted, or powdered, throughout.) Several shades of blue wool were used for the embroidery, but the exact distribution of the colors is no longer clear. The ground fabric is cotton and linen twill. The bordering floral motifs were arranged so that the opposite corners have the same design, only reversed. The middle motifs on the top and bottom are identical. Outlines for the motifs were made in closely worked stem stitch. Solid fillings in spot-like areas on petals and leaves were made in satin stitch. Solid fillings in long shapes were embroidered in closely worked herringbone stitch. Veins in the leaves were embroidered in back stitch. The dotted lines adjacent to the stems of the flowers were worked in running stitch; curls were worked in back stitch. Buttonholing was used for birds' wings and flower petals. The man's hat was done in herringbone stitch. The lettering is a combination of buttonhole and running stitches.

Contemporary adaptation

Reproducing this pillow cover embroidery is a simple task. Trace the individual motifs and, if desired, enlarge them. The motifs on the right side of the pattern correspond to those on the left side but must be reversed for the left side. Using dressmakers' carbon, transfer the designs to linen twill or other ground fabric. The work

This diagram shows only part of the pillow cover because the same motifs are repeated on the other half.
Notice in the photograph that the upper right-hand motif, diagrammed here, is repeated in the lower left-hand corner of the pillow cover.

PILLOW COVER
England; 1689,
21 in. x 19 in.

This flower appears in the upper left-hand and lower right-hand corners of the pillow cover.

need not be mounted in an embroidery frame; a hand hoop can be used. With two or three shades of blue crewels (woolen yarns) embroider the designs according to the description of the stitches. Detailed instructions for all stitches can be found in the Stitch Directory at the back of the book. When the embroidery has been finished, the two sides of the pillow cover can be joined (usually only the front was embroidered), and tassels can be added in the corners in keeping with the original. (Tassels were one of Marot's innovations.)

Without revisions this pillow cover could be used nicely in many rooms today. The individual spot patterns that comprise this design could be used separately in various ways on other household articles. The floral motifs might be used for clothing. The designs would be equally attractive in other colors and in a scale slightly different from the original.

Bed cover

During Queen Anne's reign (1702-1714), English trade with the Orient increased after the East India Company monopoly finally was broken. At the same time, French and Dutch influence (see page 93) declined. France was developing the rococo style, which was to become popular everywhere on the continent. In England, though, the rococo impulse manifested itself primarily in lighter colors, smaller designs, and more delicate fabrics. As the preference for embroidery in colored silks with gold and silver grew, needlework shifted away from the long-familiar worsted embroidery made on twills woven with linen warps and cotton wefts. Experiments with new weaves were undertaken, and utilization of textiles composed entirely of cotton or linen was begun.

The uses of needlework changed too. Needlepoint embroideries on canvas for upholstery purposes were made more frequently. Settees, wing chairs, pole screens, and card table tops were decorated with oriental, classical, or biblical themes. Furnishings became more restrained and sober. The merriment of Charles II's court and the pleasant domesticity of the reign of William and Mary had passed. Anne, who lost one child after another, worried over the problem of succession and had little time for the arts. She dressed in Venetian silks and lace.

Patterned weaving became fashionable, but embroidery, though declining, was still made. Garments, royal portraits, pictures, samplers, and maps with lettering were rendered in needlework. White openwork and drawn-thread embroideries were used for women's aprons, which had been long and worn for practical purposes but now were newly modish. For articles that required greater durability, such as men's waistcoats, women's caps, bedcurtains, and coverlets, quilting or white surface embroidery that had a knotted or corded effect was popular.

Knotting had been a pretty pastime for idle hands throughout the seventeenth century. Sedley wrote of Queen Mary:

> Whene'er she rode in coach abroad
> Was always knotting thread.

Many portraits of ladies of the day show them with elegant knotting shuttles poised in graceful fingers. Various sorts of knots were made at intervals along cords that ostensibly were meant to be couched in designs on garments, bedcurtains, or other needlework. But miles of knotting were made simply as busywork with no definite use in mind. In the bedspread shown on page 98 the dainty outline design made in coral stitch resembles knotting (see photograph of detail on page 99).

The central stem of the design is outlined in coral stitch, in which the knots are so closely arranged as to create the effect of a row of small French knots. Within the stem is a design of five French knots in a rosette and a serpentine line of French knots spaced slightly apart. The smaller stems attached to the flowers are outlined in coral stitch as is the large central stem, but their filling texture is large single French knots. All

BED COVER
England; 18th century,
62½ in. x 76 in.

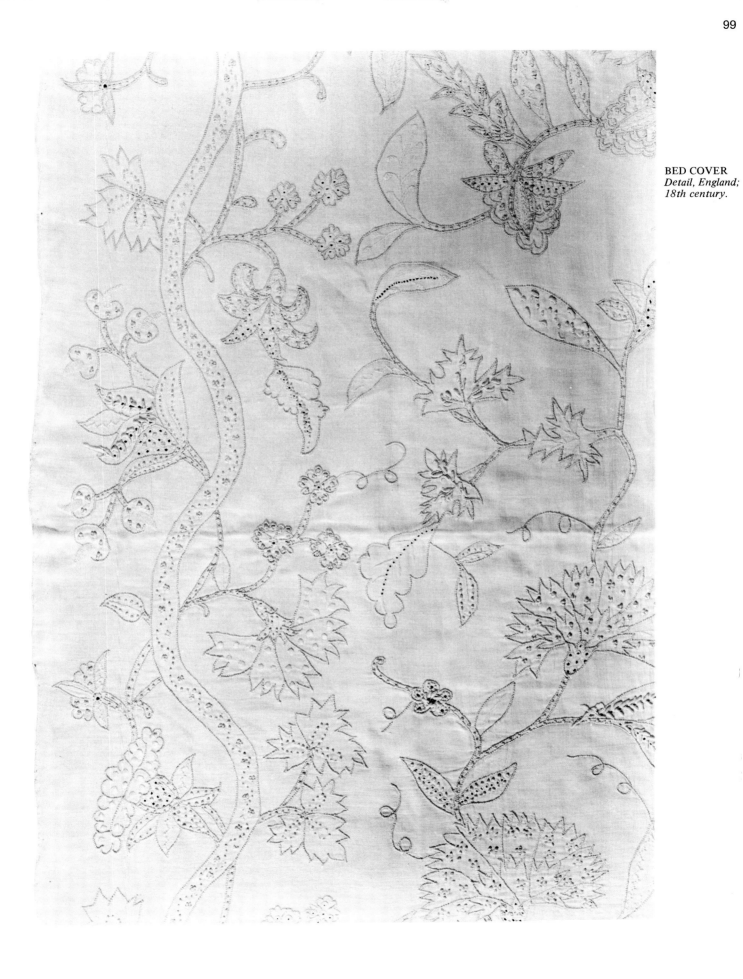

BED COVER
Detail, England;
18th century.

*This diagram
of the left side
of the bed cover detail
can be used same size
or englarged
for a more elaborate work.
Several tracings
of this pattern can be
joined together and used
as a continous border.
See the M&T section
at the back of the book
for a description
of the procedure for
changing scale.*

*In this diagram
the heavy, wavy stem line
has been removed to make
a simpler single-unit pattern.*

the flower and leaf motifs also are outlined in coral stitch, and each has accents in a variety of other stitches.

The portion of the design diagrammed is part of an end border. The side border design is similar to the one shown. The total effect of the bed cover is of allover white embroidery with no central, dominating motif. If you could inspect the total design closely, you would notice that it is made up of borders and rectangular units placed in such a way that background spaces are uniform throughout. The textural details within motifs vary slightly within the repeats. Stitches selected for filling designs are not consistent in every repeat. Not visible in the portion diagrammed, but used elsewhere in the embroidery, are hemstitching, feather stitch, and overcast eyelets.

The embroidery thread is white linen of varying thicknesses. The thinnest thread was used to make the buttonholed eyelets; the heaviest thread was used for some of the French knots.

Contemporary adaptation

Linen or cotton ground fabric can be used for white embroidery, but the material should be slightly bulky and soft. Linen thread or good, dull-finished cotton should be used for the stitching. The design transfer could be made with dressmakers' carbon; however, if the diagram is to be repeated many times make a pricking for transferring by pouncing. (See M&T.) This embroidery can be accomplished without difficulty in a hand hoop. Directions for all the stitches of the original can be found in the Stitch Directory at the back of the book.

If you decide to repeat the design several times in your project, the filling stitches of flowers should be alternated or varied. The diagrammed border pattern can be turned into a single unit design by removing the heavy, wavy stem line.

The openness and simplicity of this border design make it a practical choice for a large-scale project. It would be ideal for decorating the edge of a table linen or skirt. In a slightly smaller scale this embroidery would be beautiful in color for a belt.

The historical background information and the patterns for the following color embroidery masterworks are on the following pages:
Child's poncho-shirt, 1;
Last Supper, 8;
Nativity, 25;
Coif, 43;
Beaded basket, 48;
Multicolored panel, 76;
Bed cover, 115;
Chasuble, 124;
Gentleman's coat sample, 135;
Bed valance, 152;
Towel ends, 162;
Ship design, 156;
Mola², 187.

CHILD'S PONCHO-SHIRT
see pages 1-4

LAST SUPPER
see pages 8-14

NATIVITY
see pages 25-27

COIF
see pages 43-47

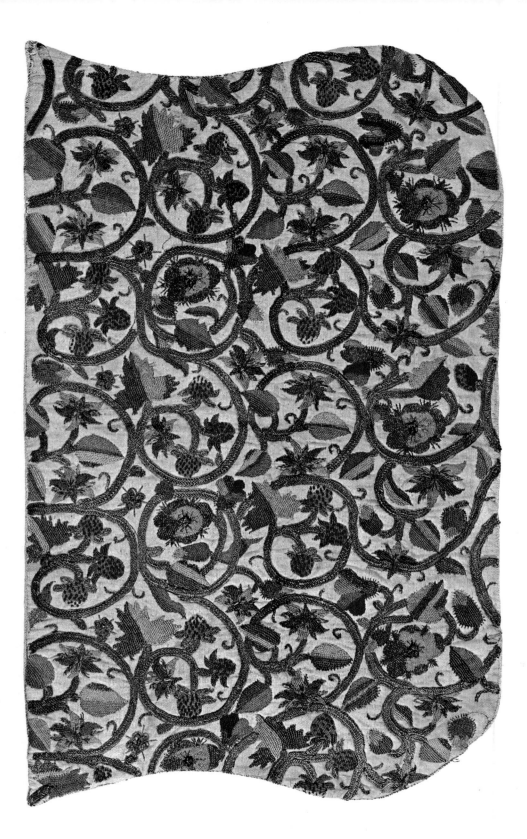

BEADED BASKET
see pages 48-52

MULTICOLORED PANEL
see pages 77-82

BED COVER
see pages 115-120

CHASUBLE
see pages 124-130

HALF BOOTS
see pages 140-143

GENTLEMAN'S
COAT SAMPLE
see pages 135-139

TOWEL ENDS
see pages 162-165

SHIP DESIGN
see pages 156-161

MOLA
see pages 187-191

Bed cover

multicolored chain stitch/England

color plate, page 108

The early Georgian period (1720-1740) brought a noticeable change in decorative style. New ideas are evident in the design of this quilted, wool-embroidered cover, or bedspread. Flowers still dominate the design, but they are less florid in color and smaller in scale than seventeenth-century designs. Some of the floral patterns in covers like this one originated in the stylized patterns of Persian coverlets; others are as natural as flowers in a garden. The effect of the flowers here is delicate and intimate.

The layout of this coverlet is typical of the new daintiness of the era. It has a central medallion and four quandrants, with small motifs scattered on the rest of the ground. The design of bedcurtains changed, too, in the Georgian period. The pattern, although still predominantly floral, consisted of a border with rather small sprays powdered throughout the rest of the panel.

In the bedspread shown here the significant new features are the Persian character noticeable in the border of the medallion, the sparseness of embroidery over much of the area, and the more reticent use of lighter colors. The coverlet is linen embroidered with wool, but silk embroidery was growing increasingly more fashionable during the Georgian period, and bedspreads worked in silk on silk also were being made.

The term "counterpane" derives from the French word *contrepoinct,* meaning back stitch or, for the French at least, quilting stitch. Quilting also is done in running stitch. Quilting—an ancient art that originated in the Orient and existed in England, according to the earliest known example, from the tenth century—had begun to come into vogue in the time of Elizabeth I. In the first half of the seventeenth

century there was a craze for embroidered and quilted Indo-Portuguese coverlets, and Spanish quilting was also popular. Curtains and garments of all sorts were made with ever more intricate quilted effects. For embroidery worked irregularly over the surface of rather lightweight material, such as that of the bed cover shown here, quilting was helpful in providing a measure of stability and uniformity to the ground.

The technique in which the needlework itself was made for the bed cover also reflects influences from the East. Rendered almost entirely in chain stitch, this embroidery duplicates the effect of imported Indian and oriental cloths that were made entirely in chain stitch or tambour, an almost identical stitch made with a hoop and hook. In addition to chain stitch, buttonhole, wheat ear, flat stitch, and link powdering were used, but only for flower centers and small accents. In general, the color was handled so that large forms have gradations of one color, from very light to dark (see the color plate on page 108). On small flowers and leaves, sharp contrasts and accents of unrelated colors were used. The leaves, including those in the medallion border, are shaded from yellow to deep bluish green with dark green outlines. In a few leaves no yellow has been used, so that they have a cooler tonality. Roses are pink-to-maroon with some tiny touches of yellow. Other flowers have yellow-orange-brown petals with yellow and green centers. The birds are green, rose, and yellow. The flower on the side that the bird faces is yellow and orange. The flower on the other side is a shade of rose. Leaves are shaded green.

Contemporary adaptation

This embroidery can be worked in a frame if desired, but a hand hoop will work equally well. Most of the embroidery should be made with rows of chain stitch placed closely together. Use

BED COVER
*England; 18th century,
67 in. x 54 in.,
center medallion has
a 24-in. diameter.*

*To make a tracing
of the center medallion,
copy this diagram twice,
fitting the two sides
together according
to the photograph
of the original. See
the M&T section
at the back of the book
for the procedure for
changing scale.*

The bird on the original bed cover measures 10½ in. x 8 in. This diagram is almost actual size.

The flower
on the bed cover measures
8 in. x 5¼ in.
If you measure
this diagram, you will
notice that it is
slightly larger
than the original.

the plate on page 108 to guide you in color selections, or create your own color scheme. When the decoration is completed, a lining and interlining should be basted to the needlework panel. Begin in the center and work outward to each side, basting the interlining and lining to the embroidered ground. Interlining can be made of cotton flannel or a very thin layer of dacron; the total of top layer, interlining, and lining should not be bulky. The original cover was not very thick. The quilting design is a simple, diamond-shaped checking (long sides of the diamonds run horizontally). Whether back stitch or running stitch is used for quilting is a matter of choice, depending to some extent on the thickness of the coverlet.

Aside from its beauty as a bedspread, parts of this design are adaptable for other household furnishings and as decorative accents for clothing. The center medallion would work well for a cushion cover.

This eighteenth-century silk-embroidered panel for a sconce shows a typical mixture of influences: floral designs from Persia, older English embroidery, and an oriental vase design reminiscent of chinoiserie objects, which were the rage of the day. Mounted wall ornaments became fashionable in the late seventeenth century. Among these wall ornaments, which in time developed various forms, were carved and gilded shelves, intended to display choice pieces of porcelain, and the girandole, a branched candelabrum. These objects were made in pairs to fit the symmetrical room schemes of the time. The embroidered panel that appears here was until recently mounted in a scroll-cut, veneered frame equipped with two candle branches. The panel is one of a pair; the other one has a parrot as the central motif rather than the peacock shown here. Embroiderers of the time seem always to have found a needlework equivalent to any lavish decorative item that appeared. This piece is an embroidered version of the rich mounted wall ornaments popular in the eighteenth century.

The original embroidered panel, now exceedingly fragile, has a satin-woven silk ground. In a few places it shows the black, brushed-ink line of its original drawing. Silk floss and threads of

Panel for a sconce

silk embroidery/England

varying thicknesses, some of them slightly twisted, were used to embroider the piece. There are accents of darned silk pile, and the vase has ornaments of silver thread. The needlework measures seven and one-half by seventeen inches.

The color of this embroidery is now faded. The back of the embroidery shows that some of the flowers that appear brownish on the front of the work were once rose colored or yellow. All the leaves were shaded in long and short stitch from deep bluish green to pale yellow-green. In most motifs the shading began with the outer contour. Each color of thread in the shading was used for one row of long and short stitch. A careful study of the color in the shading of a motif as it deepens or grows paler will help you to understand the way that the stitches were laid in. Many were made in a radiating fashion.

The following general description of the coloration in the flowers will aid you in making your embroidery. The central upper flower was shaded from blue to white. The flowers to the right and left of it were shaded in rose to white. There is more and deeper rose color in the flower on the left. The flowers to the right and left of the peacock were shaded from pale yellow to brown and have accents in shades of green. The carnation-like flower below the peacock is in shades of rose, tan, and white. Below and to the left of it is another flower in the same general colors, but paler in tonality, with green-to-yellow leaves at the base. Just above the vase is a rose-like flower in rose, tan, and white. Some of its rose tones are quite deep; this flower and the blue one at the center top have the strongest colors among the flowers. The drooping tulip at the bottom left is pale yellow, tan, and white. The tulips on the right are rose (or possibly they were lavender), tan, and white. Small flowers are pale pink or yellow shades, pink where they are next to yellow flowers, yellow where they are near rose. The peacock has a blue head, and his feathers are brown-to-gold. The "eyes" on his tail feathers are blue, and he has a red eye. The butterfly is shades of blue. The vase was shaded in blue with accents of deep rose, white, and silver. Scallops and buds across the center of the vase were made with silver passing. The clipped silk pile behind the vase is blue shaded with brown on the right, and brown shaded with blue on the left. At the base is an area shaded blue-green-yellow.

Contemporary adaptation

This design can be transferred to satin with dressmakers' carbon or sugar solution. The work should be mounted in an embroidery frame. (See M&T.) If the satin is lightweight it can be backed with lawn or fine linen. Most of the embroidery is carried out in long and short stitch, and the shading is made to follow a principal contour or to accent a characteristic detail. The first row of long and short stitch in a given area is arranged along this contour line; then rows of lighter or darker colors are arranged to create a shaded effect or in some places to create a pattern of stripes.

There are accents of darned pile behind the vase. The pile is made with looped running stitches placed closely and clipped. Working rows of loops over a needle laid on the surface of the fabric may help to keep the loops even and high. The few silver threads, such as those along the contours of the vase handles, were couched or were worked like satin stitch. Stems are silk in stem or outline stitch.

This sconce panel has a somewhat architectural flavor and might be used suitably behind the glass doors of a small cupboard or in shutter panels that have open sections for the insertion of small curtains or some other decorative treatment. If this embroidered panel is used in this type of shutter, it should be mounted over a flannel-covered panel of thin plywood, hardboard, heavy compo (heavy board made of paper), or mat board. The flannel and embroidered panel both should be stretched on the backing and secured with strong thread and long stitches worked from side to side and from top to bottom on the rear of the backing panel. (The embroidered panel should be large enough to wrap around the backing.) When the needlework is secured in place, the backing panel can be lined with cloth or felt, or a piece of colored mat board can be positioned behind the backing panel when it has been put in place in the shutter.

PANEL SCONCE
England; 18th century,
7½ in. x 17 in.

*If you wish
to enlarge this diagram
to its original scale,
refer to
the M&T section
at the back of the book
for the correct procedure.*

Cope and chasuble

gold embroidery and coral beading/Italy

color plate, page 109

The lovely, but not so ecclesiastical-looking, embroidery of the vestments shown here is a hybrid of elements from the baroque (beginning about 1600) and rococo styles. How such light-hearted patterns came into religious use was neither accidental nor arbitrary, but a reasonable development in the ever-changing relationship between the church and the faithful.

In the late Gothic period (which in painting began about the beginning of the fifteenth century) artists set aside the symbolic expression of ideas in favor of optical views of the natural world, although symbolism persisted in meanings ascribed to plants, animals, and objects of everyday life. The climactic Renaissance that followed emphasized analysis of the problems of anatomy, perspective, and chiaroscuro (effects of light and shade in imitation of nature).

Then came the period of the Reformation, and for the short time that began during the deliberations of the Council of Trent (1545-1563) and ended at the final determination of counter-reformation policy there emerged an art of new religious fervor based on exaggerations of principles gleaned during the objective Renaissance. An appreciation of this art, called mannerism, depended heavily on the spectator's conversance with the principles involved. Mannerism was not easily understood, and counterreformation policy required a persuasive art that appealed directly to the senses rather than to the intellect in order to reinspire the doubting and draw them with renewed confidence back to the church. The baroque style, with its rosily robust figures lightly floating heavenward, was the answer. It was an overwhelming style, giving impressions of infiniteness that were not to be taken in at one glance, and it set the stage for monarchy as effectively as it served the purposes of the church. The advent of Louis XIV's monumental refurbishing of the hunting lodge at Versailles

in the second half of the seventeenth century caused the center of art for the secular world to be moved from Italy to France. In time, as the saddened old king's reign came to a close (September 1, 1715), the carefree baroque style grew dark and sober. In a few years it was replaced by the rococo style, a light-hued, asymmetric confection of fantasy and intimacy that reflected the taste of two ladies—Madame de Pompadour and Madame du Barry.

The Italian cope and chasuble shown here are transitional in design; their style lies midway between the stately, symmetrical baroque and the tantalizingly pastel, s-curved rococo. These vestment patterns are as light in color and as small in scale as patterns of the rococo, but they share with baroque design a boldly scrolled compartmentalization and frontal, symmetrical arrangement. Most copes and chasubles in the baroque style have floral designs of much larger scale. The gold work frequently has a heavier look. Copes and chasubles in the rococo style quite often reflect a contemporary taste for Chinese things as well as taste for imaginative design based on commonplace objects of nature, such as rocks and shells. As they had been in the past, vestments were sometimes cut from garments worn by the wealthy. Many vestments of this period were made of textiles that seem as appropriate for a party as for the pulpit. On the ones shown here even the ecclesiastical symbols do not announce their meanings assertively. (The peacock symbolizes immortality; coral deflects evil.)

If you look closely at the flowers on these vestments it is apparent that the designs are no more botanically accurate than are those of earlier embroidery, but their dainty shading presages the nodding naturalism that was to come in the eighteenth century. It has been noted that in England and in northern Europe an interest in naturalistic flower motifs began in mid-sixteenth century. Botanical gardens already existed in Italy at Pisa, Padua, and Bologna before France's "Jardin du Roi" (King's Garden) was established in 1608. In 1585 the Robin brothers had interested Henry III of France in their idea for a botanical garden in Paris. They collected well over a thousand plants from such far distant places as Africa and America. Pierre

CHASUBLE
Italy; late 17th-early 18th century, 45 in. x 26 in.

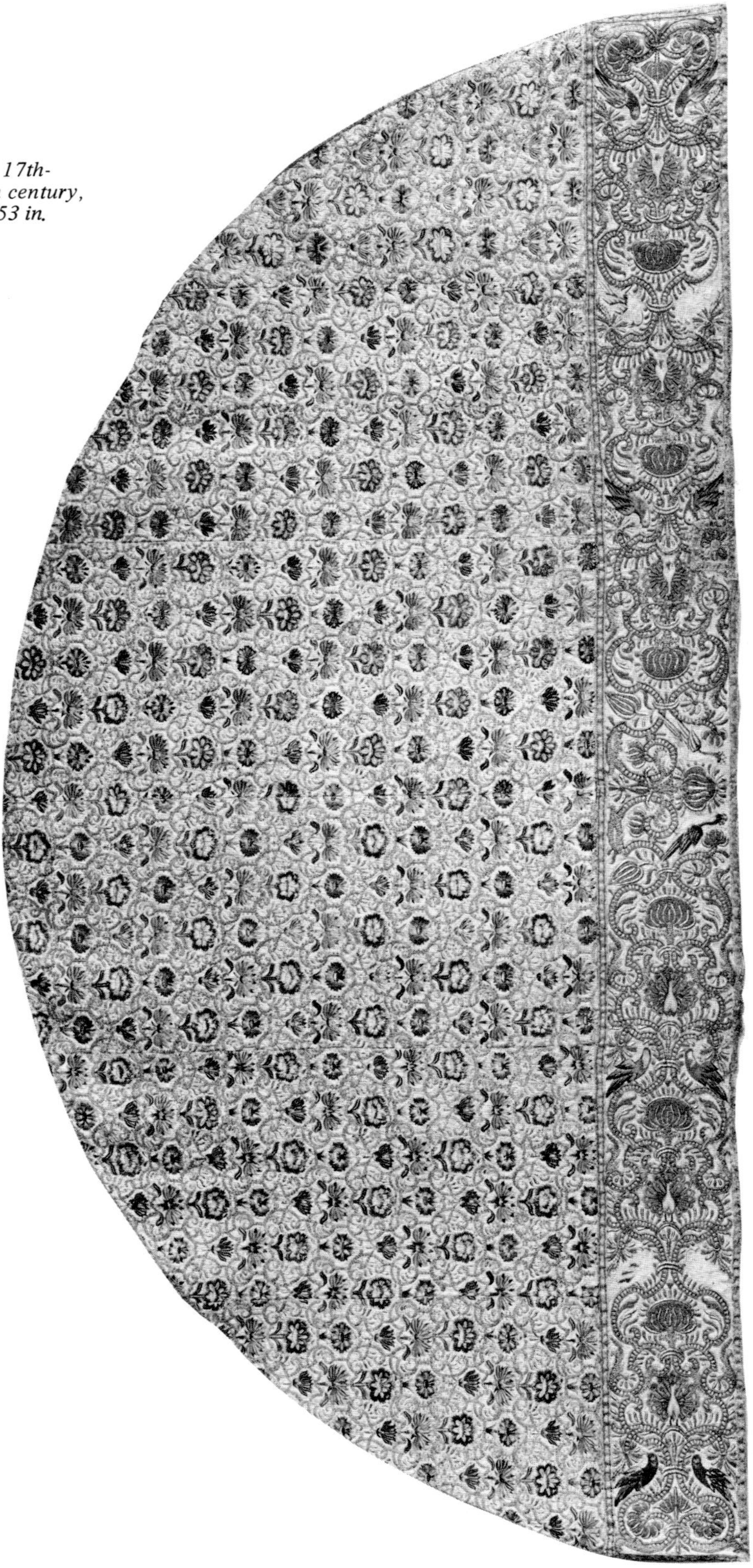

COPE
*Italy; late 17th-
early 18th century,
118 in. x 53 in.*

Vallet, a royal embroidery designer, joined in the botanical garden project, and between 1608 and 1650 he created a series of fine engravings of horticultural subjects that were, according to the title he gave his work, "exactly drawne."

In keeping with the trend Henry IV established gardens at Fontainebleau and elsewhere. When Perelle laid out the Jardin des Plantes in Paris in 1635 he had the Robins' garden in mind. The close alliance between gardens and embroidery is apparent in the French name for formal flower beds laid out in geometric and arabesque designs—*compartiments de broiderie.* The vestments shown here carry with them the spirit of intricately designed formal gardens of the kind one sees, most often in bird's-eye view, in engravings by Vallet, Perelle, Callot, or Van de Passe.

This cope and chasuble were made of white, satin-woven silk over a stabilizing layer of linen. The silk floss embroidery—the repeated flowers in the body of the vestments, the peacocks, and the other birds—are presumed to have been made first. Long and short stitch was used throughout the work in a variety of shaded color combinations: wine with white; brown, coral, and white; shades of blue, coral, and yellow. The bodies of the birds and peacocks were worked in shades of blue in long and short stitch. The peacocks' tails were worked in single satin stitches of green, brown, and gold. The eyes of the peacocks are blue and gold. Brown and white stripes were worked on the legs and wings in satin stitch.

These needleworks are good examples of how different kinds of metal threads were used in harmony with silk embroidery and various ornaments. The gold threads are of two types— passing and plate. Passing is metal strip wound on a fiber core. Plate is a flat strip of metal, in this case almost one-eighth of an inch wide. To make flat leaves and coils (shown in the diagram with broken lines across the shapes) many rows of double strands of passing were laid parallel to one another the length of the band. Each double strand of passing was couched at regular intervals to secure it to the ground. The couching stitches of each successive pair of passing threads were made at exactly the same intervals as the previous pair, so that a pattern of stripes was

built up across the passing. Areas treated this way have borders of large coral beads. Large leaves, indicated in the diagram by allover broken lines, were made in the same way, except that the couching stitches were arranged brick fashion, and the shapes were edged either with beads or metal cord. Small leaves, indicated in the diagram by solid lines drawn horizontally across the figure, were padded and covered with plate folded back and forth, zigzag fashion, across their width. The folds were caught at each side with couching stitches. The edges of the padded leaves are covered with couched gold two-ply cord. The photograph of the detail shows that some of the motifs are filled with beads. These were sewn into place individually with back stitches. Slight variations in the treatment of motifs occur as the pattern repeats along the border of the cope.

Contemporary adaptation

To make a silk and gold version of the portion of the design diagrammed, first press a sugar solution transfer onto the ground satin, which, supported with an underlayer of linen if necessary, can then be mounted in an embroidery frame. (See M&T.) Work should begin with the silk floss areas—flowers, peacocks, and other birds. When these have been completed, passing threads can be couched into place. Then the padding for shapes to be covered with plate should be made. Using gold-colored silk floss or some other heavy thread for the padding, build up lengthwise stitches until sufficient padding is in place. Plate and coral beads should be put on at the end of the work. Plate is fragile, and the coral beads, once in place, are hard to work around. Therefore, when you sew on the beads, begin with the areas to be embroidered

ORPHREY
*Detail from cope, Italy;
late 17th-
early 18th century.*

This diagram can be
enlarged easily
for a more detailed
embroidery. See
the M&T section
for changing scale.
The accompanying legend
is a key to the way
in which various sections
should be worked.

Gold plate—padded
and couched—couching
stitches should be only
at the outer edges
of the motifs.

Gold passing—couched
brick fashion using
pairs of threads
running lengthwise
on the motifs.

Gold passing
lengthwise
pairs of threads—
couched with
tying stitches
arranged in rows
across the ribbonlike
motifs.

Coral beads—sewn on
with back stitches.

at the center and work out to the sides. Completed gold work can be protected by keeping a soft cloth under your hands.

The most astonishing feature of this needlework is its coral beadwork. These beads are irregularly cut and quite large. To duplicate these extraordinary beads today you would probably have to disassemble a necklace made from similar beads. Nothing approximating their quality can be found in any needlework supply store. Before you start an equivalent beaded needlework it would be wise to experiment with the beads you plan to use, so that any needed alterations in the diagram can be planned from the beginning of the work.

The design of this embroidery could be worked with threads and grounds other than silk and metal. In chain, Van Dyke, herringbone, Cretan or other fancy line stitches, the design would work well for woolen embroidery. French knots or bullion stitch could substitute for beads, or wooden beads could be used. Lovely French knots result when strands of different colored threads are combined in the needle. Leather strips could be substituted for pairs of passing threads. First, slightly dampen the leather strips by rolling them for a few hours in a damp towel; then curve the strips into place, allow them to dry, and couch them. Braid or cord also are possible substitutes for metal in this design.

The pattern can be adapted for costume use, and it could be modified for sleeves on an evening gown or for a decorative accent on an evening bag. The design also would be suitable for embroidered panels in shutters, as was suggested for the English sconce panel (see page 121), or as a cushion or chair back if worked in soft materials. Enlarged, this design could be used for a screen or wall hanging.

Man's cap

long and short stitch/France

Although the long-lived, round-topped man's cap (see page 38) continued to be worn in the eighteenth century, a new type, rather Chinese in style, developed out of interest in Eastern cultures. This cap's simple peaked crown was made from two pieces, and it had a two-piece brim. Sometimes a crease was pressed along the center of each side of the finished cap, so that it gave the effect of being four-sided, not so different from the earlier style. The oriental features of this cap are its flaring brim and tasseled peak. Its embroidered borders are typically French, identical to those transferred or painted onto porcelain and lacquered furniture at the time. Caps of this new design were also made of pattern-woven silk. Some were made of damask-woven or brocaded fabrics especially produced for the cap. These fabrics had small borders in the basic design that were woven in the pattern shape of the cap and exactly fit the cap edges when assembled. The designs of the woven borders often were similar to the design of the embroidered border shown here.

In the eighteenth century imitations of lace appeared in many patterns for embroidery and weaving. The merchant's sample shown on page 136 is one example. Embroideries of the time had replicas of all sorts of luxurious costume trimmings; of these one of the most popular, after lace, was an effect of ermine worked in chenille. In general, eighteenth-century embroideries deserve careful study for their technical ingenuity, especially for subtle effects achieved with underlying layers of cardboard, wire, or other paddings, and for their grace in transition between the woven design and the

embroidery, in the choice of both threads and stitches. Sometimes the line of demarcation between weaving and embroidery is not discernible on the face of the works of this period.

This cap is made of white silk satin with an underlayer of linen. The lining is rose-colored silk. The embroidery pattern differs on the two sides of the crown; the side not shown has a naturalistically colored rose as the central flower. On the side seen here a large carnation and bud were worked in silk floss in long and short stitch (used for all flowers and leaves) in shades of purple. A tulip, just below the carnation, was shaded from pink to deep rose. All the leaves were shaded green, darkest at contours. The stems were made with three rows of outline stitch in gold-colored silk. The colors used on the crown also were used on the brim. However, while the design for the brim is symmetrical, the color arrangement varies on the two sides; the four-petaled flower is in shades of rose on one side and in shades of yellow on the other. Lace-like designs along the edges were made primarily with gold-colored silk in line and stem stitches, but a few touches of pale yellow and rust appear here and there. From crown to headband the cap measures eight and one-quarter inches. One side of the cap measures twelve and one-half inches across from brim tip to brim tip.

Contemporary adaptation

The diagram shows the cap in its original size. To make it you should cut a trial pattern first, and reduce or enlarge the original pattern to fit the head of the intended wearer. Once you have decided on the proper size, baste tentative cutting lines for each half of the cap onto the silk ground, allowing a five-eighths-inch seam allowance all around. Do not cut the silk. Within the basting line, position a sugar solution transfer of the design on the silk. After the design has been transferred, mount the silk over linen if necessary, and put the work in an embroidery frame. Using silk floss, embroider the piece in colors and stitches that correspond to the description of the original. Check the basted cutting lines,

MAN'S CAP
*France; 18th century;
from crown to headband
this cap measures 8¼ in.;
one side measures 12½ in.
from brim tip to brim tip.*

This diagram shows
the carnation side
of the cap design.
Only half of the brim
has been shown because
the design is symmetrical
and is repeated
on the other half.
In order to give you
as large a diagram
as possible, repeated
designs are not shown.

and readjust them if the shape has altered during the embroidering. Cut and join the halves of
the crown; then join the brim ends. Line the
brim, which in this case is made separately, and
join it to the crown. Put the crown in place,
turning the raw edges of the hat, brim, and lining under it, and finish the crown lining by
turning it under and overcasting. There is no
headband ribbon to reenforce this cap, which
has frayed rather badly. A ribbon of purchased
milliners' grosgrain can be added, if desired.
Dampen the ribbon by rolling it in a damp
towel for a few hours to absorb moisture.
(Putting towel and ribbon in a plastic bag will
hasten the process.) Shape the moistened ribbon over a pattern that shows the curve of the
cap edge, and allow it to dry. Then sew the ribbon along the lower inside edge of the cap. Do
not join the upper edge of the ribbon to the
cap. A tassel made of twisted passing threads
trims the peak of the crown on the original.

Timelessly attractive, this cap, exactly as it
was originally made, could be used today for
evening wear. It also could be made for daytime wear in wool or soft leather, using threads
appropriate to those ground materials. The designs of the cap could be rearranged for use on
a handbag or covered box, or for chair backs,
seats, or cushions. An ensemble effect in keeping with eighteen-century style could be created
by using these designs for painted decorations
as well as for needlework. Chairs, shutters,
small tables, lamps, or other household items
could be ornamented in this way. Painted designs under several coats of clear lacquer would
give an authentic eighteenth-century effect.

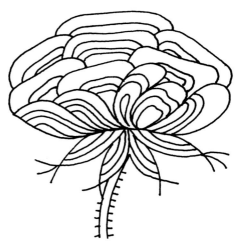

*This rose is the only
varying motif on the side
of the cap not shown.*

Gentleman's coat sample

satin stitch/France

color plate, page 110

In the eighteenth century men's dress clothes were richly trimmed, as were women's garments, with fine laces and embroidery and silk, and, in the first part of the century, gold and silver as well. The taste for embroidery was revived in France when Catherine de Medici came to Marseilles to marry the duke of Orleans, who later became Henry II, in 1533. In 1662 Colbert purchased the Gobelin workrooms in Paris, to be used for the production of furnishings and textiles for Louis XIV. Embroidery ateliers were established at Gobelin. Quantities of dainty, precisely made needlework were produced. In addition, Chinese and Japanese embroideries were imported. Suits were so richly decorated and expensive that by 1745, at the time of the Dauphin's marriage, it was not unusual to rent rather than buy a suit for a special occasion. Cost apparently did not inhibit demand. Henry Algoude relates in *Philippe de la Salle* that embroidery was so popular that 20,000 embroiderers were employed at Lyons.

To decide on a proper embroidery for a suit, a man chose from a set of samples submitted by a salesman, who very likely limited identification of the sample to a single number in order to protect his position as the middleman. The design shown here was intended for embroidery to be used as the borders on a man's coat and waistcoat. It comes from a set that includes smaller and simpler designs, but all are similar in that they have small flowers in rather natural colors interspersed with lacy or ribbonlike designs, and many have dark backgrounds. On other borders the designs might be more capricious. Gardening tools, wheelbarrows, dwarf gardeners, and monkeys playing musical instruments—subjects familiar in other crafts as well—were embroidered on clothing. Border designs were revised to fit pocket flaps and elaborated for borders surrounding pockets. Circular designs were made to cover buttons, which did not always function, and were sometimes used to border sleeve cuffs. In addition to samples of actual embroidery, the salesman carried painted patterns for embroidery as it would appear on particular garments. One of these painted samples is shown here.

Garments were worn for long periods, and today the ones that have survived are often faded and show all-too-evident signs of wear. For this reason collectors covet merchants', or salesmen's, samples; such sets are usually clear, clean, and bright even now.

The ground fabric for this sample is a voided velvet; that is, a design has been woven into the fabric in such a way that a pile surface appears in certain areas, while the basic ground weave shows in the remaining areas. (In the photograph the voided areas appear lighter against the black background.) In this sample the pile is black, the voided areas are purple, and an additional pattern of tiny pale green or gray dots is woven into the small, geometric design. The original sample measures eleven and three-eighths by seven and one-half inches, which will give you an idea of the scale.

The use of a rich ground fabric with a woven pattern of its own is usual in embroidery of this period. Like most characteristic embroidery of the time this sample is almost entirely satin stitch, sometimes called flat stitch, which is worked perfectly flat. Contours of the precisely drawn design are carefully worked. The thread most frequently used for these eighteenth-century needleworks is silk floss virtually untwisted, but tightly twisted silk threads, silk chenille, and metal threads are not unusual. Light-against-dark designs are typical, and a great deal of white is used. On cuffs and at necklines such embroidery made a graceful and harmonious transition between stiff silken garments and soft lace used as neckwear and sleeve frills.

In this sample, small white flowers have varying center color schemes and single straight stitches radiate from the colored center which is composed of two minute satin stitch circles. Each tiny flower center is two of three colors—pink, rose, pale green. The center of the upper, satin stitched rose is black with tiny back stitches around a satin stitch center. The white rose has a bronzy gold oval in the center surrounded by small knot stitches, which are gold and dark green. The upper inner petals of this flower are not satin stitch but are textured with

**GENTLEMAN'S
COAT SAMPLE**
*Detail, France;
18th century,
overall measurement is
11-3/8 in. x 7½ in.*

GENTLEMAN'S
VEST PATTERN
France; 18th century.

strands of floss laid across the area to form a checked, or lattice, design; the strands are caught with tiny stitches at the points where they intersect. The outer side and top petals on the rose are made with two rows of radiating straight stitches, which are made like long and short stitch; in the outer row the stitches are placed close together, while in the inner row they are spaced slightly apart so that the dark fabric shows through. The petals at the bottom of this flower are white satin stitch; the direction of stitches differs on each petal so that each reflects the light differently.

The border of the design is composed of solid bands of slanted satin stitch, a white row in untwisted silk floss and a blue row in silk in two-ply twist. These rows of satin stitch cover the edge of a mesh border made in tulle stitch.

Contemporary adaptation

Do not make the mistake of thinking that contemporary velvet or velveteen can be substituted for the velvet that was used for this needlework. Most present textiles have a pile that is coarser and higher than the pile of the original fabric. You must find a textile into which you can work a fine, flat stitch—perhaps a supple piece of silk rep, a damask-woven silk with a design that is not too outspoken, or a compound weave with a small geometric pattern. The original sample has a small, geometric, striped pattern that works in perfect counterpoint to the freely curving design of the embroidery. The formality of the simple lace-embroidery band along the edge functions to unite the two types of design.

When you have selected a fabric, carefully make the transfer. The method for transferring designs to velvet and the sugar solution transfer to be used with other fabrics are described in the M&T section. This embroidery should be mounted in a frame over an underlayer if necessary. Begin by embroidering the stems in outline stitch or diagonal satin stitch; then make

the leaves and, finally, the flowers. The stems and leaves are worked in satin stitch in five shades of green, from bluish to very pale. The direction of the stitches can be seen quite well in the photograph. When you are not sure, use your best judgment. Note that there is no long and short stitch (except as a single decorative row on a petal of the white rose), only flat satin stitch. Any effects of shading occur because shapes of related colors are juxtaposed, but the piece has no shaded areas. There is a clear line of demarcation between individual areas of solid color. Worked in silk floss this procedure produces in the work a maximum satiny sheen and exceedingly rich color; satin stitch produces a more glittering effect than does long and short stitch.

To make the border stripes, work twigs, feathers, and dots over mesh in line and satin stitches. To simplify the making of this border you can sew a strip of tulle or net in place; work the twigs over it in line stitches; then work the feathers (radiating long and short stitches), dots (satin stitch), and stripes (slanted satin stitch).

Although this design may be put to its original purpose of ornamenting clothing, it also may be considered for use on a small purse, a table linen, or a cushion. For the cushion a mirror image may be made from the design. The lacy border can be used alone as a simple decoration. For table linens and washable articles, the design can be worked in cotton or linen, or if enlarged it can be worked in wool, perhaps for a hat or evening coat.

*This diagram
of the merchant's sample
can be repeated
for a border design or
can be embroidered
as a single motif. The
pattern here is only
slightly smaller
than the original.
See the M&T section
at the back of the book
for changing the scale
of the pattern.*

Half boots

chenille embroidery/England

color plate, page 110

Over the years boots and shoes have been subject to as many vagaries of style as any other article of dress. Not infrequently they have served as a mark of status, as did the pair from Noin Ula (see the Introduction) on which even the soles were decorated. Shoes that had pointed toes of extraordinarily impractical length were called cracowes, after the Polish town of Cracow. In England the length of these shoepoints was officially limited in a 1464 edict that inveighed against the wearing of shoes with toes extending two inches or more beyond the normal length of the foot. The penalty included public damnation by the clergy as well as a fine. All manner of shoe shapes, many of them little related to the shape of the foot, have been tried. One of the most astonishing had a squarish toe with two little horn-like shapes extending from it. A broad-toed type of German origin was called *kuhmaul* (cow's mouth). In the last part of the sixteenth century a Venetian stilt-like shoe called *chopine* had a sole height that at times exceeded the length of the foot. Short Madame de Pompadour favored the *chopine* even though she, like everyone else who wore them, needed help in walking.

Every sort of decoration that can be applied to leather has been used for shoes. Leather has been pressed, carved, plaited, braided, molded, painted, ornamented with metal and gems, appliqued, and embroidered in every imaginable fashion. Shoes of cloth have been decorated in at least as many ways. Until recently pairs having identical right and left shoes had been made; the differentiation of shoes for the two feet can be traced back to medieval times.

Half boots, called startups, were fashionable over a long period. The pair shown here dates between 1840 and 1860 and probably was professionally embroidered. Laced or buttoned, boots were worn universally until about 1900. By this time machine-made laces and embroidery could be obtained (the first embroidery machine was invented in France in 1828 and patented in England in 1829), but despite the availability of ready-mades, hand embroidery continued. Quilting, patchwork, Berlin wool work (needlepoint embroidery with heavy woolen yarn), smocking, beading, and lace-making went on apace amid Victorian aspidistras and the antimacassars. For those more interested in profit than in beauty, "drizzling" was a satisfying hobby. Drizzling consisted of picking apart old embroideries that contained gold threads, then reducing the metal to dust so that it could be sold.

Too many domestic embroiderers relaxed into listless technique and thoughtless design during the nineteenth century, but needlework as a cottage industry reached remarkable levels of intricacy and precision. Programs to raise economically depressed conditions in rural areas frequently involved the production of one or another kind of whitework embroidery. Prices paid for the work were pitifully low, though, and many women went blind or had eye problems at an early age because of the exacting work. Designs of merciless detail were carried out without deviation from the marked pattern; precision was expected.

Embroidery manuals of the nineteenth century seem to assume that the worker would not innovate, and there was little new in the way of technique. An "oriental" type of embroidery was made in flat satin stitches without shading and with outlines kept in reserve; that is, a narrow line of background fabric was to show between areas of different colors. Another popular kind of embroidery, called needle-painting, was distantly akin to the great ecclesiastical embroideries of the thirteenth to sixteenth centuries. Needlepainting was done with flat stitches, usually long and short, shaded and carefully arranged so that the direction of the stitch helped to explain the forms of objects depicted in the needlemade "painting."

Fortunately, the nineteenth century produced some maverick needleworkers who did not always go by the book. The decoration of these

HALF BOOTS
England; 19th century.

boots is a potpourri of techniques. (See the color plate on page 110.) The lilies of the valley and their leaves were worked in the precisely contoured satin stitch of the oriental method. The roses were couched in chenille thread in several pink-to-maroon shades plus some rosy browns, and their leaves, also chenille, were worked in greens. Leaves with serrated edges were shaded with greens in long and short stitch. Some of the fuschia flowers have all-white outer petals with rose-colored inner petals. Others are half rose and half brownish wine. All were worked in long and short and satin stitches. (Mauves, magentas, and related colors were favorites after Perkins's discovery of aniline dyes in 1856.) Slender flower stamens were tipped with tiny gold metal beads, which also were scattered in clusters along the stem. Some of the stems of the flowers and leaves were worked in gold passing, two strands twisted and couched into place.

A striking note in this design is the handling of the lilies of the valley. Each flower is set against a broad green leaf, which is shorter than those in nature. This scheme solves the problem of trying to show a white flower against a white background fabric. The stylization provides a necessary astringent note in a design of sweet, full-blown blossoms.

In the nineteenth century no flower was more popular than the rose with its accompanying leafy buds, but the fuschia was a close second. Here the rose, fuschia, and lily of the valley are combined. Another popular, and symbolic, combination was the rose, thistle, and shamrock.

Contemporary adaptation

The diagram shown here is in the exact scale of the original design. It represents one half of the embroidery on one shoe. In the original, because of its relief the chenille rose is much more prominent than are other parts of the design. If the design is to be adapted to a new context, perhaps a border, the thread and stitches used for the rose may need to be changed to give the rose the same effect as the rest of the embroidery. Silk chenille is seldom to be found today, but cotton chenille can be obtained from weavers' suppliers. An excellent substitute for silk chenille can be made with a loose darning stitch pulled up and clipped to make pile. Hooking, as it is done in rug making but with a small hook, is another possibility. Small hooks are available in craft shops.

A sugar solution transfer should work well for this embroidery, which need not be framed if the pile, metal, and beads are applied last. The metal and beads could be put on without any tension after the rest of the work has been finished. The description of the original embroidery can be followed in doing the stitchery. Specific directions for the stitches can be found in the Stitch Directory at the back of the book.

This pattern would make a fine decoration for a fur-banded hat or jacket. It could be used in combination with velvet ribbons to make a cushion cover. Reversed repeats would make interesting designs on a shopping bag or at a neckline. And this design is still fine for boots or evening shoes.

*This diagram
is in the exact scale
of the original design.
It represents one half
of the embroidery
on one shoe. You will
probably want to put
the design to a new use:
a border on a hat
or shirt. Directions
for changing the scale
of the diagram
can be found in the M&T
section at the back
of the book.*

Cap back

white embroidery/France

From the fourteenth century on, when a French girl married she received a bonnet. To say she was bonneted was the same as saying she was married. Through the years, small caps have been made and worn by women in many countries, and they are seldom without decoration. Quilting, cutwork, drawn thread, and other embroideries and laces all have been used to decorate these caps. This nineteenth-century cap was bonnet shaped. It may have tied under the chin, and it may have been trimmed with a ruffle, most likely of bobbin lace, around the face. The cap was made of two pieces of embroidery—a back like the one shown here and a long rectangular piece fitted along the arc of the curved section to make the whole. The cap clearly reflects the design of the coveted laces of France and Flanders.

The northern countries developed beautiful and expensive laces that had graceful leaf and flower designs with miniscule fillings of intricate patterns and dainty mesh backgrounds. In contrast to these, the forerunning early laces of Italy were bold, either geometric or sculptural. They developed from drawn thread embroideries *(punto tirato)*. The threads that were drawn out of the ground fabric were used to work patterns into the fabric in hemstitching, weaving stitch, or buttonhole stitch. In a variation called *punto tagliato* parts of the ground were cut away. When drawnwork became so elaborate as to leave virtually no ground fabric other than the few threads that served as a base for the overlying embroidery, a lace called *reticello* was formed.

The next step was to dispense with the ground fabric altogether. Threads were basted to parchment over two layers of cloth in a design that was no longer tied to the horizontals and verticals—warps and wefts—of a ground fabric but could arch and curve according to fancy. This work was called *punto in aria,* point in the air. Buttonhole stitch was worked over the meandering lines; little bars joined the elements of the design. These little bars, or "brides," were worked solidly in buttonhole stitch. The development of *punto in aria* freed the design of laces from the geometric character that earlier techniques had imposed. Scrolls and botanical subjects could be worked, and extra threads were sometimes added to thicken and emphasize contours. All this work was done on a parchment and cloth base. When the stitching was finished and the lace complete, the basting threads of the initial outlines were snipped between the two underlying layers of cloth, and the lace was lifted from the parchment and linen ground. The delicate French and Flemish needlepoint laces, with their shaded flowers and *trompe l'oeil* (eye-fooling) effects, developed later in the same way as *punto in aria.* Whitework embroidery makers and lacemakers increasingly refined the subtleties of transparency and relief in their work. By the nineteenth century both needlework and lace were exceedingly intricate.

This cap is typical of those made in the nineteenth century, but it is relatively simple in technique. Its floral design relates both to the classical appliqué from Seo de Urgel on page 130 and to the bed valance from Skyros on page 153, but its meshy background and the various shadowy geometric fillings of its flowers are boldly simple statements of the same kind found in the intricate designs of needle lace. The symmetrical design (a cap back without a symmetrical design does not come to mind) consists of heavy buttonhole and satin stitch leaves and scrolls. Much of its lacy effect was achieved by working the entire background area in squared ground stitch, so that an overall mesh-like texture was created. Most of the flowers have fancy fillings. Notice that one has a large checkerboard pattern. The "whitest" of the squares in the checkerboard

CAP BACK
France; 19th century,
4¾ in. x 8-1/8 in.

were made with crossed back stitch. Crossed back stitch is always used on sheer fabrics, because only half of its effectiveness is the result of what happens to the stitch on the front surface of the fabric, where it looks like two parallel rows of back stitch. The manner of working these back stitches produces crossed stitches on the back of the fabric, and these can be seen as part of the design if the fabric on which they are worked is sheer enough to see through. Hence, what is happening on the back of the embroidery ground becomes a part of the lacy texture that one sees on the front. This stitch creates a white of middle density, halfway between the thinness of the ground and the thickness of the satin stitch and buttonhole stitch embroidery. The broad contours of flowers and scrolls were made with satin stitch and buttonhole stitch. The smaller, simpler flower fillings are geometric designs created with faggoting and squared ground stitch, by skipping stitches in rows or along diagonals in order to form a pattern.

Contemporary adaptation

The best fabric you could find to duplicate this cap back would be a linen that is sheer but has a good deal of body. Whatever you chose, it must be a plain-woven fabric. If you are working on a sheer fabric of light color and are intending to make a background of squared ground stitch, the design should be transferred to the back of the work in such a way that it can be seen on the front surface of the material. Making the transfer on the back is doubly advantageous, because the first embroidery to be worked should be the background (squared ground stitch is worked from the back), and because a tracing on the back of the ground fabric eliminates the possibility of smudges from it on the face of the work. White, of course, requires a delicate transfer.

To keep the two sides of this symmetrical design precisely the same, you may want to mount the ground fabric in a frame before making the transfer. Carbon transfer should work well. (See M&T.) The squared ground stitch embroidery will progress more easily if a rather large tapestry needle is used. When the background is finished, remount the work with the face side upward; then in crossed back stitch work the areas that have checkerboard designs. Some of the smaller fillings of the original are faggoted in geometric patterns; others are squared ground stitch. Your fabric and the scale of your work probably will differ from those of the original, so fillings probably would have to be redesigned for your use. The photograph will give you an idea of the type of simple, geometric pattern that was worked out for the original. The heavy part of the embroidery—the scrolls and flowers in satin and buttonhole stitch—should be put in last. These will cover any irregular edges that result when the threadcounted faggoting and squared ground stitches are made. Notice that in most places the buttonhole stitches are diagonal rather than at right angles to the contour, as is usual. Satin stitch appears in only a few small areas. These areas can be recognized because no little ridge exists along the edge of the areas embroidered in satin stitch. Stems and curlicues should be done in chain and outline stitch.

The thread used for this embroidery will affect the appearance of the work in a crucial way, so you should choose linen thread or cottons of special quality (made for this type of work). Weavers' threads in linen are more generally available than are linen embroidery threads. Experiment with both warp and weft types. Warp threads, tightly twisted for durability during the weaving process, will not break but may tend to twist unpleasantly as they are used; weft threads, which have a lovely sheen, may break or fray when used for embroidery. However, each is at times a better choice than a coarse mercerized cotton. Weft threads, used in short lengths, can look quite beautiful in embroidery.

This design would make a pretty cap for members of a wedding party. A border for a front section could be improvised from the motifs of the back. In miniature it would make

This diagram shows half of the cap back pattern. Since the design is symmetrical, trace this diagram twice, turn over one of the tracings, and butt the two halves so that the overall design matches the photograph. See the M&T section for changing the scale of the pattern.

a lovely christening bonnet. Worked on wool or leather in crewels with laid work in place of lacy filling stitches, the design could be used for a cold-weather cap. (For an idea of how to cut the front section of this cap see the accompanying illustration.)

The design on this cap can be adapted easily for other types of projects. To make the design into a square, repeat in the upper corners the rosette and leaf motif that appears in the lower corners, adding a second leaf on the other side of the rosette. As is or revised, this design would look handsome as a runner or as scarf ends. Upended, it could decorate a neckline or pockets. Translated to quilting, the shape would need little revision for use on a handbag or tea cozy. With corner motifs removed, the design could be used for a little round boudoir pillow.

This type of design also looks charming worked in colors. Traditionally it is seen in heavy padded satin stitch in wool of gay hues. The basic design, with the complicated fillings and background eliminated, is simple enough to adapt to stitches and materials of many kinds.

This diagram gives you some idea of how the back was sewn to an over-the-head piece of embroidered fabric to make the cap, which was tied under the chin with drawstrings.

In general American needlework followed English work, but those women who had limited leisure time and few pieces of fabric to give to the art produced, from necessity, a variation that differed in the proportion of ground to motif—more background was left open—and in the seemingly deliberate choice of stitches that put most of the thread on the front of the work. Imported materials were available in towns, but in the country fabric and thread were most often homespun and home dyed. (After 1787 mechanically spun yarn did become available.)

The first settlers in America found hemp growing wild in Virginia. Lord Delaware wrote: "Hempe better than English [grows] wild in abundance." (See Frances Little's *Early American Textiles.*) Flax growing was encouraged, because the English found that the linen made from colonial flax was excellent, and flax raising provided good employment for the poor, thus assuring a constant supply of raw materials for English industry. However, tobacco was a more profitable crop, and flax raising lagged behind it. Silk production also was encouraged in the colonies, because attempts to raise mulberry trees in England had been abortive. Although silk was produced successfully, its culture on a large scale proved to be impractical, so efforts ceased. Sheep raising for wool production was discouraged by the mother country, where

Tablecloth

competition with a thriving English industry was not wanted. When the cotton gin was invented in 1794, cotton became the leading American textile fiber.

The American needlewoman liked rich, full-bodied color. Red was derived from madder roots. Onion skins boiled in a brass kettle produced a lemon yellow. Purples sometimes were made by boiling the dye out of paper in which sugar was wrapped. But at the time indigo was the only dye that was washfast without the use of a mordant. (Mordants are agents such as aluminum hydroxide or tannic acid that combine with the dye to make it insoluble. In some printing processes the mordant is printed with blocks or other devices onto the textile, and the whole is dyed; then after washing, that part that has no mordant-print appears "white" because the dyestuff has dissolved in those areas.) The easily grown indigo plant was brought to South Carolina in the eighteenth century by Mrs. Eliza Pinckney, daughter of the governor of Antigua. Soon every household had a vat of ill-smelling, fermenting indigo in some well-ventilated spot. Making the dye was a lengthy and disagreeable process, but several good blues could be produced, and with an overdyeing of yellow, greens also were possible.

American design sources were similar to those used in England. Where available, pattern books, herbals, ladies' magazines, samplers, wallpapers, lining papers, and pattern-woven textiles yielded designs, and itinerant artists provided patterns. In towns needlework technique was taught in private schools. Polly Balch's establishment in Providence, Rhode Island, was a famous one.

This American tablecloth from the eighteenth, or possibly the early nineteenth, century was made of tabby-woven linen, part natural, part dyed blue. The cloth was carefully pieced together from 108 natural colored squares embroidered in blue linen. Between the squares, which measure about five and one-half inches, are two and one-quarter inch bands of blue embroidered with white cotton designs.

The stitches are simple: stem, buttonhole, long and short, and tied herringbone. (Note that in the diagram repeated areas, such as the four leaves that extend from the central flower and the curved shape in the border, have been drawn in detail once. The other sketches indicate the basic shape of each motif.) The central floral motif has a center circle worked with stem stitch; a row of buttonhole stitch is on each side of this stem stitched circle. The petals are outlined by two rows of stem stitch. Four sprigs of buds and leaves emanate from the center circle. They are edged with one row of stem stitch, and outside that row is one row of buttonhole stitch worked so that an edge of picot-like spines surrounds all. The bottom side leaves, indicated by cross-hatching on the diagram, are filled with tied herringbone stitch, making a lacy, zigzagged design in them. The middle leaves, indicated by long broken lines, are filled with long, straight stitches. Blue border areas embroidered with white have stem stitch and buttonhole stitch leaf edges with tied herringbone fillings. The rosettes were made with stem and buttonhole stitches; the outer edges of the petals have three rows of stem and one of buttonhole.

Contemporary adaptation

This patchwork embroidery might be carried on a trip to work at odd moments. For such a purpose you could cut small, separate squares, transfer the design to them, and embroider them in a hand hoop. For convenience in handling the small squares you could baste them into a larger square that has a five-and-one-quarter-inch square opening cut in the center. (The five-and-one-half-inch finished measurement of the patches should be increased to about six and one-quarter inches to allow for a small hem.) With the patch basted into the supplementary square, the work will be large enough to be held securely in a hoop so that excess fabric need not be left on each patch for this purpose. When the embroidery is finished, the basting threads

TABLECLOTH
*America; 18th
or early 19th century,
72½ in. x 94½ in.*

are removed, and another patch is basted into the supplementary square.

To work the patches on intact fabrics, pull threads out of the ground linen at six-and-one-quarter-inch intervals in each direction to indicate the squares. Work an embroidered motif in each square and cut them apart when ready to make the patchwork.

Prepare a pricking for pouncing. (See M&T.) When a simple design is to be repeated several times, a transfer made in this way is worth the trouble. Work the embroidery in a hand hoop, according to the description of the stitches of the original. The blue fabric is prepared and worked in the same way as the natural fabric.

If the tablecloth will be unlined, as is the original, all patches should be hemmed. If the embroidery will be lined, hemming the patches is unnecessary. The patches are joined with tiny overcasting stitches.

In making this needlework, you might consider that the effect of hand-dyed blue is sufficiently important to undertake the dyeing of ground fabric and thread. Weavers' supply companies and some artists' suppliers can provide dyes and directions for their use, which will vary according to the type of dye.

This design would make a good tablecloth or bed cover in the scale of the original or in a slightly enlarged scale. It also could be used for quilting. Single motifs could decorate for pockets, potholders, hotpads, napkins, or other small projects. Greatly enlarged and worked in heavy threads or yarn, a single motif with four bordering patterns would make a pillow cover. A change of thread and fabric will give this design a contemporary look. Consider the possibility of using a small print or stripe in conjunction with an embroidered border of these designs to make a skirt or apron.

*This diagram shows
the repeating square and
border motif
for the American
tablecloth. The size
as diagrammed is exactly
like the original. See
the M&T section
at the back of the book
if you wish to change
the scale of the pattern.*

Bed valance

darning stitch/Greece

color plate, page 111

Until the nineteenth century, pirates scourged the Aegean Sea. Inhabitants of the Greek Islands, too poor to construct walls around their settlements, built their houses close together with backs connected so as to form a barricade around the village. Women stayed in safety on the islands and had little opportunity to exchange ideas with people from other places. Much of their spare time was spent in embroidering. A family's status depended to a surprising degree on the quantity and quality of the needlework it possessed. Mothers and grandmothers handed down designs of their work; there was little conscious innovation. Thus needlework patterns remained virtually the same over a period of 150 years. When new ideas did appear, they were prompted by foreign designs that came to the islands during periods of Turkish or Venetian occupation, or by patterns on some new object brought home by a seafaring man. Many embroideries reflect the designs on faïence from Isnik, Kütahya, or Chanakkale.

Island embroideries contain a wealth of motifs, but a freely drawn, illustrative composition is a rarity. The embroidery of each island is recognizable by its distinctive motifs, color, and stitching. Among the often-repeated schematic designs are diamond and hexagon arrangements, pairs of geometric leaves set at forty-five-degree angles ("kings"), branched arrangements within diamond shapes ("queens"), and compact, flower-like designs seemingly derived from ancient patterns that show confronting or addorsed animals with a tree of life between them ("glastras"). Rose sprays, which arrived from **Persia** through Turkey, were popular. Stylized peacocks, griffins, dogs, and other animals appeared. The double-headed eagle was a staple motif of Cretan embroidery, which was deeply influenced by Venetian and Turkish art. The motifs of Turkey and Italy intermingled in Cretan design; the Turkish carnation appears alongside the double-tailed Italian siren.

The Greeks produced their own linen and silk, from raw material to finished goods. Certain colors identified needleworks as having come from a particular island known for its special dye. The presence of pale blue and lemon yellow identifies Skyros embroidery. These colors, which suggest the embroideries of the neighboring Turks, have a pastel quality that plays little or no part in needlework of the other islands. Many embroideries made in the Greek islands are monochromatic or are limited to two or three colors worked out in a one-to-two or a one-to-three ratio.

The embroideries of Skyros and the northern Sporades make much use of human and animal figures. A well-known one is the Skyros cock with its flowering tail; it has counterparts in much other folk art and seems also to be related to the flower-sprouting cocks of the ancient Scyths, for whom the cock represented the sun god. Skyros motifs also include a large female figure that appears to be related to the Scythian Great Goddess. That the needlework of the Greek islands is tradition-bound and conservative becomes clear when it is compared with the domestic embroidery of England. There needlework always clearly reflected the political and social interests of the moment, and frequently the embroiderer disinclined toward politics, simply looked at nature for inspiration—and that never seems to have entered the head of her Greek sister.

It has been said that much of the islanders' wealth lay in costumes and furnishings, for ritual and daily use, that their families accumulated through the generations. Greeks took pride in the richness and exquisite workmanship of the embroideries they brought out on the festal occasions that marked the milestones

KÜTAHYA WARE
Detail, Turkey;
18th century.

of their lives. The bed tent door, the most re-markable and sustained effort among all the forms, was used at marriage, shortly thereafter, and on only a few other occasions in one gener-ation. The people that made these embroideries intended them for use within their own families. Each girl received some of the family embroidery from her mother, and she made a good deal her-self. When girls no longer showed interest in providing the needleworks for their own dowries, chagrined mothers sometimes separated im-portant large pieces so that more than one daughter would have at least a part of a really impressive embroidery.

The bed valance shown here comes from the island of Skyros. It was worked entirely in darning stitch, except for a few outlines in out-line stitch. The silk threads used for the em-broidery are fairly thick, so the one thread of the ground fabric that was picked up in the darning stitch hardly shows. The bulging stitches of the rows that lie on each side tend to crowd the space. The ground fabric, of medium weight and rather loose plain weave, was well adapted to the requirements of threadcounted darning. The motif seen here was repeated with only very minor variations along the edge of a wide valance. Each motif is twelve and one-half by fifteen and one-half inches and is set about six or seven inches away from the adjacent patterns. The colors vary: red alternates with yellow from one design to the next.

Contemporary adaptation

To duplicate this embroidery obtain an open, plain-woven linen and fairly heavy silk thread with a slight twist. Two-ply thread would work well. Embroiderers' evenweave linen would

ISNIK WARE
Detail, Turkey; c. 1545.

COCK
Greece, Skyros;
17th century.

BED VALANCE
Single motif,
Greek Islands, Skyros;
17th-18th century,
12½ in. x 15½ in.

*This diagram
may be repeated
along a border and used
much as it was
in the original Skyros
bed valance, or it
could be enlarged for a
more elaborate embroidery.
See the M&T section
at the back of the book
for enlarging procedures.*

count easily and would be perfectly appropriate, but it is a denser fabric than that used for the original. Suppliers of drapery fabrics sometimes stock linens that approximate the texture of the material on which this needlework was made.

This embroidery need not be mounted in a frame; a hand hoop is adequate. Care should be taken that the design, as it is transferred, is as symmetrical as possible. Variations will occur inevitably as the needlework progresses, so there should be as few deviations as possible at the outset. Sugar solution or dressmakers' carbon can be used for the transfer. (See M&T.) As darning stitches are made, the threads of the ground should be picked up in such a way that a brick-like pattern builds up with each successive row.

Consult the color plate on page 111 for color arrangement. A black outline surrounds most yellow and white shapes. A red outline surrounds shapes next to green in the central motif. The heads are not filled with embroidery, but the hands are white. Note the curling of the pointed serrations of leaves and petals, suggestive of Turkish design. Note also that most of the shapes have no outline, and that much of the charm of this technique lies in its carefully made edges.

A bold, large spot pattern of this type has many uses. Only one repeat would make a handsome pillow cover, shopping bag, towel end, or panel for a glass cupboard door.

Among the embroideries in the collection of Burton Yost Berry is a large square that has a corner detail showing a ship. In an article in *Embroidery* magazine (June 1936) Mr. Berry wrote, "In Turkey weaving and ornamentation of textiles was regarded as one of the fine arts." He pointed out that since the Moslem interdiction against depicting humans and animals in art precluded the decoration of mosques with painting and sculpture these arts failed to develop as fully as they did under the sponsorship of other religions. The result was that some of the best creative energy in the country was expended on the making of knotted carpets, pattern-woven textiles, and embroidery.

Among nomadic people textiles are an appropriate vehicle for artistic expression. In medieval times tapestries and other textiles were carried from house to house as feudal lords moved about to oversee the affairs of their vast estates. Possibly, decorative textiles have gained popularity in our own day because we, too, are on the move and appreciate an art form that can be rolled up and transported without fear of damage. The Turks were true connoisseurs of fine textiles. They even carried embroidered tents to the battle fields.

There are two major divisions of Turkish embroidery. One is clearly related to woven textiles and is always large in scale. Wall hangings, screens, prayer rugs, and floor coverings belong to this category. An article sometimes identified as a bedspread is, in fact, a sort of lap robe. (Turkish beds were rolled up and placed out of sight during the day.) Embroidered rugs were practical because shoes were customarily removed before entering a house. The designs of these large embroideries relate to woven textiles that were made at Brusa and Scutari.

The other major group of Turkish embroideries consists of smaller items. Although these needleworks vary greatly in size and shape, they can be classed as "squares" (chevré) and "towels" (peshkir); a long form of the towel became a

Ship design

reversible embroidery/Turkey

color plate, page 113

SHIP DESIGN
*Single motif
from a square, Turkey;
18th century; square
measures 52 in. x 52 in.;
the ship motif measures
12 in. x 16 in.*

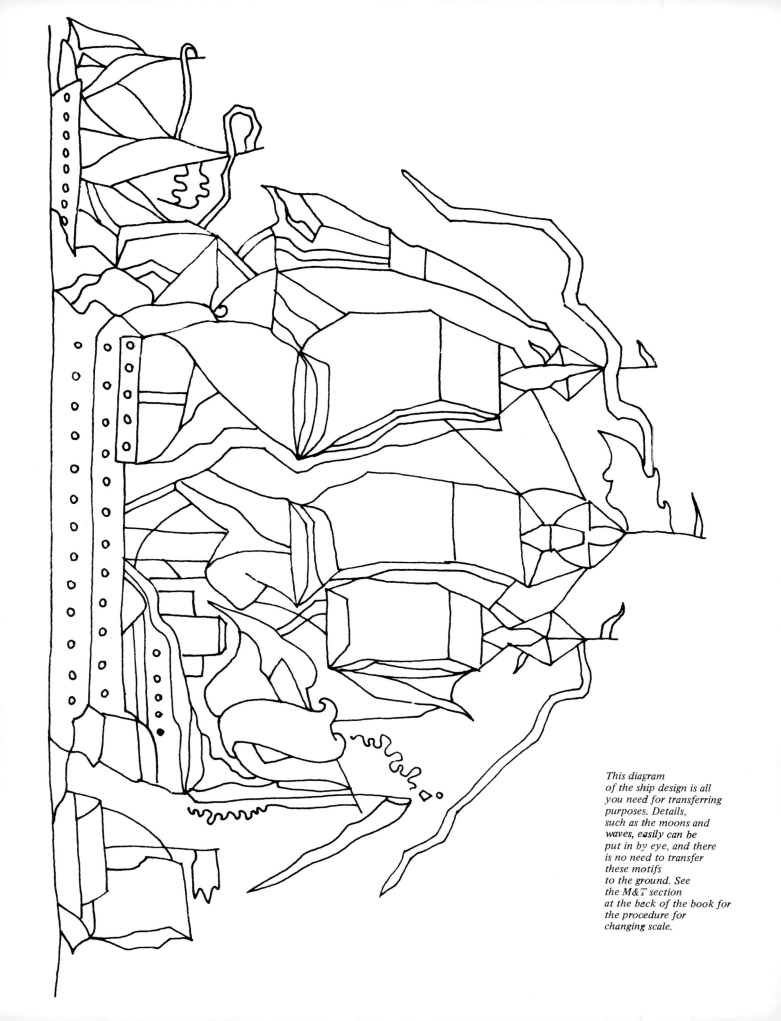

This diagram
of the ship design is all
you need for transferring
purposes. Details,
such as the moons and
waves, easily can be
put in by eye, and there
is no need to transfer
these motifs
to the ground. See
the M&T section
at the back of the book for
the procedure for
changing scale.

sash. Squares were used as handkerchiefs, napkins, or towels, depending on the need of the moment. The towel served as a sash, headdress, or napkin. This ambivalence of function is characteristically Turkish. In a Turkish house a room had no one particular function. To bring in a tray was to make the room a dining place.

Squares were made of cotton, linen, silk, or combinations of fibers. In Stambul, jewels were worked into the embroidery. Occasionally, human hair was substituted for black thread; the usual threads, though, were silk and metal. In the sixteenth and seventeenth centuries, squares had ogival patterns in light tones of red, blue, yellow, green, and brown; stronger colors and new designs were introduced in the late seventeenth century. Flower sprays, cypress and kiosk landscapes (presumably to represent a particular garden favored by the harem woman who made the embroidery), and calligraphy were used. Mosques and minarets appeared infrequently. The Bosphorus is seen in many of the landscapes, and ships and fish appear in others.

The pastel colors of this Turkish embroidery are not the result of fading. When threads are separated to reveal fibers never exposed to the light, little fading can be detected. A great many squares of embroidery were made for special occasions, and when the day had passed they were tucked away for safekeeping and never used again.

The lace edging on this embroidery was worked in an interesting technique called bebilla. It is found on Greek, Turkish, and Armenian textiles, but its exact origin is not known. It can be traced to Syria 600 years before Christ and seems related to ancient rugmaking. Its likeness to fishermen's knotting is obvious. Another suggestion is that it may have been developed as an alternative to the perishable wax flowers that Turkish harem women wore in their hair. Flowers worked in colored bebilla were more durable. A simple geometric design is seen here, but some very intricate work was done in designs that included the extremely popular floral motifs, as well as fish and animals. Colored or white silk thread of fine texture was used most often, but in some locations a heavy white thread was chosen. In the first quarter of

the twentieth century, old bebilla designs were copied in crochet and in a technique that involved sewing cords together.

The square shown here is a large one, measuring about fifty-two by fifty-two inches. Eight ship motifs were worked along the edges, each measuring twelve by sixteen inches. The ship's hull, worked in gold passing, blue, tan, and cream silk, was embroidered in double faggot stitch. This stitch also was used for the triangular-shaped motifs in the wavy sea and the upper sections of the sails. The faggoting is finished so as to be reversible. The embroidery of this square is identical front and back.

The crossed stripes in one of the accompanying diagrams indicate areas in which plate (gold) has been used. The other diagram is intended to show only the essential parts of the drawing that must be included in the transfer. Stripes worked in sturdy plate were made by pushing the metal strip through the loosely woven ground fabric, wrapping the threads of the ground as in overcasting stitch. The rest of the design was worked in silk in double running stitch. Long, narrow, straight shapes, as a rule, were embroidered with double running stitches. For example, the large flag at the top of the highest mast has blue stripes worked in double running stitch in the direction of the stripes, and gold stripes worked in double faggot stitch. All the stitches are very tiny. Double running stitch was worked with two-ply twist silk.

Contemporary adaptation

Because of the difficulty in obtaining materials similar to the ones used in the original, you should not attempt to work this ship exactly like the original. The gold passing threads are exceedingly fine, and the plate has a much more

workable texture than does currently available material. An embroidery in the same stitches and in gold supplies now on hand could be successful if the scale of the design was increased, and it still would be a challenging project. With dressmakers' carbon or sugar solution, transfer onto a fine, plain-woven linen as much of the design as is needed; then mount the material in an embroidery frame. Silk stitching in double running stitch should be done first. Double faggoting with gold passing should be worked next, counting threads. Plate should be put in last. Since most sources now carry only narrow widths of plate, you may find that you can work the plate into the ground by using a large needle that will open a hole in the fabric large enough for the metal to pass through without abrasion.

An edging made with detached buttonhole stitches would stand in very well for the bebilla edging of the original, or a crocheted edge could be used. Bebilla-making is very taxing to the eyes, and some authorities point out that it was made only in countries where the light is very strong. Since the most incredibly delicate of needle laces were made in northern countries, this argument hardly seems justified, but it is true that the bebilla stitch requires dexterity and close looking, so little points of detached buttonhole stitches would be much simpler to make.

This rather mystical ship and small caïques, according to Turkish custom, have no sailors aboard. The same ship may be found in Greek embroidery, where it is fitted out with checkered and dotted sails, and teems with sailors, animals, and birds. These motifs even fill the sky.

Much of the charm of this embroidery results from its naturalistic design and extensive detail worked in threadcounted techniques. These techniques slightly abstract the shapes, giving them an angularity that intrigues as they force the shapes into surprising configurations and compromises with the curves of nature. This design certainly could be rendered in needlepoint, and it would be greatly enriched by working tent (petit point) stitches along with larger (gros point) stitches, using silk, gold, and wool. Naturally, some simplification of the design would be necessary.

The design also could be worked much more simply by using double running stitch with Italian cross stitch. For these stitches the design would have to be enlarged, but the resulting embroidery would be reversible. Although the large original square very likely was draped, most people today probably prefer to see a design like this kept flat, possibly as a picture or wall hanging.

The striped areas in this diagram show the sections in which plate gold has been used.

Towel ends

double running stitch/Turkey

color plate, page 112

Squares and towels were the work of harem women. Sometimes they based their needlework on designs that male draftsmen supplied, but more often they copied old work. They also had samplers, some of them outlines only, which were handed from house to house. The designs were transferred to the ground fabric by copying freehand or, in some instances, by beginning immediately with thread. Print no. 52 in *Les 100 Estampes de Ferriol,* published in Paris in 1714, shows a Turkish woman seated cross-legged before a low, table-like embroidery frame. She appears to be working on a towel, and she is using her left hand on top of the work and her right hand from below. (This is a reversal of the usual position of the hands, but it may have resulted from the printmaker's failure to reverse the original drawing.) The frame is of interest because it shows no detail to indicate whether it was adjustable either in height or in the working area.

In *Turkish and Greek Island Embroideries,* Margaret Gentles provides an insight into the functions that these needleworks served.

> Writers of the Byzantine period mention the ceremonial use of the towel or napkin, as it is variously called, being thrown by the emperor from the imperial box at the Hippodrome to start the races. In 1652 De Busbecq, a traveler in Turkey, describing an archery contest held on a plain above Pera, wrote that the prize was an embroidered towel. Modern novelists have dramatically described how a sultan would select a beauty to be his queen for the night by presenting her with an embroidered towel—an event that happens also to be historically accurate. A bride normally was given a distinctively embroidered towel to be used on her wedding night and preserved thereafter as proof of the consummation of the marriage.

Commemoration of special occasions provided a continuing use for towels. Imperfections were intentionally worked into them to ward off the Evil Eye.

The unrealistic, fantastic nature of the cornucopia in the example shown here seems vaguely related to a group of woven fabrics, being made at the same time, that are now called bizarre. (See page 77.) Unlike Greek embroidery, the Turkish embroideries, no two exactly alike, were subject to influence from many places. Residents of the harems were themselves of various nationalities, and they brought embroidery designs from their homelands. There was a great deal of movement, both voluntary and because of the practice of exiling leaders out of favor, which added to the comingling of styles. It is through the differences in stitching rather than in the motifs that work of various districts and towns usually is identified.

On Turkish towels and squares some of the embroidery was threadcounted. Frequently, when tent stitch was used rows of back stitches were inserted between the rows, making the embroidery denser. Pulled stitches or openwork was used as background or filling. In the earliest Turkish embroidery double running stitch was used only for outlines. Later, used as a filling, double running stitch became one of the most favored stitches. Because it appeared identical on the front and back of the work, the reversible embroidery ideally suited the uses of squares and towels, a great many of which are exactly alike on both sides. Diagonal stitch also was used in these embroideries. It is interesting to observe, however, that while the popular rose usually was worked in double running stitch and the pink (dianthus) in diagonal stitch, when the two flowers were used together the two stitches were not combined, which indicates the preference of the Turkish needleworker for very few varieties of stitching within one piece. Towel ends were finished in several ways. Fringes made from warp ends, lace, or special hems with fancy stitches were made. Bebilla, the knotted buttonholing that appears on the square in the Turkish ship design on page 158, was also used for edging.

Towels had floral, geometric, or landscape designs. The florals might be single flowers with stems, sprays, fruit designs, cornucopias, or vases. Landscapes had various arrangements of leaves, trees, tents, houses, gardens, villages, and rivers. Rose, pomegranate, dianthus, hyacinth, pear, and tulip designs were favorites. It was from Turkey that the graceful tulip spread to Western Europe.

By the eighteenth century, when the towel seen here was made, it was customary to use rich colored silks in combination with gold plate and passing. The plate was wide and had to be pulled through the loosely woven fabric. Black was seldom used. The front-facing full-blown rose was very popular. Worked in stitches that, except for their random direction, resemble weaving, the Turkish towel embroidery looks very much like delicate tapestry. The tapestry effect was heightened by the system of shading that was used; a few tones were blended coarsely with sawtoothed joinings exactly like the "hachures," or short lines that indicate shading, of early tapestry. Allowing large areas of the few colors used, because the shapes were not broken by the continuous modification of the hues in gradual shading, this simple system was more successful than more complex blendings of color in retaining the maximum intensity of pure color. The excitement was augmented by adding to harmonious light, medium, and dark shades of rose the dissonance of a brownish maroon and a purplish pink of medium value. The bold, large scale adds to the drama of this piece and many others similar to it.

In this towel each repeat measures eight and one-half by twelve and one-half inches. Two

TOWEL
*Turkey; 18th century;
each repeat measures
8½ in. x 12½ in.*

kinds of gold thread—plate and passing—have been used in addition to silk floss. This reversible embroidery was worked almost entirely in double running stitch. Plate was pulled through the cloth after the fashion of satin stitch. The towel is edged in gold bobbin lace.

Contemporary adaptation

Because this embroidery is made on a sheer fabric and is quite heavy, tension will be kept most even if the work is mounted in a frame. Choose sheer linen in a natural ecru shade. Transfer the design to the linen using dressmakers' carbon. (See M&T.) The silk portion of the embroidery should be worked first, using double running stitch. If the embroidery is to be reversible, work each new thread under a previously embroidered area. Where that is not possible start the knotted thread a little apart from the place where the embroidery is to begin,

make two back stitches at the beginning point, and continue the work in double running stitch. The knot can then be clipped off. Follow the color plate on page 112 for an indication of how to arrange shaded areas. When the silk embroidery is finished you can begin the gold work. Some of the leaves and scrolls are filled with pairs of gold passing threads in double running stitch. These stitches can be made without too much injury to the passing if you use a large tapestry needle; but the eye of the needle must be large enough to open a hole so that the threads can pass through with ease. The plate can be handled in the same way if it is sufficiently supple and not too wide. The original embroidery has a gold bobbin lace edge, but crochet or a border of detached buttonhole stitches in a small, fancy pattern could be substituted.

This motif, made in reversible gold and silk embroidery, would be beautiful on a stole. In the proper setting the design also could be used for a cushion cover, a skirt or apron border, a box or book cover, or a carryall. The pattern probably would be more useful today as a wool-on-wool embroidery.

This diagram showing one repeat of the Turkish towel end can be used as a single motif or combined with many repeats and used along a border. This pattern is slightly smaller than the original embroidery. If you want to enlarge or reduce the scale of this motif, see the M&T section at the back of the book for the proper procedure.

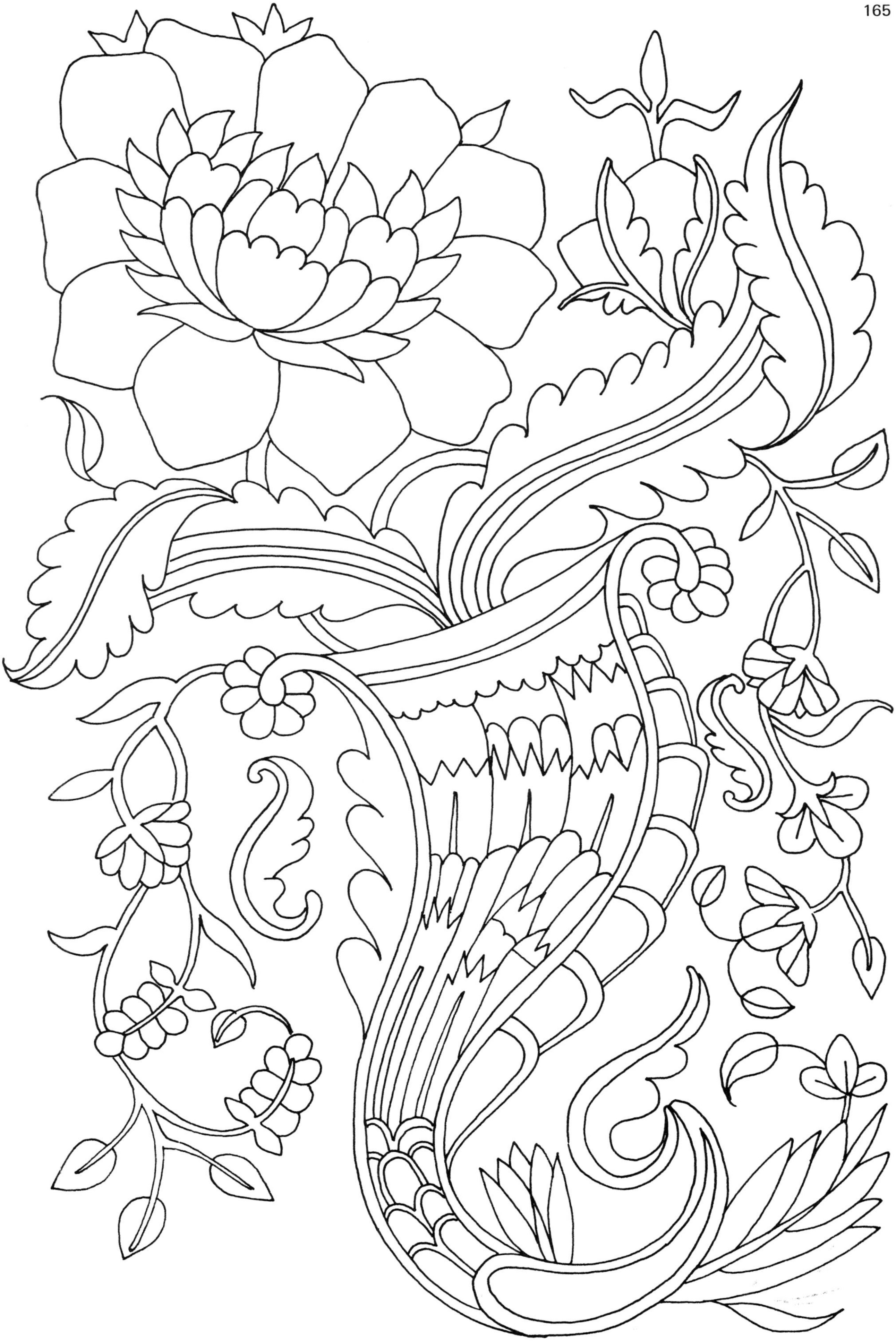

Sash

double darning stitch/Turkey

Most of the needlework designs in this book bear clear indications of the time and place of their origin, but the design and technique of the embroidery shown here are not easily placed. Early in the twentieth century researchers began systematic efforts to identify the geographic origins of different embroidery styles and techniques of the Mediterranean and the Near East, but regional variations of Turkish, Persian, and other Levantine needlework, long inaccessible to curious Western eyes, are not, in the West at least, so fully understood as those of Greek embroidery. The lack of records concerning domestic embroidery compounds the problem, which becomes even more confusing in needlework made after mid-nineteenth century, when French knots, satin stitch bows, and other Western motifs began to be used.

This embroidery clearly belongs to the Mediterranean area. The color, style, and materials of this long sash suggest that it is Turkish work, probably of the nineteenth century. Its pastel colors (coral, rose, soft brown, and turquoise) are more characteristic of Turkish than of Greek work. This sash was originally as light in color as it is now. Separation of the threads to reveal those hidden from light shows little fading has taken place. The use of gold thread and metal strip is also more characteristic of Turkish embroidery than of that in other Mediterranean regions. In this piece both passing and plate have been used. The presence of passing usually indicates an "early" embroidery —that is, from the seventeenth and eighteenth centuries—but the broad handling of this abstracted design makes it difficult to be sure it was made earlier than the nineteenth century.

A long sash made of loosely woven fabric is a typically Turkish object. This one is nine inches wide and eighty-seven inches long. It has been folded and sewn together along one side to form a headdress.

In this design the sawtooth petals and bold concentric bands on flowers are suggestive of Tetuan (Moroccan) embroidery, but the strong color schemes of Tetuan needleworks, although sometimes now faded, included much red and blue; in fact, the backgrounds were often red or blue, and this embroidery does not have these colors. The design does not fit any of the formulas for pomegranate or rose spray patterns. It defies efforts to associate it with the Greek "glastra"—a symmetrical, highly abstracted arrangement of flowers (a "tree of life?") with vestigial, sometimes animistic shapes in the lower corners (confronting animals?).

A drawn thread border from Niji-Novgorod (Russia) correlates with this sash pattern in a more satisfying way (see illustration). In the Russian piece an arrangement of geometric flowers, positioned between facing, rearing horses, is obviously intended as a tree of life.

The ambiguity of this sash-headdress argues for Turkish origin. Women in Turkish harems came from Greece, Persia, Russia, Tunisia, and Algeria, and their cultures and crafts surely must have intermingled.

This embroidery is reversible. All thread ends have been worked into the stitching, and

SASH
Detail, Turkey;
probably 19th century,
9 in. x 87 in.

BORDER
Niji-Novgorod, Russia.

the needlework has an identical appearance front and back. The flowers and leaves were worked in double darning stitch, running vertically. There are some double running stitch contours and some straight overcasting where thicker lines along the border were wanted. Metal strips were worked in and out of the loosely woven ground.

In the center flower of the design the colored circles, beginning at the center, are arranged as follows: gold (metal), silver, brownish rose, pale peach, and rose on the outer edge. In the upper right-hand corner and lower left-hand corner of the embroidery the color scheme for the flower, from the center, is: gold (metal), brownish rose, pale peach, no embroidery next row, and turquoise. The lower right and upper left flowers' color scheme, starting from the center, is: silver, gold (metal), brownish rose, white, no color, deep coral. The double running stitch stems of the flowers and leaves now appear brown; originally they were deep brown or black. Circular buds are rosy brown, and small, tulip-like blooms are peach with gold (metal) spots. Leaves adjacent to the small blooms are gold, and the downturned, somewhat triangular shapes are gold (metal). There are brown-black lines throughout. The lower border is yellow and black satin stitch.

Contemporary adaptation

Since this embroidery was threadcounted, you will need a loosely woven plain weave for the ground material if you plan to make a piece like the original. The design can be transferred onto fabric with dressmakers' carbon or by any other preferred transfer method. (See M&T.) The gold portion of the embroidery must be accomplished with the fabric mounted in a frame, but silk embroidery may be worked in a hand hoop, if preferred, before the gold is worked. Plate can be threaded into a large needle and sewn into place. The needle should open a hole in the fabric large enough to allow the plate to slip through the opening without injury. The design as it appears in the diagram is the same size as one repeat in the original. Duplicate the pattern for the other half of the design to make a facsimile of the original.

Made reversible, this design would be lovely on scarf ends or as a panel for a small window. It could be used for a cushion cover, chair seats, or a handbag. Repeated, it would make a handsome bed or table cover; enlarged in scale, it could be used for appliqué.

Most of one repeat for the Turkish sash has been shown in this diagram. On one edge the motifs are not complete, but these are simple to finish by hand when you are tracing. Considerably enlarged this pattern would make an interesting wall hanging. See the M&T section at the back of the book for enlarging procedures.

Sleeve

black wool embroidery/Spain

Because Spain was isolated from the most used trade and travel routes in Europe, and because Spanish art assimilated Islamic forms over a period of eight centuries, the folk textiles of Spain are of particular interest to embroiderers. Many are unlike the folk embroideries of the rest of Europe, which share many common characteristics. The Moslem restriction against depiction of human figures in art led to superior development in Islamic decorative arts (see page 163). Moslem formalization of floral patterns, to be restated in the handsome Italian damasks and velvets with their geometrized, two-dimensional, or visually flat, fillings (often simple checkerboard designs), eventually also appeared in Spanish rural embroidery.

The black dog afloat in the design of the Salamancan sleeve shown here assumes a pose also found in woven textile designs of the thirteenth and fourteenth centuries. His lapping tongue extends in the same sweeping arc as those of the basilisks and dogs on ancient silks. Other Spanish embroidery designs seem to have originated in the Persian schools of manuscript painting, where in early times Arab artists had studied. Thus it is in large part an Eastern influence that accounts for the designs that appear on Spanish needlework as well as on Spanish pottery, with which embroidery designs seem so closely associated.

Black and white embroidery has long been traditional in Spain; possibly it, too, was introduced by the Moors. It makes one of its most striking appearances in the costumes and furnishing linens of the charros (peasants) of the Salamancan region. Wool and flax are abundant in Spain, and one of the fine characteristics of the black and white needlework of the Salamancan region is the natural color of the black sheep's wool, which was used undyed and tightly twisted for embroidery. Silk or linen thread also were used, but wool was more usual.

In the Salamancan region colored embroidery on a black ground also was made, using patterns very similar to the ones shown here. Sleeves, shawls, shirts, and aprons were made of colored embroidery on black wool and were trimmed with black wool bobbin lace or with gold fringe. Salamancan garments were not always so elaborate. An engraving of a charra of 1777 shows her wearing a simple costume with sleeve embroidery much like the designs shown here. In such sleeves the heavy, homespun material was expertly manipulated into a small, neat wristband worked in smocking in herringbone pattern and edged with a ruffle of woolen bobbin lace.

Sleeves often had smocking patterns more intricate than this one. Allover fretwork or interlacing designs in the smocking appear frequently. The use of a strict geometric design with the rambling arabesques of the embroidery makes a handsome counterpoint. Covers and wall hangings made with black and white embroidery of this type often include areas or bands of all-white drawnwork and bobbin lace.

In this Salamantine sleeve, as in most embroideries of this type, flat silhouette shapes were filled with flat stitches, such as satin or

DOGS
*Detail from
pattern-woven silk,
Italy; mid-14th century.*

SLEEVE
Spain, Salamanca;
probably 19th century,
25 in. x 9 in.;
entire sleeve
is 18 in. wide.

DOG
Detail of sleeve.

Roumanian, arranged in bands in chevron or basket-weave designs. Arabesques—scrollwork patterns—with conventional flowers and curled lines were worked in stem stitch. The half sleeve design shown here measures twenty-five inches long by nine inches wide; the entire sleeve is eighteen inches wide.

Contemporary adaptation

A supple, fairly heavy linen or cotton homespun that is not too soft would serve well as a ground material for this embroidery. To prepare the designs for transfer to a sleeve section, consider that the vase of flowers at the bottom of the design and all motifs above it represent the center of the sleeve as it is worn. The photograph of the sleeve gives you an indication of

where one design should be placed. Transfer the diagrams to cloth with dressmakers' carbon or other transfer method. (See M&T.) The diagrams shown here include both left- and right-hand motifs of the pattern; the center of each pattern is represented by the midpoint of the vase. The entire center section is included in one diagram because, as you will note, the pattern is not symmetrical throughout. The pattern with the serpentine figure should be placed on the other half of the sleeve to correspond with the dog design. This embroidery can be worked in a hand hoop.

Everywhere in the original embroidery satin stitch was used for shapes except where "necks"

Only the outlines of this diagram need to be transferred. This motif can be used to embroider other parts of a garment. It would be quite suitable for the yoke on a shirt or for a collar if it were reduced. See the M&T section for the procedure for changing scale.

of some petals narrow, and then Roumanian stitch was used. In the diagram white lines on shapes indicate how rows of satin stitches were arranged. By outlining certain areas with stem stitch, the contours will be sharper. Stem stitch also was used for the curling lines of the arabesques.

This overall design could be used for costume parts like the ones it originally decorated—sleeves guimpes, and yokes. The design would be nice for a blouse worn under a jumper or pinafore, or it could be rearranged for use on a jacket or skirt of woolen ground fabric. Each of the two halves of the design can be made "square" by moving the lower right and left motifs slightly upward and to the right or left, and by repeating them at the top center of the design. The right-hand tier of motifs should be reversed, of course, and repeated on the left. As a square this design could be used for a shopping bag or cushion. The design could be painted on a door wall panel in a room where cushions or curtains that have the same pattern will be used.

Although this design is most exciting in the black on white of the original, the pattern could be worked on black with colored threads for an equally authentic look. If you do not care to hold to tradition you will think of numerous combinations: multicolors on various colors or white, gold or silver on white, colored embroidery to match the tiny dots of a printed or woven dotted ground, or embroidery on man-made suede, to mention only a few.

This serpentine figure appears on the side of the sleeve not photographed.

Cover

The cover on these pages is a nineteenth-century Russian embroidery, probably made in the southwestern Ukraine, where naturalistic floral embroidery prevailed, and where quiet colors on dark linen grounds were typical. Such embroidery clearly contrasts with the frequently all-white central Ukrainian types, and with northern Russian embroidery in which red is a prevailing color and a highly geometric arrangement is a usual design. The whole of the Ukraine tended to be preoccupied with the floral idea. By contrast, Moscovite needlework of the north took a variety of directions in design: purely geometric patterns, animals, birds, and landscapes.

Embroideries like the one shown here identify closely with the patterns of Ukrainian tapestry weaving and are related in some ways to the Oltenian and Bessarabian tapestries and carpets of neighboring Roumania. The difference between the sharp angularity of the tapestries and the soft contours of the embroideries can be explained by technical factors, but the designs are similar. Alike, too, are the conventions of color distribution. For example, leaves and stems may be uniformly one color throughout, except for an occasional leaf that may be embroidered or woven in another, often more neutral, color. Variations are apparent in the borders of embroideries and tapestries from the Ukraine and Roumania, and many are highly decorative. The cover seen here, though, has a simple border composed of the same flowers, fruits, and leaves that appear in the ground, but they are arranged in a continuous band. Inside this border is a stripe worked in Roumanian stitch in a dull gold shade.

A pitch black field is characteristic of Ukrainian embroideries. To eyes accustomed to the bright hues of much domestic embroidery made in rural areas, the tints chosen for these pieces may seem dull and washed out. A look at the back of this needlework or in between the threads shows that the color was always pastel and neutral, never very bright. The color of the leaves and stems is a somewhat pale medium green with an occasional gray-blue leaf. Gray, white, and gold were used for fruits and flowers.

The cover shown here measures seventy-five by one hundred and five inches, and the motifs measure twelve by fourteen inches. The entire cover was worked in Roumanian stitch and Roumanian couching, which were worked both vertically and horizontally. Placement of the motifs can be determined by comparing the diagrams to the photograph of the cover.

Contemporary adaptation

The embroidery of this cover is uncomplicated and could be finished in a reasonably short time compared to many other embroidery projects of similar size. If you plan to repeat the pattern in your project, it would be worthwhile to make a pounced transfer, reenforcing the design with dilute tempera in a light, related shade. (See M&T.) If only one repeat is to be made, a sugar solution transfer will suffice. The work may be mounted in a frame if you like, but it also could be accomplished by using a fairly large hand hoop (large enough to encompass the largest single unit to be couched in the design). Roumanian couching and Roumanian stitch are variations of the same stitch; the stitch version is used to make a broad line (stems, tendrils, borders), and the couching is used to cover larger areas. The original embroidery was worked with heavy, tightly twisted wool. The shapes are not outlined, and the edges appear slightly rough and irregular because of the weave of the ground fabric. This "nervous" contour of the shapes accounts for a great deal of the charm of the needlework. The original cover had no lining but simply was hemmed.

A beautiful table or bed cover could be made from the two patterns shown here. However, single design units could be used for cushions or chair seats. The designs also could be adapted easily for weaving, rug hooking, or needlepoint.

COVER
*Detail, Russia, Ukraine;
19th century,
entire cover measures
75 in. x 105 in.*

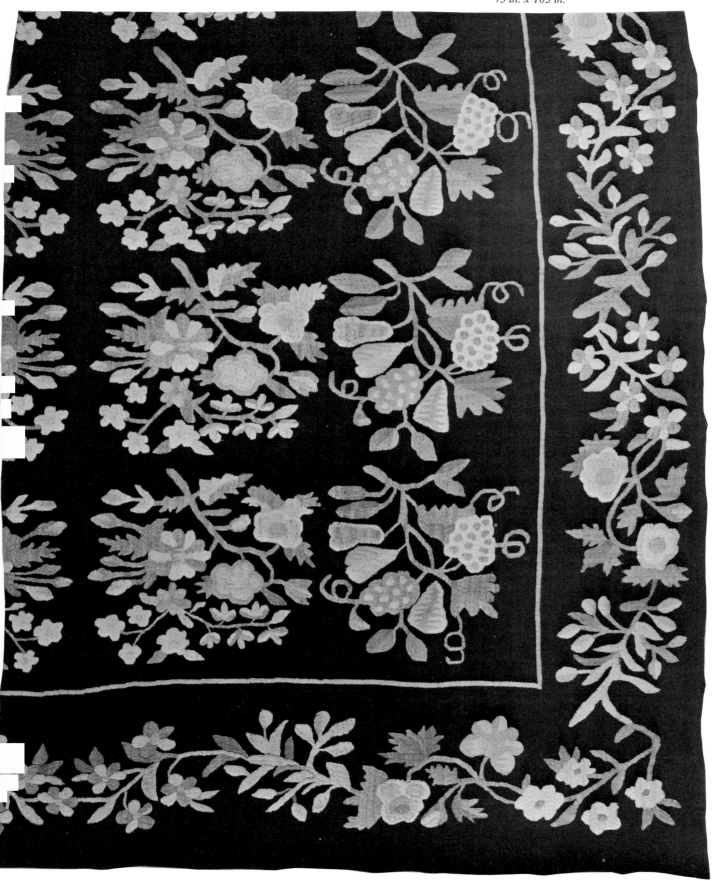

The diagram of this motif is somewhat smaller than the original, which measures 12 in. x 14 in.

Although this motif appears to be smaller than the preceding one, it is actually the same size in the original. The diagram here is somewhat smaller than the original 12 in. x 14 in.

Border

colored drawnwork/Russia

To the present day such crafts as miniature painting, metalworking, woodcarving, ivory carving, embroidery, and lacemaking are taught in Russia, and, in addition to more contemporary motifs, designs found in works of the sixteenth and seventeenth centuries are still used. Russia, like much of Europe, has had Byzantine and oriental as well as Western influences in its art. The motifs used in Russian embroidery do not differ greatly from those found in popular art all over the Western world. A few of these motifs are mermaids, griffins, double-headed eagles, heraldic lions, and fantastic birds, some of which are partially in the form of women. Though these designs originated in mythological or religious symbolism, they have lost their meanings through the years and have become purely decorative. A design may show delightful confronting bulls that seem almost to smile and dance, not at all like their forerunners, the austere beasts that confronted each other on ancient Persian textiles. From the time of Peter the Great, Russian designs that show public events and landscape with architecture have appeared. Some of these motifs are specific in nature, and besides known buildings they include trees, animals, and human figures. Patterns of this sort may be found on the bedcurtains and bedstead base panels made by the needlewomen of St. Petersburg and Moscow.

The great quantity of embroidery produced in Russia can be explained in part by the long winter isolation of country needlewomen and in part by Byzantine teaching, which led to the practice of secluding females within the home.

In addition, Russian tradition required that as evidence of perseverance and skill young girls should complete a number of embroidered linens and articles of clothing before marriage, and many embroidered wedding gifts were made for others.

Designs like the border shown here, with thick stems, rudimentary leaves, and stylized, tulip-like blooms made in a profusion of intricately textured stitches, come from Yaroslavl. On this border there are fabulous fowls with tails trailing tulips that seem like modern versions of the ancient and ubiquitous flowering cock. Peasant woodcarvings have birds with the same magnificent tails.

The lower section of the background in this border design was worked entirely in heavy pink linen thread in single faggot stitch. Carefully omitting areas where motifs occurred, the embroiderer prepared the upper background by withdrawing four threads, then leaving the next four threads; this pattern was continued both horizontally and vertically. Over the remaining threads, interlocking stitch—familiar in drawnwork and filet lacemaking—was worked in fine pink linen thread. Most of the textured fillings were worked in pattern or damask darning. (Some of the filling designs have been diagrammed here.) The outlines, dull blue linen in stem stitch, were worked last. Some of the fillings were made over drawn threads, but so much thread has been added to the areas that they do not have the appearance of openwork. Some of these fillings are made up of more than one stitch. For example, the heavy upper part of the wing on the bird at the left, the central motif in the photograph, was worked in green in weaving stitch, and the largest feather in the tail of the bird on the right also was worked in weaving stitch, but in purple thread. Then, in both areas, interlocking stitch was worked diagonally throughout, and the loops of the interlocking

BORDER
*Detail, Russia; late
19th-early 20th century;
this half-section
measures 36 in. x 14½ in.*

This diagram is all you will need to transfer the border design. Work each section according to the following numbered diagrams and corresponding patterns on pages 182 and 183. If you want to change the scale of this design, check the M&T section at the back of the book for the proper procedure.

*This numbered diagram is
a key to the way in which
different sections
of the Russian border
are to be embroidered.
After transferring the
pattern, choose an area
in which to begin.
Embroider the area
with the pattern that
corresponds to the number
located in that section.*

stitch were worked over the crossings of warps
and wefts that remained in the ground.

There are two pairs of birds in each of the four
sections of this border. In each pair the bird on
the left has been embroidered in shades of warm
and cool green, chartreuse, and gold. The bird
on the right has been embroidered in shades of
blue, lavender, purple, and rose. No shade of
either range of colors was used anywhere except
on its own motif. The half section shown in the
diagram measures thirty-six by fourteen and
one-half inches in the original.

Contemporary adaptation

This is a simple design, but the embroidery,
as originally worked, required a great deal of
care and perseverance. It seems doubtful that today anyone would have the time to complete
more than a single repeat—the pair of birds—but
one motif would make a handsome wall hanging. The work would be especially effective hung
in such a way that light could be seen through
the openwork. The birds also would be effective on
a valance.

This design should be transferred (using carbon, transfer pencil, or sugar solution) to the
ground fabric of plain weave so that the threads

could be counted for embroidery. Hardanger
cloth or evenweave linen would facilitate the
work. The background stitches probably should
be put in first. It is not necessary to remove all
the threads from the ground before beginning
to work interlocking stitch areas; in fact, it
would be better to remove the threads a section
at a time, and finish each area before weakening
the fabric by removal of additional threads.

In this design threadcounted fillings like those
in blackwork were used, but here they were
embroidered in color. The geometric patterns
fill shapes that make up the bodies and wings
of birds. Interspersed with shapes worked in
filling stitch are areas of heavily filled drawnwork.

This flat, simple design could be worked in
other filling stitches and without the use of
drawnwork. It even could be rendered as blackwork. For a totally different effect, different
stitches could be used. The long horizontal
shape of the design recommends it for use as an
overmantle or overdoor piece or as a valance.

Pattern 1

Pattern 2

Pattern 3

Pattern 4

Pattern 5

Pattern 6

Pattern 7

Pattern 8

Pattern 9

Pattern 10

Pattern 11

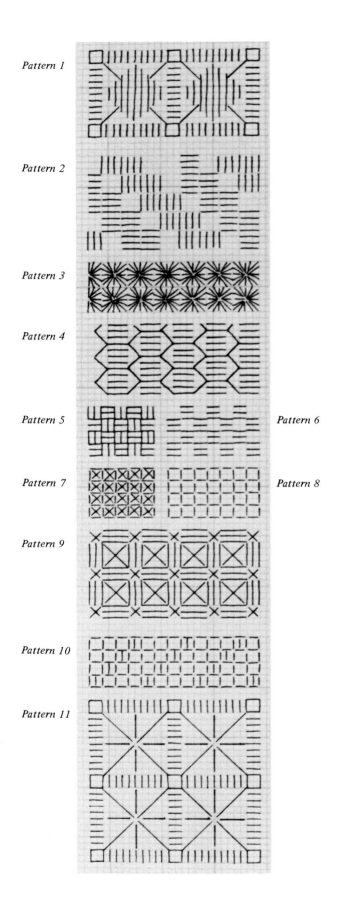

Mola[1]

reverse appliqué variation/Panama

The Cuna Indians of the San Blas Islands of Panama make a distinctive type of appliqué needlework, which because of its popularity in recent times has proved to be an economic boon to their communities. Originally these rectangular needleworks were the lower front and back portions of blouses worn by island women. The procedure by which they were, and still are, made is now called reverse appliqué. One supposes that this term was devised to explain that in the San Blas appliqué the usual method of appliqué is reversed: the fabric is cut away from, rather than added to, the ground. However, this definition does not fully explain the complexity of the technique as it is actually practiced.

All Cuna appliqués begin with two or more layers of fabric, almost always tabby-woven cotton, basted together, probably, to hold the layers in place. While it is possible that some workers begin by drawing designs on the top layer, many start a needlework without having drawn a pattern on the fabric. The design begins to appear as the worker cuts a line or slit, little by little, through the top layer only, and folds back a hem on each side of the "line" as work progresses, finishing the hem with tiny stitches. If there are more than two layers of cloth, the second layer is cut and hemmed in the same way, revealing the color of the third layer. Many variations of reverse appliqué are practiced, and while the design shown here could have been made by the method just described, it was made, in fact, in a completely different way. A red (top) and orange (bottom) layer were finished; then a black layer, representing the background in the design, was added, and its hems were turned in such a way that the orange appears as a narrow outline separating main motifs and background.

The colors of the San Blas molas are strong, but they are usually arranged with sensitivity. Frequently the sequence of color in layers involves colors of similar values or adjacent analogous hues—orange or pink next to red, for instance. Handling much of the color this way tempers it brilliance so that a few combinations of strong contrast (orange or white with black, for example) stand out as accents. These bold juxtapositions, plus the fact that the most frequently used color for the top layer is red, rank San Blas molas with the most brightly hued of all needleworks. Neutrals are seldom seen; pastels are substituted for them.

The Cuna Indians used extremely varied motifs. Some are entirely geometrical and non-objective, but double-headed eagles, heraldic lions, and fantastic birds are to be found. Demons and monsters from Indian lore also appear, and infrequently there is a paisley pattern or a floral design of European ancestry. In addition to all of these motifs, some needleworks deal with the life and times of the Cunas. Fishermen, hunters, medicine men, dancers, and, recently, even television viewers appear in the compositions. In the mola shown here a ship with human and animal passengers is the theme. Whether it derives from the Old Testament story of Noah or from some ancient symbolism like "the ship of the dead," or whether it simply represents daily life among the Indians is impossible to decide.

The islanders practice one method of design, similar to the pattern shown here, that makes use of the ambiguity of motif and background characteristic of this technique to produce bird, animal, and hunter designs that are beautifully abstract. In these designs background and subject are handled alike, without emphasis on the principal motifs. The result is an allover, camouflage-like effect. There is a striking similarity between these molas and Panamanian pottery decoration.

The design example shown here is from Isla Tigre; its technique is sometimes called linear duotone. In it, three colored layers were used. The outline of the design has an incised (slightly indented) effect because its color (orange, lightest value) is the bottom layer of the needlework.

Contemporary adaptation

This needlework measures fifteen by twenty and one-half inches. The red and orange layers should be basted together, the red layer on top. Because of the complexity of the design, a dressmakers' carbon or sugar solution transfer on the top (in this case red) layer is recommended. (See M&T.) The shapes should be drawn "full" so that

MOLA 1
Panama, San Blas Islands,
Isla Tigre;
probably 20th century,
15 in. x 20½ in.

the line of the transferred design can be turned under and concealed as work progresses. First the red layer is cut little by little, allowing about one-eighth of an inch for a hem. When the hemming has been completed, the black layer is basted into position on top of the work. The black fabric is cut and hemmed carefully so that all red shapes show with narrow borders of orange surrounding them. By pressing firmly on the right side of the work before beginning to cut, you can mark the black fabric enough to show where the appliquéd areas lie under the uncut black layer.

The pictorial nature of this composition limits its use to a wall decoration. With adjustment the attractive design could be worked as a satin stitch or chain stitch embroidery. It would also make an excellent felt appliqué.

In transferring this design, make sure you transfer all the dotted lines. These lines represent the top hemmed layer. To enlarge this pattern see the M&T section at the back of the book.

Mola²

reverse appliqué/Panama

color plate, page 114

The twentieth-century mola shown here comes from the Panamanian island of Mandinga Niranjo. Its design represents the sky spirit. It is an example of a type of reverse appliqué that is more complex than the one seen on page 185, and it has details of standard appliqué, embroidery, and commercial rickrack trim, as well as a many-hued color scheme dominated by red, green, and black.

Scrutiny of several molas will reveal that among the numerous technical variations are some interesting types that appear repeatedly. One type involves working out a design in two or more layers, using a single color for each layer. An additional layer is made up of a multicolored patchwork and is added to the top. Over this another single-color larger, usually red, is added. This layer unifies the composition because it is worked so that the multicolored layer shows only as a border around other shapes. Sometimes more appliqué or embroidery then is added.

Whether instinctive or intentional in mola design, the use of red as a binding color is interesting. The neutral spatial quality of red has long been appreciated; in *Concerning the Spiritual in Art,* Wassily Kandinsky graphically explained its action in relation to other colors: "The glow of red is within itself." Kandinsky also demonstrates in his book that red does not reach out toward the spectator as yellow does, nor does it move away from him, like blue. The most satisfying molas seem to be those dominated by red.

Very often the background areas of mola designs are filled with small slits, one to two inches long, which when opened reveal a patchwork layer beneath. At other times small, jewel-like triangles of bright colors set against slightly larger triangles of black ornament the design. Small devices powdered over an area are the rule.

San Blas designers, like so many others, abhor a vacuum in their needlework, and they may have a sound technical reason for sewing in an allover manner. Allover sewing produces a needlework of uniform substance and a bulk somewhat similar to quilting. If you remember that these needleworks were intended to be worn and laundered, the practicality of the method can be appreciated.

Contemporary adaptation
To make this mola in the original size, begin with three layers of cotton cloth, each twenty by twenty-four inches. The mola is smaller—

MOLA 2
Panama, San Blas Islands,
Mandinga Niranjo;
probably 20th century,
16½ in. x 20 in.

*This diagram shows
the direction
of the stitching and the
various layers
of the mola. Use it only
as a guide for completing
the details of
the embroidery.*

sixteen and one-half by twenty inches—but an ample margin will prove helpful while the appliqué is being made. Part of the design, the simpler of the two diagrams, should be transferred to the top layer of the fabric. In the original color scheme the top layer is red, the middle layer green, and the bottom layer black. After the transfer has been made, the layers should be basted together so that they will not shift during the work. In making the transfer, draw the shapes just slightly larger than they are to be when finished so that as hems are made the transferred line will not show when it is turned under. Dressmakers' carbon should make a satisfactory transfer. If necessary, the tracing can be reenforced with dilute white tempera, since the line eventually will be hemmed under.

Check the color plate on page 114 to determine which hems are to be made first. All red edges bound by green lines should be turned first by cutting the red fabric about an eighth of an inch from the edge of the design, thereby allowing for a narrow hem, cutting the material a few inches at a time, and then hemming. Working this way keeps everything in its proper position and prevents buckling or puckering. When some of the hems have been completed, red pieces of fabric will fall away from the work. So that there will be no difficulty when it is time to put these shapes back into place, it might be wise to number them. When all red edges with green borders have been finished, the green layer is cut and hemmed in the same way as the red layer, making the stitches for the hem as tiny as possible. In the end a narrow border of green should appear around all red shapes.

The next step is to make the serpentine (wormlike) filling designs in the outer edge shapes that surround the sky spirit. In this step the green layers are replaced by layers of various colors. If you have saved and numbered your green scraps as they fell away from the work, you can use them as patterns on top of the substitute colors you will use to replace them. Working clockwise and beginning at the upper left-hand corner, the replacement colors are as follows: hot pink, lemon yellow, purple, orange-blue-white print (a printed rather than plain fabric was used), hot pink, orange-yellow, royal blue, lemon yellow, purple, orange, royal blue, orange-yellow, purple, hot pink, lemon yellow, royal blue, red only, and orange. Each of these sections is worked in the same manner as the red and green outer gridwork; only the nar-

row borders of each color should show. The green layer is replaced with orange in the area of the star surrounding the sky spirit. All red edges next to orange are then turned, leaving the little leaf-shaped designs within the points of the star flapping and free. These designs are backed by yellow, hot pink, and green (top, left to right), and yellow, green, and hot pink (bottom, left to right). In the area of the arms the orange layer is replaced by yellow. Small pieces of angle-shaped cloth are appliquéd in the corners of the triangles. The orange layer is cut away in the area of the head. No second color appears around the oval of the head, but a row of small yellow rickrack is sewn on. A white underlayer is used for the mouth. A pink underlayer serves for the nose and eyebrows. White eyes are appliquéd onto the red face. Details of running stitch and chain stitch plus some additional slits in the red background areas complete the design.

Once the principle of designing for reverse appliqué has been grasped, one will understand how molas can be made without prior drawing. A few simple cuts in the top layer lead to complex and unusual effects in the second and third layers. For example, it is really not necessary to transfer this design. One could begin by folding the red layer in fourths and cutting the central star. When the center motif's position is established, the rest of the design can be worked out by eye, helped, if necessary, by a few simple guidelines sketched freehand in white pencil or dressmakers' chalk.

Today molas are used as wall hangings, framed pictures, and cushion covers. Reverse appliqué would still be very exciting in its original use as a blouse decoration, and it need not have an ethnic, or peasant, look. Colors less eye-catching than those the Cunas use for their molas also produce fine effects.

Reverse appliqué would be appropriate for a slipcover for a small chair, a typewriter cover, a handbag, or any other decorated fabric article that must be fairly substantial. Reverse appliqué is well suited to large-scale work, can be used for large wall hangings, and would make a superb bed cover. Dedicated short-cutters can use felt to achieve effects similar to the San Blas appliqués without the bother of turning hems, but careful, tiny stitches still are recommended. In times past unusual appliqués were made with dyed leathers, and these look especially splendid as upholstery. Mola designs could be used for appliquéd leather work.

For transferring purposes you will need to trace only the portion of the design shown here. To enlarge this diagram, check the M&T section at the back of the book for the proper procedure.

M&T | materials and techniques

In this section materials and techniques
for all the types of embroideries discussed
in this book are described, along with kinds of needles
and threads and transfer methods for different types
of embroideries. Most department stores and
all needleworkers' boutiques and specialty shops
carry the supplies that you will need to complete most
of the embroideries in this book. When certain supplies
are more difficult to come by, suggested places
for finding these materials are given
in the following sections.

NEEDLES

Good technique requires proper tools. Having a selection of needles appropriate for various types of embroidery will facilitate your work. Crewel needles come in various sizes and have sharp points and large eyes. Blunt-pointed tapestry needles are used for embroidering on needlepoint canvas and for such stitches as detached buttonhole, Ceylon, or ladder. These stitches are worked in such a way that the needle rarely pierces the ground fabric, and the yarn or thread can accidentally split if a sharp-pointed needle is used. Besides sewing needles of all sizes, tapestry and crewel needles, a seamstress's needle case should include darners, straw (long), and chenille (sharp, large eye) needles. Other types of needles, such as the curved and straight bodkins that are made for leather and upholstery work, may be used occasionally. Glover's needles also are useful in sewing leather.

The choice of a needle depends on the weight of the thread, the texture of the ground fabric, and the stitch to be made. Usually a needle should make a hole in the fabric big enough to allow the thread to slip through the cloth without dragging against it. This is especially true of needles for use with metal embroidery, in which the needle acts as an awl to make an opening for the metal thread. There are times, though, when a needle that seems too small should be used—for example, when using woolen threads that look attractive when they appear to be "squeezed" into the cloth. For this type of embroidery, the yarns may have to be pinched together to get them through the eye of the small needle. As a general rule, if you are a needleworker bent on fine sewing, you should use a needle as small as is practical for the weight of the material on which you are working.

THREADS

Mercerized cottons and crewels (woolen yarn) are widely available for needlework. Silk and metal threads must be searched out, and you may even want to order them specially from needlework suppliers. For unusual or hard-to-find items check the telephone directory or inquire at the specialty shop or notions department of the store where you buy other sewing supplies. Embroidery and handweaving periodicals also list up-to-date sources for needlework supplies. In addition, local embroidery guilds usually assist their members in obtaining materials, and they sometimes have supplies for sale.

Wool

Crewels—woolen threads made for embroidery—are among the most popular embroidery yarns. They are widely available and come in an extensive range of colors, including shaded tones of particular hues, variegated skeins (also available in cotton and silk threads), yarn-dyed colors (mottled), many neutrals, and strong colors of poster-like vividness. Crewels often are composed of three strands of two-ply yarn loosely plied together. These can be separated and used singly if you want to work with greater delicacy than can be achieved with two or three strands. When crewels are threaded into a needle, a downward stroke of the thread should feel smooth as the hand goes "with the grain." If the strand feels rough, as if it is stroking against the grain, the other end of the strand should be threaded into the needle. If the work requires two strands, use two strands of yarn, not a single strand doubled.

Any attractive yarn is a candidate for needlework. The most nubbly bouclé or the most fragile angora presents no more problems than a metal thread; all can be couched. Fingering, baby yarns, and all sorts of synthetic materials are easy to handle and give good results in embroidery, and you may find that in some cases woolens or synthetics intended for weaving or knitting give results superior to crewels or other embroidery threads.

Cotton

Cotton embroidery threads are available in all dry goods stores. Their quality varies greatly, so you should be alert to differences in color, sheen, and texture when selecting them. Almost all cotton threads are mercerized, a process that makes them stronger, more receptive to dyes, and glossier. The most familiar type of cotton thread is six-strand floss. This thread may be separated into individual strands, and one or more may be used, depending on the nature of the stitch to be made. Chain stitch worked with two strands of cotton thread, for example, gives a neat, distinct line. Stem stitch made with one strand makes a fragile line. Six strands of cotton may be used when preparing a padding for satin stitch. Some especially fine qualities of cotton floss are produced for making

whitework and neutral monochromatic embroideries. Heavier cotton threads, two-ply twists in various weights, called pearl cottons, are smooth, easily worked, shiny. Chenille threads, velvety strands larger and coarser than those used in embroideries in this book, can be purchased from weavers' supply houses.

Linen

Linen threads are not as easy to find as cotton. Like metal and silk threads, often they must be specially ordered. They are usually two-ply twists that look very much like pearl cotton, except that the thread is not so shiny. Linen is used commonly by weavers and may be found at weavers' supply houses. You can use warp and weft threads of linen for embroidery if you understand their specific characteristics and drawbacks in relation to the work you are attempting. Warps must be strong, so warp threads are tightly twisted. In the weaving process wefts do not take the beating that warps do, so weft threads are more floss-like and therefore shinier. Weft threads fray easily, so they should be used in short lengths, and when fraying begins, a new thread should be started. Weft threads look pretty in stitches like satin or buttonhole, which ordinarily look their loveliest in floss treatments. Warp threads can be used for chain, stem, interlacing, and other stitches in which the best effect is a clear, even line. Linen threads also are used for lacemaking; threads specially made for lacemaking are fine and tightly twisted and can be used for lacelike stitches in embroidery, too.

Silk

Silk thread is not so generally available as wool or cotton, and neutrals and muted shades, now sometimes referred to as tapestry colors, are dwindling. This is unfortunate, because silk, with its marvelous sheen that is more softly lustrous than cotton, often needs the quietude of such colors so that the excitement of its silky texture can be exploited to the fullest without producing a garish result.

For some kinds of embroidery, silk buttonhole twist, a thread intended for buttonhole making, can be used, but because it is twisted it is not a good substitute for embroidery that is better made with floss thread. Floss, which is barely twisted at all, is used for satin, long and short, and various cross stitches, either because the

sheen of the thread is maximized or because the detail
of the stitch is not confused by additional twistings
in the thread itself.

Silk threads intended for weaving can be purchased
from weavers' suppliers. These threads are equally suitable for embroidery; the only disadvantage in ordering
them from a weavers' supplier is that usually you must
purchase a quantity larger than the amount you need.
This may not be a problem if you are making a monochromatic cross stitch piece, but if you are making a
multicolored design it may mean a rather large investment and a lot of overage. It is encouraging, however,
that weavers' suppliers increasingly are putting up small
quantities of threads for use in needlework.

Metal

Metal threads can be purchased from suppliers who
specialize in materials for gold embroidery or from
firms that make ecclesiastical vestments. Several types
of metal thread are made. Two types, which come in
various weights, are made by winding a strip of metal
around a fiber core. One, called passing, is wiry; the
other, a type commonly used in oriental embroidery and
called Japanese gold, is very pliable. Also available are
cords made by twisting together two or more gold
threads. These cords come in a variety of sizes, colors,
and combinations. Plate is a flat metal strip, but the
imitation metal plates that many shops sell in sizes
intended for knitting, crocheting, or weaving are too
narrow to be useful for needlework, which requires a
width of at least one-sixteenth of an inch. All these
threads—passing, Japanese gold, and plate—are quite
often couched. Horsetail is a strong, thin silk thread
especially intended for couching metal threads. It
should be waxed before use.

Purl, which looks like a dainty coil spring when you
buy it, is a tubular material that is purchased by the
foot or yard and is intended to be cut into pieces and
sewn in position on the work like beads. Purl is made
by winding a wire around a cylindrical form in the
same way that a spring is made. The wire may be of
various textures. It may be angled so that it has little
facets that catch the light like a cut gem—check purl—
or it may be convex and give the effect of a string of
beads—pearl purl. Purl also may be smooth or even
cloth-like in texture.

Spangles and other types of metal ornaments are
used on needlework, too. In old embroideries spangles
are always smaller than most of the sequins sold today.
They were made of a small twist of wire that was beaten
flat. Pearls, beads, and jewels also were used in much
old gold embroidery.

GROUND FABRICS

When you plan your embroidery project you will
probably have in mind a certain type of ground fabric
that will give to the work the look you want it to have.
You should also consider whether the fabric will be
functionally practical. Theoretically an embroidery
ground should be substantial enough to carry the
weight of the embroidery that is worked on it. In
practice most heavy embroidery has been worked into
unsupported fabric too fragile to stand the weight, and
it is the ground, not the embroidery, that gives way
first. Silk garments trimmed with metal needlework
and crewel embroidered bedcurtains lead the list of regrettable losses. The matter of selecting a suitable
ground for the embroidery to be done should be considered in the planning stages of the work. Of course,
if the embroidery is always to lie flat, the problem is
not so critical. And there are times when a heavily
embroidered, unsupported sheer fabric is wanted,
perhaps for a garment. This sort of needlework obviously
should be stored flat, not hung on a hanger in a closet.

For needleworks that are to hang vertically for long
periods, a delicate fabric may be used if it is supported
by an underlayer of a more substantial fabric and if
the stitches are worked through both layers. The underlayer chosen for a ground fabric that does not have
sufficient stability of its own should be a material
that takes the needle with ease and is not drastically
different in texture from the upper layer. In other words,
the characteristics of the visible ground should be preserved as much as possible. It would be a mistake to put
a stiff, heavy linen under a supple, lightweight silk. A
handkerchief-weight linen would be a better choice,
two or more layers if necessary.

Linen

As a ground material for needlework linen has always
been more widely used than any other fabric. Most
linens have a desirable combination of firm body and
soft texture. Their natural colors are neutral and attractive, and they have a dullness of surface that provides
an unobstrusive background for embroidery.

Certain dressmaking and high-count table linens are
less useful as grounds for embroidery because of their

outspoken sheen and, in some instances, because they are so densely woven that it is difficult to pull embroidery thread through them.

For crewel embroidered work of the type made in the sixteenth and seventeenth centuries a linen twill is available that is lighter in weight and stiffer than the cotton and linen twills of the original embroidery, but it is a satisfactory material for such needlework. Its dense weave is not unpleasant to work into, and the weave makes it possible to achieve a degree of accuracy with the needle (in long and short, stem, and other surface embroidery stitches) that is not possible with more loosely woven materials, which are more appropriate for threadcounted needlework.

Threadcounted embroideries require plain- or tabby-woven fabrics. A linen called evenweave is made especially for this purpose. Unlike most linens, its warps and wefts are exactly the same size and are spaced at exactly the same distance apart, so that if cross stitches are made in the linen, perfectly square stitches result. The threads of this cloth are even and smooth and do not interfere with the correctness of the stitching. Slubs and irregular threads, so attractive in linens used for other purposes, are often a detriment in embroidery. Another characteristic of linen that should be taken into account is its tendency to stretch. If sagging or buckling seems likely to present a problem in the future, linen can be lined (tacking at intervals) with cotton.

Wool

Woolen fabrics make highly acceptable embroidery grounds except when they are too limp and irregularly woven, and even these can be used if they are improved with firm linings. The soft surface of most wool textiles renders their colors, even when very strong, less shrill than they often appear in other fibers. Care should be taken so that the texture of the woolen fabric chosen as an embroidery ground is not too coarse for the threads and stitches that are to be applied to it. Flannels and homespuns gracefully accept embroidery threads. Gabardines and other similar hard-surfaced materials, intended for tailored clothing, have a mechanical look that must be carefully considered when designing embroidery for them. Usually a textile with the look of handweaving coordinates pleasantly with embroidery, which is a handmade decoration. Some printed or pattern-woven woolens look very rich in combination with needlework.

Silk

All sorts of silk weaves have been used for embroidery in the past: plain, satin, damask, twill, leno, and velvet. (Velvet weaves that are difficult to embroider directly often have applied embroidered motifs.) In times gone by the most sumptuous and complex combinations of weaves were further enriched with needlework, often so subtly blended that one cannot readily detect where the woven decoration leaves off and the embroidery begins. Sometimes it is a moot point whether a motif has been incorporated as brocading, which takes place while the weaving is in process, or in embroidered darning, which is worked after the weaving is complete. The effect is identical; not even knots on the back are a real giveaway as to which is which, because some weavers, such as the Guatemalans, occasionally knot their brocading threads.

Cottons and synthetics

Many cottons and mat-finished synthetics are so closely woven with threads of such fineness that the added embroidery threads seem unpleasantly coarse by comparison. The case may be put the other way around: next to the warmth and richness of handmade needlework, some cottons and synthetics seem cold, mechanical, and uninteresting in texture. However, homespun types of cotton and other weaves that have comparatively large threads adapt well to embroidery.

Hardanger cloth is a cotton fabric woven for threadcounted needlework, specifically the Norwegian drawnwork embroidery of that name, which is worked in geometric designs in weaving, overcasting, interlacing, and other stitches. Like evenweave, this fabric is woven in such a way that cross stitches make perfect squares, and pairs of threads are easily counted.

Needlepoint canvas

Stiff grounds, plain woven with paired or single threads, are woven for needlepoint embroidery. These are made with various numbers of meshes per square inch. Tent stitch or petit point requires fine meshes;

cross stitch or gros point requires fewer meshes per square inch. Florentine and Hungarian stitch also are worked on needlepoint canvas. Many threadcounted embroidery designs can be translated for use on needlepoint canvas.

SCISSORS, THIMBLES, VISUAL AIDS

Embroidery scissors are small and short-bladed and have sharp points. For cutwork and types of embroidery that require close snipping, the size and shape of the point of a pair of scissors is a critical factor in the quality of the work, but for much other needlework any pair of scissors will do.

A good thimble is essential. Although many people find a thimble awkward when first worn, once they are accustomed to wearing it, they usually find it indispensable. A thimble greatly facilitates sewing on heavy fabrics, because a finger shielded with a thimble can push harder and more precisely than a finger without one. It also permits the healing of a finger that is perforated with dozens of little needle-end punctures.

Good light is an absolute necessity when doing needlework, and a magnifying glass is a great help. A large glass with a long goose neck or other adjustable type of construction is a good investment if you intend to engage in close work for long periods of time.

MOUNTING AN EMBROIDERY

Most embroidery is more easily worked if the ground material is held in tension. Embroidery stitches tend to draw up grounds unevenly, and unattractive buckling results if the warps and wefts of the fabric are not held straight and taut. Embroidery frames, including the round types called hand hoops in this book, serve this purpose. Hoops that are held in the hand allow the embroiderer to sit more restfully than is possible when working at a large frame, but a good-sized rectangular frame has the advantage of keeping a large expanse of ground fabric in tension. Every type of frame is made in versions that either clamp to a table or stand independently on the floor. Embroidery frames free both hands for stitching.

The choice of a frame is a matter of practicality, not rule—a matter of choosing the tool that will give you the best chance for good results on the particular job

at hand. For example, traditionally, gold embroidery is mounted in a frame. The gold threads of these embroideries are vulnerable to damage through breakage, abrasion, or simply too much handling. They also are tricky to manipulate, so having two hands free is an advantage. It would seem, therefore, that gold embroidery really always ought to be framed. But there are times, when gold is just as successfully, and more easily, worked in a hand hoop. A very small motif intended for application to a larger embroidery or a design in which gold and silver details are small and widely spaced may be worked just as well in a hand hoop. You should simply keep in mind that gold and silver threads should be the last threads worked into an embroidery and that they should not be forced between hoops.

There are times when an embroidery that may not normally require framing may need to be mounted in a large frame. If the needlework is good-sized, it may be less cumbersome to work on when it is framed. There also are times when you may need no frame at all. For example, after an amount of heavy embroidery has been worked into a piece of cloth, the needlework itself may be rigid enough to make framing superfluous. For a busy person who embroiders only when already tired, the way in which an embroidery

Embroidery hoop or ring mounted to stand on a table

is mounted for work may be a salient point in choosing the needlework to be made; if you use a hand hoop you can sit in an easy chair with your feet up.

Hand hoops

Embroidery hoops consist of two wooden, metal, or plastic rings, one of which fits snugly inside the other. In the best type the outer ring has a thumbscrew construction that allows it to be made larger or smaller. This screw-type construction permits the worker to gently close the hoops on a piece of needlework, rather than having to drag one tight hoop down across the embroidery. Thumbscrew hoops also hold the needlework more securely than do spring types or types that have no adjustment feature. Hoops from about four to ten inches in diameter can be purchased at specialty shops or department stores, as can wooden hoops too large to be held in the hand. The large wooden hoops can be used for quilting, but they are not satisfactory for precision embroidery. Some hoops are equipped with stands and clamps for mounting on a table. In past days beautiful floor-standing types were made, and these can still be found occasionally in antique shops. Table- or floor-standing hoops leave the hands free for work.

A good feature that not every hoop has is a grooved inner ring that accommodates a strip of felt. This felt feature can be improvised by wrapping the inner ring with a strip of soft cloth. Modified either way, the hoop will "grab" the fabric more tenderly. Tissue paper or a scrap of sheer cloth can be put into the hoop along with the ground fabric and will serve the same purpose as the felt. The paper or cloth put into the hoop with the ground should be cut away in the area where stitching is to be done. If an embroidery is small the ground can be sewn onto a larger piece of fabric that can be held in the hoop; then the hoop need never touch the actual embroidery ground. The larger fabric can serve as a backing or can be cut away in the area where needlework is to be made.

Rectangular frames

A rectangular embroidery frame that has no stand must be rested against a table or chair back during work. Floor-standing models can be adjusted for height, and the working surface can be tilted to the desired angle. Both types of frames come in various sizes; the floor type generally is larger than the table type. The size of the working area is adjustable to the size of the embroidery by means of two threaded, screw-like side members or by pegs fitted into holes drilled at close intervals along two sides.

Whether the screw-like mechanism or pegged holes are used, the other two sides of the frame are dowel-like or round and have sturdy cloth tapes to which the embroidery ground fabric is sewn. If the piece to

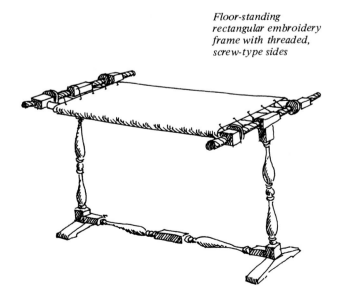

Floor-standing rectangular embroidery frame with threaded, screw-type sides

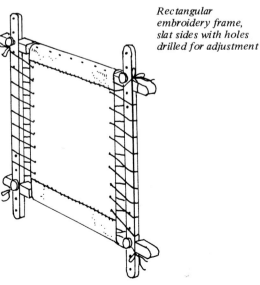

Rectangular embroidery frame, slat sides with holes drilled for adjustment

be embroidered is longer than the frame, the excess, or part not being embroidered at the time, can be wound around one or both taped sides and secured in such a way that the section to be completed is exposed on the working surface of the frame. When the ground material, which is exactly centered on the two sides of the frame to keep the grain of the fabric straight (this is important), is sewn to the tapes and wound around the dowels if necessary, the drilled or threaded sides are fitted into the dowel sides. If the frame is the kind that has screw-type threadings, it will have discs (nuts) that turn along the threaded sides to hold the taped sides, to which the embroidery fabric is attached, at just the right distance apart to keep the fabric taut. If the frame has holes drilled along the sides, prior calculations will be helpful. Determine the approximate length of ground fabric plus the width of the cloth tapes that are attached to two of the frame sides. Measure distances between peg holes on the ends of the other two sides to find out into which holes the peg should be put. Baste or pin the ground fabric to the two frame tapes, being sure the grain of the fabric is straight and the cloth is taut. The frame should be assembled when the basting or pinning is done. When the ground fabric has been correctly positioned, it should be sewn securely to the tapes, but you should remember that at the end of the work the stitches will have to be removed.

The two sides of the ground fabric not wound around the dowel sides should be turned under and hemmed or temporarily bound to strengthen them. You should do this before you begin to mount the fabrics in the frame. These edges should be laced to the frame with long, sturdy threads or string worked back and forth between the sides of the frame and the cloth. Lacing should begin at the center of both sides (both sides should be worked at the same time). Then ease, pull, and temporarily tie the supporting strings until the piece is in position, with the grain of the cloth straight in both directions; then secure the string. If you prefer, the design can be transferred after the ground fabric is stretched. This procedure is preferable when a symmetrical pattern is involved.

If the embroidery to be worked is substantially smaller than the frame, or if it is to be rendered on a delicate fabric, or is to be backed, then a second, sturdy piece of fabric may be required. Cut away the backing fabric behind the area to be embroidered if you do not want the worked area backed. When you roll extra lengths of fabric around the dowel sides of the frame, you should roll sheets of tissue paper between the layers for the protection of the embroidery and the fabric. Folds of cloth can be basted over the edge of the frame to protect the embroidery from soil as you handle the needlework, and a cloth should be kept under your hands as you work. Whenever work is not in progress, framed needlework should be covered to keep the dust off.

CHANGING SCALE
Most of the patterns in this book are necessarily either larger or smaller than the original needlework. As presented some are practical for embroidery, but if a close reproduction of the original effect is the aim, the pattern may need adjustment. The pattern can be accomplished in several ways; the easiest is simply to have a photostatic copy made in the larger or smaller dimension required. For only a few dollars a photostat house will copy your tracing of the pattern from the book in the new measurements that you request. The photostat then can be traced and transferred to the ground fabric.

A second method, practical for those skilled in photography, and excellent for large-scale work, requires that you photograph the pattern and have it developed as a slide. This slide then can be projected onto a sheet of paper on which the desired dimension is marked. The projector or the paper can be moved forward or backward until the image is the correct size. Then it can be traced.

The third and more conventional way to change the scale of a design is slower but requires only simple tools. To begin, trace the design on thin paper; then draw a gridwork of squares over the pattern. If the embroidery design is to be larger or smaller, determine the length and width of the pattern in the new scale, and draw a rectangle based on the new measurements.

*Method of enlarging
designs; dotted lines
are trial estimates
of positions of parts
to be drawn in relation
to the lines
of the gridwork*

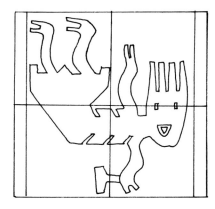

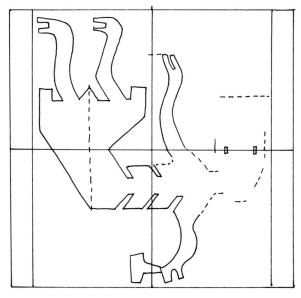

Draw within the rectangle a second gridwork that contains the same total number of squares as the first. Then, referring to the position of lines and shapes within each small segment of the original, make a copy in the new scale. Many details may be eliminated in changing the scale of a design because they can be added freely later, as the work progresses.

TRANSFERRING

When a drawing of a design in the appropriate scale has been finished, it is transferred to the ground fabric in one of several ways. The time-honored method (described in *II burato, libro de recami,* published in 1527) requires that the drawing, on thin layout or tracing paper, be pricked from the back with either a tracing wheel or a needle, and pounced with powdered chalk or charcoal. A pad for pouncing is made by rolling up a strip of felt, perhaps one and one-half inches wide, to make a coil one-half to one inch in diameter, and securing the coil with stitches. Then if the pouncing is to be made on a dark-colored fabric, the end of this pad is dabbed in light-colored chalk; if the pouncing is to be made on light-colored fabric, charcoal is used. The chalk or charcoal is patted through the pricked design onto the ground fabric, which is secured under it with pins, thumbtacks, or drafting tape. The pricking should be made on the back of the thin paper design so that the paper will lie perfectly flat over the ground fabric during the pouncing process, thereby producing a clear image. When the pouncing is finished, the design should be made permanent immediately by redrawing it delicately with pen or brush and India ink or tempera. If you are embroidering something that will be laundered, make sure you use a permanent tempera or ink.

It is also possible to transfer designs by using dressmakers' carbon paper. A color that offers contrast to the ground fabric should be chosen, and the paper should be fastened between the drawing and the ground.

NEEDLEWORK PATTERN,
*England, 17th century;
linen with design
in pencil*

The drawing is then traced with a blunt-pointed pencil or similar instrument to avoid punctures in the drawing.

The hot transfer method is easier than either pouncing or dressmakers' carbon, but it requires care and a little practice. First, draw the design on tracing paper; then redraw it on the back of the tracing sheet with a hot transfer pencil. Then fix the drawing in place over the ground fabric with the hot transfer side next to the cloth. Press a hot iron over the paper, and the design is transferred in a red color from paper to fabric.

It is very easy to make a smudgy, unusable transfer, but you can avoid smudges if you have a sharp point on the hot transfer pencil and you use it lightly but accurately. You cannot make corrections when you use the hot transfer pencil because these inevitably will transfer to the fabric, and no erasure ever is sufficiently thorough. If you make a mistake in a place that will show in the finished work, you should start your transfer again. By keeping a sheet of paper under your hands, you can prevent accidental smudging, which will transfer to the fabric. Some practice in handling the iron is helpful in making a neat transfer. It should be hot and should not be moved back and forth from place to place but lifted. If the iron is held on the fabric too long, the transfer line may bleed on the cloth. The hot transfer method, correctly used, is quick and satisfactory. Hot transfer pencils are stocked by embroidery suppliers who handle a wide range of materials.

Another transferring method, based on transferring directions in old embroidery books, is good for delicate fabrics. First, mix a small amount of tempera paint (light-colored temperas are used for dark fabrics, and colors of darker value for light fabrics) with two parts sugar dissolved in one part water to make a thin syrup. The solution can be cooked to dissolve the sugar quickly, or very hot or boiling water can be added to the sugar, which is then stirred quickly so that it dissolves. Although the sugar must be dissolved, the solution should be boiled only briefly, because the small amounts of sugar and water used will very quickly become too thick to flow easily. If the mixture is cooked, it should be painted onto the design immediately, before the syrup starts to thicken, as it will when it cools. With a brush handled delicately but accurately, paint over the lines of the pattern on the back of the tracing paper. The way you handle the brush is most important—a broad line transfers as a broad line. Allow the painted

side of the pattern to dry thoroughly (about one hour). Then secure the pattern over the ground, with the painted side touching the fabric. Transfer the design by pressing over the paper with a hot iron. The iron should not be pushed from side to side, but should be lifted, brought down, and held motionless for a second or two, but not long enough to scorch the fabric.

Transferring a design onto velvet can be accomplished by basting along the essential lines of the paper design, which is positioned on the velvet in such a way that the basting goes through paper and cloth. When the basting is finished, tear away the paper design; the basting threads will indicate the design on the velvet. You can use this method for other materials, but it is especially useful when you embroider directly onto velvet.

THREADCOUNTED EMBROIDERY

Most of the embroideries in this book are surface embroideries, so-called because the stitching is made without reference to the weave of the material it is worked on. For surface embroideries the design is transferred to the ground material or drawn directly on it. The needlework is made by using a variety of stitches that typically includes long and short, stem, outline, chain, back, laid, coral, Cretan, feather, split, satin, and various kinds of speckling and couching.

A few of the needleworks in this book are threadcounted embroideries. To make threadcounted embroideries, one usually counts the stitches of a diagram worked on graph paper, or works on a ground canvas on which the design has been specially painted. A few threadcounted embroideries that require stitch-charted diagrams have been included in this book. Only one pattern is entirely threadcounted (see page 69). Several other patterns require a combination of surface stitching and threadcounting.

There are numerous types of threadcounted embroideries. One of them is needlepoint, the general term for several types of canvas embroidery such as gros point (large stitches), petit point (small stitches), Hungarian, or Florentine (long, straight stitches), flame stitching, or Bargello, and combinations of large and small stitches, sometimes with surface stitching or raised work included. Today needlepoint is rarely worked on a ground other than the canvas that is especially made for this purpose, but in earlier times needlepoint was worked on tabby-woven linen. The canvases used for needlepoint today come in meshes of many sizes and are stiff and woven so that there is an easily seen space between each thread or each second thread of the weave. Tent and cross stitches are the most commonly used needlepoint stitches, but many others, including some that also are worked in surface embroidery, are employed: Italian cross, long-armed cross, herringbone, satin, Hungarian, and rococo. Directions for these stitches can be found in the Stitch Directory, but many other stitches also may be used for needlepoint.

Assisi embroidery is another type of the thread-counted needlework (see page 65). This embroidery, like the pattern-darned example on page 8, the mesh-grounded examples on page 144 and page 179, and the blackwork pillow cover on page 33, is a combination of surface stitching and threadcounting. Of these, the Assisi embroidery is the simplest because it requires only that the design be drawn on ground fabric and traced with back stitches, and that the background be filled in with long-armed cross stitches, all worked the same size and in the same direction. In this book the mesh-grounded and pattern-darned embroideries have diagrams accompanied by linear geometric graph patterns. The graph squares are comparable to threads in the fabric. As shown, each stitch passes across the same number of threads that it passes in the original embroidery, but if your ground fabric is very different from the original, you must adjust the pattern for your fabric. For example, the linen used for the pillow cover on page 33 is quite finely woven. If you try to work the filling patterns for this design as they are charted, on a coarse linen, you will probably find that the filling designs are very large in comparison with the flowers and other shapes they are intended to fill. To work the pillow cover design on a coarse ground, either enlarge the scale of the flower-coiling stem design or simplify the filling patterns so that they are small enough to look pleasing in the original scale but on the coarser fabric.

Drawn threads or threads pushed out of alignment are the distinguishing element of another type of threadcounted embroidery. Often drawnwork is all white, but examples on pages 8 and 179 show that this is not necessarily always so.

The easiest way to learn how to draw threads out of a piece of fabric is to use a plain-woven (tabby-woven) fabric that does not resist the removal of threads. Smooth, tightly twisted threads come out more easily than those with slubs or other irregularities. You can use hardanger cloth, evenweave linen, and other special fabrics (although some of them are too inferior in quality to merit the time and effort that will be spent on fine embroidery). Using a small pair of embroidery scissors, clip one thread of the ground fabric at the edge of a shape that is to have drawn thread work. Using a tapestry needle, lift out this first thread, working between each two or three crosswise threads until you come to the opposite edge of the shape. After making sure that the fabric is lying flat and is unpuckered, clip off the thread. Draw the threads out of the ground in the proper sequence. For example, if you are to draw out every fourth thread, then count very carefully from the first thread and draw out the fourth; repeat this sequence throughout the shape. Work all the threads in one direction, horizontally or vertically; then work in the opposite direction. You will find that after the first few rows of threads are removed the process of drawing them out eases considerably. In most embroideries the raw clipped-thread edges will be worked over with embroidery at some later stage, but they should be overcast in the beginning so that there will be no stretching or distortion of the fabric.

The Stitch Directory contains several stitches used in drawn thread work; interlocking, buttonhole, faggot, weaving, double faggot, and Russian overcast. Other stitches are used for drawn thread work, but these are not listed because they are not used in any of the pieces presented in this book.

When threads are pushed out of alignment, but not withdrawn, as the stitches are made, the work is some-times called punch work. The term punch work has been applied because in certain cases the ground is prepared first by making an opening with a punch needle or other instrument between threads at equal intervals—for example, between every four threads. In finer work, such as the cap back on page 144, the openings can be made by using a fairly large needle (a punch needle if you can find one in the right size) and rather fine thread (lightweight enough so that it won't fill up the opening you make as you pull together the threads of the ground fabric).

Stitches used for punch work embroidery that are listed in the Stitch Directory are overcast, Italian cross, and faggot.

SUPPLIERS

The following suppliers are good sources for all types of needlework materials. Starred firms (*) are suppliers of silk and gold threads of the type needed to complete the metalwork embroideries described in this book. Other firms on the list supply woolen, cotton, or synthetic threads or yarns. Suppliers of dyes and linen threads are noted. All these suppliers are equipped to handle mail orders.

Appleton Bros. of London
West Main Road
Little Compton, Rhode Island 02837

Appleton Bros. Ltd.
Church Street
Chiswick
London, W4, England

Borgs of Lund
P.O. Box 1096
Lund, Sweden

Colonial Textiles
2604 Cranbrook
Ann Arbor, Michigan 48104

Countryside Handweavers, Inc.
West Elkhorn Avenue
Box 1743
Estes Park, Colorado 80517

Craft Yarns of Rhode Island
603 Mineral Springs Avenue
Pawtucket, Rhode Island 02862

Dharma Trading Co.
P.O. Box 1288
Berkeley, California 94701
(supplies include dyes)

Dryad
Northgates
Leicester LE1 4QR
England

Frederick J. Fawcett, Inc.
129 South Street
Boston, Massachusetts 02111
(linen threads)

Glen Black
1414 Grant Avenue
San Francisco, California 94133
(supplies include dyes)

Joan Toggitt*
52 Vanderbilt Avenue
New York, New York 10017

Lee Wards
1200 St. Charles Road
Elgin, Illinois 60120

Lily Mills
Shelby, North Carolina
(linen threads)

Louis Grossé Ltd.*
36 Manchester Street
London W1
England

Mace and Nairn*
89 Crane Street, Salisbury
Wiltshire
England

Merribee
2904 W. Lancaster
P.O. Box 9680
Fort Worth, Texas 76107

Mrs. Mary Allen*
Turnditch
Derbyshire
England

Nantucket Needlery*
2 India Street
Nantucket, Massachusetts 02554

Old Mill Yarns
P.O. Box 115 WA
Eaton Rapids, Michigan

Paternayan Bros., Inc.
312 East 95th Street
New York, New York 10028
(will inform you of outlets
for their product in your locality)

Royal School of Needlework*
25 Princes Gate
Kensington, London SW7
England

Small Fortune
420 South El Camino Real
Tustin, California 92680
(supplies include dyes)

Studio of Weaving and Lacemaking
319 Mendoza Avenue
Coral Gables, Florida 33134
(linen thread for lacemaking)

The Needlewoman
146 Regent Street
London W1
England

Watts & Co. Ltd.*
7 Tufton Street
Westminster, London SW1
England

Yarn Depot
545 Sutter Street
San Francisco, California 94102

Yarn Primitives
Box 1013
Weston, Connecticut 06880

Stitch directory

The stitches in this directory have been listed
in alphabetical order so that they can be
located easily. Only the embroidery stitches needed
to make the pieces in this book are discussed.

Before making a stitch that you have never used
before on your embroidery, practice the stitch on a
piece of scrap linen until you feel that you have
the right rhythm and technique and are ready to apply
the stitch to your work. By practicing the stitches
before applying them to your embroidery, you may avoid
the need to remove stitches from the needlework,
and thereby reduce the risk of accidentally
damaging the ground.

BACK
Back stitch is
used to make
lines or to
produce grainy
texture within an area. To make a line, work from
right to left. Bring the needle to the face surface of
the work one stitch length to the left of the right end
of the line. Then insert the needle at the right end of
the line to make the first stitch. Next, bring the needle
to the surface again one stitch length to the left of
the stitch just made. Repeat the stitch.

Back stitch makes a perfectly straight row of
stitches. The amount of thread deposited on the back
of the work is about twice the amount on the front.
Sometimes the stitch is used for quilting. In whitework embroidery, single back stitches frequently are
powdered over an area, giving it a seedy, grainy, or
sand-like appearance. In France this powdering of back
stitch is called *point de sablé*.

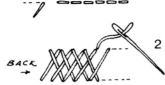

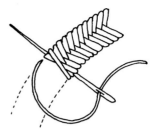

BACK, CROSSED

Crossed back stitch is worked on transparent fabric so that the crossings made on the back of the embroidery will show through. This stitch is used for small shapes or broad lines. When you transfer a design that includes crossed back stitch, indicate two lines on the pattern to show the width of the line to be worked.

As in back stitch at the left, work for crossed back stitch proceeds from right to left. Begin one stitch length to the left of the point where you want to start on the upper line, bringing the needle to the surface, and reinserting it at the starting point on the upper line. Then move the needle downward on the back of the work to a point one stitch length to the left of the starting point on the lower line. Bring the needle up to the top surface at this point and return it to the back of the work at the starting point on the lower line. At this point one back stitch has been made on the top line and one on the bottom line. A cross stitch made on the back of the work shows through the transparent material as the process is repeated, beginning a back stitch one stitch length to the left of the first back stitch on the top line.

For obvious reasons crossed back stitch is sometimes called shadow stitch. On transparent materials it provides a degree of density midway between the thinness of the material and the thickness of opaque white stitchery as in, for example, satin stitch.

BASKET

Basket stitch is used when you want a band or heavy line. It may be worked on counted threads or between two lines of a transferred design. To work it vertically, as it is shown here, begin by bringing the needle from the back to the surface at the top of the left line. Then insert the needle at a lower point on the right line to make a diagonal stitch at about a forty-five degree angle, and bring it to the surface again on the left line, directly opposite the point of insertion. Cross the needle over the first stitch and insert it at the starting point of the right line. Move the needle across the back of the work to the left side, and bring it to the surface next to, but below, the first left-hand stitch. This stitch can be placed close to the first left-hand stitch or a little apart from it, depending on whether you want an open or closed effect. Repeat the entire process for the length of the line.

The term *basket stitch* sometimes is used to define an embroidery comprised of blocks of satin stitches arranged in basket weave or brick fashion.

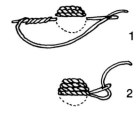

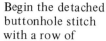

BULLION

Bullion stitch 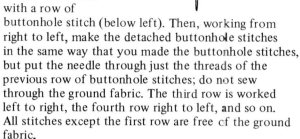 makes a small, sausage-shaped knot that lies on the surface of the ground fabric. The size and shape of the needle are important in working this stitch. The needle should be of uniform thickness and should not bulge around the eye; tight twists of thread are made around the needle, and these must pass over the eye.

Make a stitch, bringing the needle to the surface of the work to about the middle of its length, but do not pull it all the way through. Hold the thread taut with your left hand about two or three inches away from the ground fabric. With the needle held in your right hand, make several twists of thread around the needle with your left hand; the number of twists depends on the size of the stitch you want. (Fewer twists make a smaller stitch.) Keep the thread taut while you turn the needle back as if making a back stitch, and insert the needle into the cloth, drawing the thread through the tightly twisted coil as it is pulled to the back of the fabric. The length of this "back stitch" will depend on the number of twists on your needle as well as the thickness of the thread. Bullion stitches may be made to cover an area compactly, or they may be powdered in random fashion.

BUTTONHOLE

Buttonhole stitch can be either threadcounted, or worked along a transferred line or an edge that has been hemmed or turned under. To begin, bring the needle from the back of the work to the surface at the left end of the transferred line, and insert it into the ground above the line and slightly to the right. (How far to the right and how far above the line depends on the size and spacing that the stitch is to have.) Bring just the tip of the needle back to the surface on the line where you began and at a point directly below, holding the thread under the tip of the needle. Then pull the thread all the way through, and again insert the needle to the right and above the line to begin a second stitch.

If spaced apart, buttonhole stitches sometimes are called blanket stitches. The tailor's buttonhole stitch is made in a slightly different way, and it has an extra twist along the edge.

BUTTONHOLE, DETACHED

Begin the detached buttonhole stitch with a row of buttonhole stitch (below left). Then, working from right to left, make the detached buttonhole stitches in the same way that you made the buttonhole stitches, but put the needle through just the threads of the previous row of buttonhole stitches; do not sew through the ground fabric. The third row is worked left to right, the fourth row right to left, and so on. All stitches except the first row are free of the ground fabric.

Detached buttonhole stitch is the basic stitch of both stumpwork and needle lace, two techniques that are closely related. Detached buttonhole can be started over long horizontal stitches of paired threads rather than with a row of attached buttonhole stitches, or it can be worked into chain stitches (at the right).

CEYLON

Ceylon stitch is used both as a wide line and as a filling.

To make this stitch, you need two transferred lines so that you can determine the width of the line or area to be worked. Work a stitch across the width of the area to be filled by bringing the needle from the back of the fabric at the left side of the width, up through, across to the right, and down through the fabric. Bring the needle up again on the left immediately below the starting point. Around this top stitch work a series of loops—as widely or as closely spaced as desired. To make the second row of loops, bring the needle up on the left, and make loops through each of the loops above by passing the needle behind the loops from right to left but not through the ground fabric. Then reinsert the needle on the right. The thread pierces the ground fabric only at the beginning and at the end of each row.

Ceylon stitch requires a wiry thread and is often used for metal thread embroidery. Because the stitch involves a minimal amount of ground penetration, it is a good one for working metal passing threads.

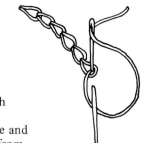

CHAIN

Chain stitch produces a straight line and is worked from right to left (or top to bottom). The needle is brought from the back to the surface at the right (or top) end of the line to be worked. The thread is held under the left thumb on the surface of the fabric; the needle is inserted at the point where the stitch began, and then it is brought to the surface again one stitch length to the left on (or down) the line. The needle tip passes over the thread, which is still held down by the thumb. By keeping the thread under the needle tip a loop is formed, and the needle and remaining thread are drawn through it. This procedure is repeated to make the chain along a line.

Chain stitch may be overcast or threaded in various ways, and it is often combined with other stitches. It also may be used in close, concentric or parallel rows as a filling. Its greatest value lies in the precise, even line it creates.

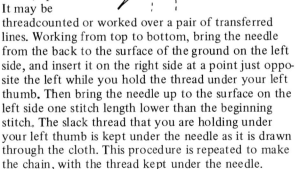

CHAIN, SQUARE

Square chain stitch makes a broad, open line. It may be threadcounted or worked over a pair of transferred lines. Working from top to bottom, bring the needle from the back to the surface of the ground on the left side, and insert it on the right side at a point just opposite the left while you hold the thread under your left thumb. Then bring the needle up to the surface on the left side one stitch length lower than the beginning stitch. The slack thread that you are holding under your left thumb is kept under the needle as it is drawn through the cloth. This procedure is repeated to make the chain, with the thread kept under the needle.

Square chain stitch is sometimes called open chain stitch or ladder stitch. In this directory the term *ladder stitch* is used to define an entirely different stitch (see page 215).

CORAL

As it is usually worked, coral stitch looks like a line of thread held down by knots. It is worked from right to left. Bring the thread to the surface from the back at the right end of the line to be worked. Holding the thread under your left thumb, make a short diagonal stitch under the transferred line, and draw the needle, with the thread held under it, through the cloth. The length of the diagonal stitch depends on the design. As the thread is pulled through, a knot is formed to tack down the thread. Make the next knot immediately adjacent to the first one or spaced a little apart from it. On the bedcover on page 97 the tiny knots are placed so closely together that the line of thread that connects them cannot be seen.

Coral stitch with widely spaced knots can be worked in zigzags or in combination with other stitches to form decorative borders.

COUCHING

In couching, one or a pair of threads is secured on the surface of an embroidery by means of a second thread. The "tying" thread is almost always smaller or finer than the couched thread, and it is pulled taut. Usually couching means overcasting with small stitches at right angles to the direction of the thread being couched. The tying stitches, often in a contrasting color, may be arranged so as to form patterns—anything from simple stripe or basket weave arrangements to complicated geometric or floral designs.

Couching is worked in all types of threads, but it is essential in goldwork because you want to keep all of the precious material on the face of the work. If the metal threads are couched with another thread, the fragile metal need not be subjected to the wear that occurs when threads are pulled back and forth through the ground fabric. Couching can be used to incorporate woolen or other yarns, leather, and fibrous materials into your embroidery when these materials are unsuitable for intricate stitching.

COUCHING, BOKHARA

In Bokhara couching, a thread is laid from left to right within an area. Then, with the same thread and needle, tying stitches are made from right to left. The tying stitches are pulled taut and slant slightly, and are arranged in such a way that they form long diagonals across the work.

Bokhara couching usually is worked in silk floss embroidery. To keep the design of the couching stitches in precise pattern, mark them on the ground fabric so that the pattern can be followed as work progresses. If the area to be filled with Bokhara couching is too large to be held within a hand hoop, the embroidery must be mounted in a frame, because the long threads to be couched must be laid in single, long stitches beginning on the left and ending on the right side of a given shape.

COUCHING, BUTTONHOLED

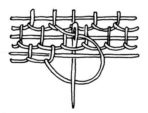

Buttonholed couching is an area-filling stitch usually used for small-sized shapes. To make the stitch, bring up the needle on the right edge at the top of the area to be worked and insert it on the left edge, thereby laying a thread across the shape. Bring the needle back to the surface on the left edge, just below the point of insertion, and couch the laid thread with a row of buttonhole stitches (see page 206). Insert the needle on the right at the end of the row of buttonhole stitches, bring it back to the surface immediately under this insertion, and again lay a thread across to the left. As you make buttonhole stitches to tie this second thread into place, work them through only the buttonhole stitches in the above row and not through the ground fabric. Only the beginnings and the ends of the rows are attached to the ground fabric.

This stitch is often worked over padding. It is appropriate for metal or other wiry threads and also is used in lacemaking, in which it is called *point d'entoilage.*

COUCHING, PADDED

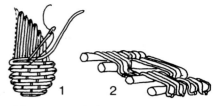

Couching stitches can be raised over padding in various ways, depending on the padding material chosen. Frequently, couching is made over a padding of long stitches arranged at right angles to the final couched stitches, as in padded satin stitch (see page 218). In old embroideries metal thread couching often was made over cords that were sewn into place in striped or other patterns before metal threads were couched over them. The gold couching stitches were pulled down firmly over the padding cords, so that their design appeared as a relief pattern. Sometimes the couching stitches pulled the threads being couched through the threads of the ground fabric. Such work was called underside couching. Of the varieties of raised effects possible in couching, this one produces the greatest relief.

COUCHING, ROUMANIAN

In Roumanian couching the thread is brought up on the left, is carried across the shape to be filled, and is brought down through the ground on the right side of the area. The needle and thread are then used to tie the laid thread; the tying stitch is long and slanting, and it is kept rather loose. Fancy patterns in the couching are not characteristic of Roumanian couching. The tying stitches are either lined up in vertical rows or staggered in brick fashion.

Roumanian couching is always made with a single thread for both laid and tying stitches, and it is an excellent stitch for woolen yarns. It is worked quickly and is therefore useful for embroideries of large scale. If shapes to be filled with Roumanian couching are too large to be encompassed within a hand hoop, the work must be mounted in an embroidery frame.

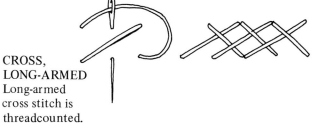

CRETAN

Cretan stitch
can be worked
as a broad line
or as bands
within a shape. In either case guidelines for the two
sides of the stitched area should be established. Small
stitches are taken alternately on the right and left; the
needle always is pointed toward the center of the
area to be stitched, and the thread is kept under the
needle as it is pulled through for each stitch. Cretan
stitch is a variation of feather stitch (see page 212).
In Cretan stitch individual stitches slant only slightly
and are kept close together, while in feather stitch the
needle is carried on a sharp diagonal as the stitches are
made. Feather stitch is more open than Cretan, which
often is referred to as Cretan feather.

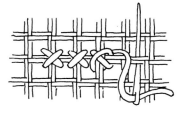

CROSS
Cross stitch
may be worked
in various ways,
but is most
attractive when threadcounted. One threadcounted
method involves working a half of each stitch across
a row of stitches to be made, then completing the
stitches on a second passage of the row. Decide how
many threads a single stitch is to cover. Bring the
needle up at the upper left-hand corner of the stitch,
count horizontally the desired number of threads,
then count vertically downward for the same number,
and insert the needle at that point. Begin the second
partial cross stitch directly above the lower end of the
slanting stitch just made, and repeat this slanting stitch
across the row. Return along the row, making a diagonal
stitch in the opposite direction across each stitch to
complete the cross.

**CROSS,
LONG-ARMED**
Long-armed
cross stitch is
threadcounted.
Work progresses
from left to right. Decide how many horizontal rows
of threads (wefts of the ground fabric) each row of
stitches is to cover. To make the first cross, count
threads toward the right side of the row, counting
twice as many threads as the number of weft threads
to be covered by the horizontal row of stitches. Beginning at the lower left corner of the cross to be made,
bring the needle to the surface and insert it into the
fabric at the upper right corner of the cross, thus
carrying the thread in a slanting direction over twice
as many vertical threads (warps) of the ground fabric
as you have passed over in the horizontal (weft)
direction. When you finish this procedure you will
have made a long diagonal stitch, one half of the cross.
Now bring the thread to the surface again at a point
directly below the upper end of the stitch just made
and between the same two weft threads between which
you began your first stitch. If, for example, you moved
the thread up four weft threads and to the left eight
warp threads in finding the position of the first diagonal stitch, you now move the thread down four weft
threads and bring it to the surface at that point. Now
count four warp threads to the left and four weft
threads upward to find the point where you insert
your needle to complete the second stitch of the cross.
To begin the second cross, count down four weft threads
and bring the thread to the surface. Now you are ready
to repeat the two stitches.

Long-armed cross stitch does not make square or
checkered units but creates a continuous band of
stitches that have a braided look. Heavy silk floss was
used for long-armed cross stitch in early Italian work;
it gives good coverage to the ground. Long-armed—or
long-legged—cross stitch is so called because one "arm"
or "leg" of the cross is twice the length of the other.

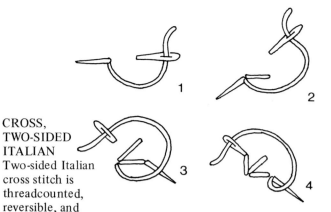

1

2

3

4

CROSS, TWO-SIDED ITALIAN

Two-sided Italian cross stitch is threadcounted, reversible, and worked on a loosely woven fabric so that as the stitches are pulled tight a mesh-like effect is created. Sometimes it is necessary to recross stitches to keep the embroidery the same on both sides. To begin, determine how many threads of the ground are to be crossed by each stitch. Ideally, the same number should be crossed in each direction. If evenweave linen is used, a perfectly "square" cross will result. A tapestry needle should be used in making this stitching, and thread and ground should be adjusted so that distinctly formed meshes are created. Make the stitch as follows.

1. Bring the needle to the face surface of the ground fabric at the lower left corner of the cross to be made. Insert the needle at the lower right and bring it up again at the lower left corner.
2. Carry the thread to the upper right corner, insert the needle, and return it to the surface of the fabric at lower left.
3. Insert the needle at the upper left, and bring it to the sufrace at the lower right.
4. Insert the needle at the upper left, and bring it to the surface at the lower right.
5. Repeat, inserting the needle at the lower right and bringing it up at the lower left, and so on, making horizontal rows below the first row.

DARNING

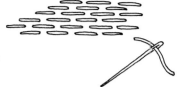

Darning stitch is used as a flat, weaving-like filling. Usually, it is threadcounted and worked from right to left, and when a hand hoop is used, the hoop is turned as each row is made. Bring the embroidery thread through from the back to the surface and pass over a selected number of ground threads; pick up one thread of the ground fabric and pass over several more counted threads before picking up another thread. In the next row of plain darning, the thread of the ground that is picked up will be midway between the "ties" of the last row. The embroidery thread chosen for darning stitch should be heavier than the thread of the ground fabric so that the stitches will make a dense covering.

Darning looks like woven brocading. It is essentially running stitch in which only one thread of the ground is picked up. It gives a damask-like effect if areas of darning are worked in opposing directions—some vertical, some horizontal. When darning is worked in patterns (at the right), sometimes more than one thread of the ground is picked up.

DARNING, DOUBLE

Double darning stitch is like plain darning, but it is worked

with floating (long, loose) threads on both the front and the back of the ground, making the needlework reversible. Running stitches—stitches and intervals the same length, as a rule—are worked in a row; then the same row is worked with stitches placed so as to fill the intervals left on the first passage. Double *darning* stitch and double *running* stitch are almost always identical.

DARNING, PATTERN

Pattern darning
is worked in the
same way as
plain darning
(at the left), but threads of the ground are picked
up so as to depict a motif, usually geometric but sometimes floral. The pattern, which will emerge as threads
of the ground are picked up in sequence, should be
drawn on the ground fabric with tailor's chalk or other
material that will wash or dust away, because the
marked threads of the ground will be picked up as
work progresses and will show in the finished needlework. For these reasons indelible transfers should be
avoided. A basting thread can be used to make the
design if a delicate, nonwashable groundfabric is used.

FAGGOT, DOUBLE

Double faggot
stitch is
threadcounted and
worked diagonally
throughout an area, creating an open effect in the
embroidery. Two stitches are made around two vertical threads and then around two horizontal threads
in a line that zigzags across the area to be filled. The
wrapping thread is pulled taut as the stitches are made
to open up the weave. Double faggot stitch is attractive from both the front and the back.

FAGGOT, SINGLE

Single faggot
stitches are
worked diagonally
across an area;
the horizontal and vertical stitches are arranged in a
zigzag pattern that becomes a square when a second
diagonal row is worked adjacent to the first. All stitches
are pulled tight as the work progresses, so that a meshy
effect is created. Usually, a fine thread of the same color
as the ground is used to make single faggot in order
to maximize the openwork effect. The upper and left
sides of the square are made first. Any number of
threads can be passed over in making the stitches, but
when fine work is made on lightweight linen or cotton,
four threads is often the best number.

To begin, working from right to left, bring the thread
to the surface at the upper left corner of the square
you intend to make. Move four threads right and insert
the needle. Next, moving diagonally to the left on the
back of the work, bring the thread to the surface four
threads below the upper left corner of the square you
are starting to make and then insert the needle four
threads above, which is the point at which you started
work. Now, you have two stitches, making a right angle.
Next move the needle diagonally across the back of the
fabric and to the left, dropping down four threads.
When you bring the needle to the surface at this point,
you will find that it is positioned correctly to make a
second pair of stitches by repeating the same procedure
you used for the first two stitches. By repeating this
procedure you make the first zigzagged line. The second
zigzagged line (below the dotted line in the diagram)
should be made in the same manner, but the stitches
should be arranged so that the zigzagged line combines
with the first row, creating a diagonal row of squares.

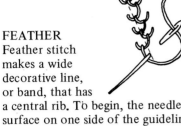

FEATHER

Feather stitch makes a wide decorative line, or band, that has a central rib. To begin, the needle is brought to the surface on one side of the guideline—which may not actually be drawn on the fabric but which represents the center of the broad line—at the beginning (top) and in the center of the band width to be made. At a point slightly below the beginning of the band and on either the right or left edge of it, the needle is inserted into the fabric and the thread is pulled all the way through except for a slack loop, which is held under the left thumb. The tip of the needle is brought to the surface again at the center of the band a short distance below the starting point and is brought through the loop you are holding with your thumb to complete the stitch. A second stitch now can be made on the other side of the band center and slightly below it. Stitches alternate from one side to the other. In many variations of this stitch, the slant and length of the lateral stitches produce different effects. Cretan stitch (see page 209), is feather stitch with the lateral stitches placed close together instead of apart, as they are in feather stitch. Closed feather, with its lateral stitches pointing downward instead of toward the center rib, and double stitch are two often-used variations of feather stitch that do not appear on any of the embroideries in this book. Feather stitch and its many variations are found most often on crewel embroidered panels and on silk patchwork coverlets (crazy quilts).

FILLING, RUSSIAN OVERCAST

Russian overcast filling is worked into a ground fabric from which some of the threads have been withdrawn. Two threads removed and two threads remaining in each direction is a usual ratio. Overcast (see page 216) the cut ends of the threads you have removed to prevent them from raveling. Drawn thread areas then are worked in Russian overcast, beginning at the lower left of the area to be filled. The overcast is worked zigzag fashion. One stitch is worked diagonally over a crossing of the ground threads, two stitches are worked vertically on the first pair of threads, a stitch is made across a second crossing of the ground threads, and then two stitches are made around a horizontal pair of threads. Work continues in this fashion—one stitch across each crossing of ground threads and two stitches around each vertical or horizontal pair—until a zigzag course has been made diagonally across the shape to be filled. Zigzagged rows are repeated until the area is completely filled—a row worked from lower right to upper left, followed by a row worked from upper left to lower right, and so on. As rows are juxtaposed, single stitches made over crossings of vertical and horizontal ground threads are paired so that each crossing has two stitches worked around it.

FISHBONE

Fishbone, a flat filling stitch, usually is used for small petal-like or lozenge shapes, but it can be made to fill larger areas as well. A central rib is drawn longitudinally through the center of the area to be worked. A straight stitch is made at the top of the longitudinal line; then the needle is brought to the surface of the embroidery on one side of the design (the outer edge), very close to the first stitch made, and inserted into the ground on the central line so as to make a diagonal stitch that slightly overlaps the first stitch. The needle then is brought up on the opposite side of the design (close to the first stitch); to make another slanted stitch that ends at the center line. The stitches are alternated from one side to the other, each stitch slightly overlapping the previous one. For a wider filling, the outer edges of adjacent bands of fishbone may be interwoven so that they have the same appearance as the central rib.

HERRINGBONE

Herringbone
stitch is worked
from left to
right, sometimes
on counted threads but more often between two transferred lines. These lines should not be transferred indelibly because they will show in the finished work if they cannot be removed. Consider using basting threads as guidelines.

Herringbone stitch makes a broad, open line. Beginning at the lower left end of the area to be worked, make a slanting stitch from lower left to upper right. On the upper line move the needle to the left and bring it to the surface at a point where the stitch length will be about half the length of the first stitch. Then make a slanting stitch from the upper left to lower right. Repeat these two stitches so that each pair overlaps the previous pair.

Herringbone stitch often is combined with other stitches to make decorative borders. It may be interwoven with a contrasting or matching thread in various ways. The stitch crossings may be tied with crossed stitches or improvised patterns of line stitches, or they may be woven around in wheel-fashion with a thread that is continuous from one crossing to the next. Herringbone stitches sometimes are placed quite close together for a plaited effect.

HERRINGBONE, TIED

Tied herringbone
stitch is made
in the same fashion
as herringbone
(see above), but the stitch crossings are tied together with coral stitch (see page 207). The tying stitches are worked from right to left. In another variation of tied herringbone, stitches are simply tied to the ground at the crossings with short straight stitches, as is done in couching.

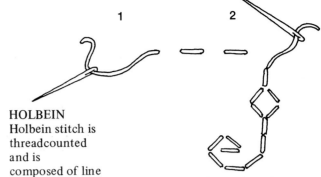

HOLBEIN

Holbein stitch is
threadcounted
and is
composed of line
(straight—vertical or horizontal) stitches and stroke (diagonal) stitches. Holbein stitch is used for small geometric patterns, and cross or satin stitches may be included (see pages 209, 218). If Holbein stitches have been handled as double running stitches (see page 218), the embroidery will be reversible.

Holbein stitch is a type of embroidery rather than a single stitch. It was commonly used for borders, many of them on garments. Holbein stitch was named for the German master painter in whose works examples of this early embroidery appear.

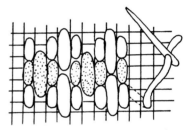

HUNGARIAN

Hungarian stitch
is threadcounted
and is worked in
horizontal rows.
The embroidery passes vertically over two, then four, then two horizontal threads of the ground to complete little diamond shapes, which are lined up in rows. One vertical thread is skipped between each diamond, and the sequence is repeated across the row. The action is the same as that in making satin stitch (see page 218). When an area has been covered with rows of Hungarian stitch, a mosaic-like effect is produced. Today Hungarian stitch usually is worked on needlepoint canvas.

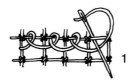

INTERLOCKING

Interlocking stitch is worked on netting to make lace or on a ground fabric to make embroidery after threads have been withdrawn from it in certain areas of the design. Possibly two threads drawn out and two threads remaining in sequence both horizontally and vertically would make a good ground for interlocking stitch. Raw edges of the shape to be worked should be overcast first to prevent raveling. Generally the embroidery will cover these edges, but it is wise to have them secured first. Begin work at the top left. Make a loop as shown in the diagram over the top threads of each square in the top horizontal row of open squares. All embroidery thread lies on top of the work except at the points where the thread loops over the ground. When you have worked the embroidery thread to the right side of the row, loop it around the ground fabric on the right of the last square, and begin to work from right to left, this time making a loop around the two bottom threads of each square in the same horizontal row of squares. In this row of loops, as you approach vertical pairs of ground threads with the embroidery thread pass it under them and above the thread that formed the first row of loops. Now you can fill the second horizontal row of squares. The procedure is the same, except that loops are always linked into the loops of the row above.

Interlocking stitch is used in open types of embroidery. In needle and filet lacemaking it is a staple filling stitch called *point d'esprit.*

KNOT, FRENCH

To make French knots, bring a thread to the surface of the ground fabric at the point where the knot is to be made. With your left hand hold the thread taut and wind it around the needle two to three times. While you maintain tension on the thread in your left hand, insert the needle in the ground fabric at a point very close to the spot where the thread emerged. As you pull the needle through the fabric, your left hand still holds the thread taut so that a tight, compact knot is formed.

To avoid confusion, all knot stitches in this book have been termed *French knot,* because now this term is commonly accepted. It should be understood, however, that in old books the term *knot stitch* usually refers to the same stitch.

LAID

Laidwork is a solid filling technique in which threads are laid on the surface of the embroidery. The technique often is used for metal embroidery or when a floss silk filling is wanted. Long threads are laid across the area to be filled, so if the area is very large the work must be mounted in an embroidery frame. Metal threads may be turned on the surface to form another row of the laid threads; then the rows are caught with couching stitches at the edges of the area that is being filled. Silk laidwork may be made by working long, closely parallel rows of stitches, exactly as in satin stitch (see page 218), across the entire area. In either case, additional threads are couched over the laid threads to hold them in place. The simplest way to work these added threads is to place them at intervals at right angles to the first laid threads and tie them down with couching stitches. Diamond shapes or other geometric arrangements of threads are used frequently. It also is possible to work out intricate scrolling designs, which serve the additional purpose of holding the laid threads securely to the ground.

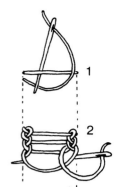

LADDER

Ladder stitch,
which makes a wide
line, is worked
from top to bottom.
Two lines should be transferred to the ground so that
the width of the ladder stitch filled area can be kept
precisely uniform. (The contour can be made to undu-
late unevenly, if desired.) Starting at the top and from
the back, make a stitch across the width of the line to
be worked. Then bring the needle to the surface on the
left, just below the top stitch, and make a loop at the
left side and then another at the right side of the band
by twisting the thread around the starting stitch; at the
same time catch a thread of ground to hold the two
loops in place. Then insert the needle on the right line
just opposite the point on the left where it emerged,
and bring it up again on the left side and slightly below
the previous stitch. Loop the thread around the crossings
of the left and right loops of the previous stitch, but
this time attach the loops to previously made loops
only; then reinsert the needle into the fabric on the
right. Repeat the process the length of the ladder. This
stitch is a variation of the Ceylon stitch (see page 206).

LINE AND STROKE

Line stitches are
simple, straight—
vertical or
horizontal—
stitches; stroke stitches are diagonal. Both often are
threadcounted and worked in exactly the same manner
as double running stitch (see page 217) or Holbein
stitch (see page 213).

LINK POWDERING

Link powdering,
an open filling
stitch, is worked
just as chain
stitch is (see page 207). However, the stitches are not
made in a continuous line but are worked separately
in a random scattering over the surface.

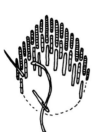

LONG AND SHORT

In making the
first row of long
and short stitch,
alternately long
and short straight stitches are worked close to one another and perpendicular to the contour of a shape to
be filled. All the stitches in subsequent rows are the
same size, but their arrangement is vertically zigzagged
because they are placed to meet the two lengths of the
stitches in the first row. Frequently, successive rows
of long and short stitch are worked in a color slightly
lighter or slightly darker than the color of the preceding
row so that a very subtle gradation of tone is achieved.
(In the diagram, different shades of color are indicated
by the number of horizontal stripes across the stitches.)
When shaded effects are wanted, long and short stitch
is the most frequent choice, whether the thread is to be
wool or silk. The direction of the stitch should be cal-
culated in advance, and stitches shortened or lengthened
to accommodate the direction of upcoming rows.
When you plan silk work, keep in mind that when silk
lies in one direction it looks darker than it does when
it lies in another. Of course, you could arrange the
stitches to adjust for this variance.

Long and short stitch often is used with satin stitch
(see page 218), but the effect of the two stitches is
quite different. The single satin stitch crosses the shape
from side to side. Although its individual stitches are
about the same length as the individual stitches of the
long and short stitch, its appearance is smooth and two-
dimensional (flat), while long and short stitch is rougher
looking and three-dimensional (making forms that
seem to have depth). When long and short stitches and
satin stitches are used together, satin stitch generally
is used for small shapes.

In making long and short stitch as much thread is
deposited on the back of the work as on the front.

OUTLINE

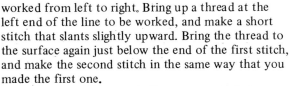

Outline stitch, sometimes called crewel stitch, is a line stitch worked from left to right. Bring up a thread at the left end of the line to be worked, and make a short stitch that slants slightly upward. Bring the thread to the surface again just below the end of the first stitch, and make the second stitch in the same way that you made the first one.

Outline stitch is very similar to stem stitch (see page 219); the difference is that in stem stitch the thread is brought to the surface above rather than below the previous stitch. Of the two, outline stitch produces the more precise line, but stem stitch is made more quickly. Quite often the two are used interchangeably—stem stitch for up-curving lines, outline for down-curving lines. Both stitches make a slightly jagged line, but straighter lines can be made with split, chain, or back stitch (see pages 219, 207, and 204, respectively).

OVERCAST

Overcast stitch is composed of tiny stitches worked parallel to one another and arranged so that they create a small, neat line. A padding thread may be laid along the guideline and overcasting worked over it; this method produces a fuller line with more relief. Overcasting also may be worked over detached threads; then the overcast stitches do not pierce the ground fabric. When overcasting is worked as a detached stitch or on the remaining threads of a ground prepared for drawnwork, the technique is nothing more than the winding of the attached threads with an additional thread.

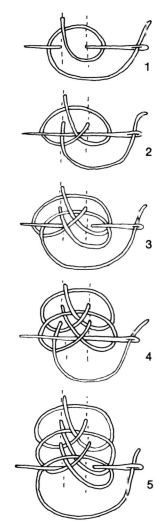

PLAITED BRAID

Plaited braid stitch makes a decorative band. It cannot be worked successfully unless the thread used is very wiry; usually it is seen in gold passing thread embroidery. Plaited braid stitch is worked from top to bottom, and two lines should be transferred as guides for keeping the braid uniform in width. Start by bringing the thread from the back at the top of the left transferred line. Make a loop, and slightly lower down, on the right guideline, insert the needle through the loop and bring it to the surface again at a point directly opposite on the left line of the band (see step 1). This first stitch should be pulled through rather loosely to form a little pretzel shape as the thread is drawn up. For the second stitch (see step 2), put the needle through a crossing of the threads but not the ground fabric. Work the stitch from right to left, and keep the working thread beneath the needle. Work the stitch that follows (see step 3) through the ground from right to left with the crossings of the first two stitches above the needle but the working thread below it. Work the stitch in step 4 as it was worked in step 2—the needle is not put through the ground but is worked under the last crossing, and the working thread kept below the needle. Step 5 repeats step 3. Work the pattern by alternating stitches first through the ground and then through only previous stitches. Take care that the initial stitches are made correctly, and do not allow the threads to get drawn up too tightly.

ROCOCO
Rococo stitch
usually is worked
on canvas that
has paired threads.
Stitches are worked over two pairs of horizontal threads
and between two vertical pairs, usually in clusters of four,
although more or fewer may be used. Begin in the
upper right-hand corner and work diagonally downward. Each stitch should be tied as it is in Roumanian
stitch (at the right) before the next is made. The
diagram shows the exact way in which the thread is
stitched around the vertical and horizontal ground
threads. As diagonal rows of Rococo are made, openings
in the ground will show between the clusters. Rococo
may be worked on tabby-woven ground fabrics as well
as on the paired-thread canvas.

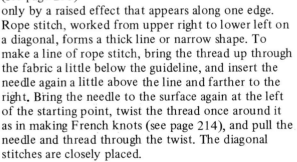

ROPE
Rope stitch can
be distinguished
from satin stitch
(see page 218)
only by a raised effect that appears along one edge.
Rope stitch, worked from upper right to lower left on
a diagonal, forms a thick line or narrow shape. To
make a line of rope stitch, bring the thread up through
the fabric a little below the guideline, and insert the
needle again a little above the line and farther to the
right. Bring the needle to the surface again at the left
of the starting point, twist the thread once around it
as in making French knots (see page 214), and pull the
needle and thread through the twist. The diagonal
stitches are closely placed.

ROUMANIAN
Roumanian stitch
(also sometimes
called overlaid
stitch, universal
stitch, or New England stitch) is used for a broad line
or narrow border stitch, and it also may be used to fill
small areas. It is worked from top to bottom of an area.
The needle is brought up at the top left side of an area
and inserted at the top right side so that a thread is
laid across the width of the area to be filled. With the
same thread the long stitch across the width of the
area is tied down in the center with a loose, oblique
stitch. Then the needle is brought up again on the left,
and the stitch is repeated.

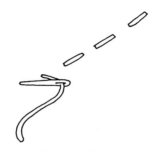

RUNNING
Running stitch is
the simplest of
broken line
stitches. When
it is used in plain sewing, it is called basting. Run the
needle under a few threads of the ground, then over
a few, drawing the thread through the ground fabric
after each two or three stitches. Running stitch may
be either threadcounted or worked freely on the surface
of the ground. It is like darning stitch (see page 210),
except that in darning fewer ground threads usually
are picked up, and the embroidery stitches on the surface are comparatively longer.

RUNNING, DOUBLE

In double running stitch, running stitches (see page 217) are made in such a way that the length of the stitch and the length of the interval are mainly equal. The line of stitches is worked from right to left; then, the work is turned upside down, and stitches are made, again from right to left, in the intervals that were left between the first stitches. To begin each new thread as work proceeds, tiny back stitches are used instead of knots, and thread ends are worked into the embroidery. Thus the work has an identical appearance front and back and is suitable for reversible embroidery. If you find it difficult to begin embroidery without a knot, you can knot the thread and enter the needle and thread into the ground at a point a little apart from the place where you actually are going to begin the double running stitch. At that point make two back stitches and then begin the running stitches. Later the knot and extra thread can be clipped off.

In most instances double running stitch and double darning stitch are terms that can be used interchangeably.

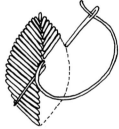

SATIN

Satin stitch is a flat stitch that can be used for complete coverage of a small area. Begin by determining the direction in which the stitches should be worked within a given shape. Keep the stitches closely parallel, and work them over the width of the shape. It is essential to keep the beginnings and endings of stitches closely aligned with adjacent stitches so that a precise contour is maintained. If large areas are to be filled, they may be divided into sections and satin stitch worked in blocks or other shapes within the area.

When satin stitch is worked flat on the surface of the ground fabric, it is sometimes called flat stitch.

SATIN, PADDED OR RAISED

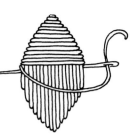

Padded or raised satin stitch is made in the same way as satin stitch (below left), except that a relief effect is created by working it over a padding of felt, cardboard, or, in most cases, layers of stitches. The top layer of padding stitches is worked in such a way that it will be at a right angle to the covering satin stitches.

SATIN, SLANTED

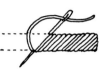

Slanted satin stitch differs from other satin stitches only in that the stitches are carried diagonally rather than horizontally or vertically across an area.

SPECKLING

This term does not define a specific stitch but indicates an area throughout which small stitches have been powdered to give a textured effect. The speckling stitches are usually individual back or running stitches (see pages 204 and 217, respectively). These stitches may be arranged in random fashion or at regular intervals. Speckling in which two back stitches make a single unit may be called seed stitch. Single back stitches placed randomly rather closely together may be called *point de sablé* (sand stitch). Single links of chain stitch, placed randomly or regularly, are referred to as link powdering (see page 215).

SPLIT

Split stitch may be used for either a line or filling. It usually is made in silk floss and is useful for rendering precise detail or making perfectly straight lines. Bring the needle to the surface at the end of a transferred line. While you hold the thread close to the line with your left thumb, take a tiny stitch backward on the line and split the held thread by bringing the needle through it a little above the point where the thread comes to the surface. Repeat this procedure along the entire line. Split stitch is easier to work in a frame because both of your hands are free. However, you can use a hand hoop if you prefer. In a finished piece it is difficult to distinguish split stitch from chain stitch (see page 207).

SQUARED GROUND

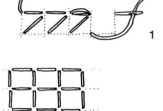

Squared ground stitch is a filling stitch worked from the back over counted threads and in horizontal rows.

Diagram 1 shows the back—the working side of this stitch—and Diagram 2 shows the front surface of the ground fabric with the stitch as it will appear in the finished work. Begin work in the upper left-hand corner of the area to be filled. Make a stitch downward over the desired number of threads from the starting point on the face side of the ground fabric. Make the next stitch upward and diagonally (thread on the fabric back, which in this case is the side you are working on). Pass the needle over the same number of warp threads to the right as were passed in making the first stitch. Insert the needle into the fabric, carry it to the left, and bring it through at the starting point. Then move the thread to the right, and repeat on the back the stitch that was made on the front. Repeat this sequence of stitches in a horizontal row for the needed width. Then work it backward from right to left; this second row completes the squares of the first row and begins the square of the second. A few line stitches must be added to complete the squares of the final row.

Faggot stitch (see page 211) produces on the face of the embroidery the same pattern as squared ground stitch, but it has a different appearance on the back.

STEM

Stem stitch is a line stitch but may be massed for a filling. It may be threadcounted or worked freely as surface embroidery.

Bring the needle to the surface at the left end of the line to be embroidered. Then insert the needle one stitch length to the right and very slightly below the guideline, making a slightly slanted stitch. Lengths of stitches will vary according to the type of embroidery being made and the weight of the thread and ground fabric being used. Begin the second stitch directly above but slightly to the left of the end of the first stitch. Bring the needle to the surface at this point, and make a stitch identical to the first. Repeat the stitch to the end of the line. If a filling is to be made, progressive rows of stitches of the same size should be fitted closely together. In making curving lines, stem stitch may be used interchangeably with outline stitch (see page 216).

STEM, RAISED

Raised stem stitch produces a border or area filled with stitches that, except for points of attachment along the edges, are free of the ground fabric. Long, straight stitches are laid across an area to be filled perpendicular to the direction that the stem stitching is to be worked. (If a pronounced relief effect is wanted, you may pad these foundation stitches). The foundation stitches should be spaced as far apart as the desired length of the stem stitches. To fill the foundation stitches, use a tapestry needle, and bring it to the surface at the lower left end of the surface to be covered (foundation stitches run vertically in the diagram). Work the thread horizontally, twisting it around each vertical foundation thread as shown in the diagram. At the end of the row, insert the needle into the ground fabric and bring it up for the next row. Turn the fabric upside down so that you can continue to work left to right, and make stitches like the ones in the first row, twisting in the same direction. Rows may be spaced apart or packed closely together.

Raised stem stitch can be worked into buttonhole stitch (see page 206), and it also can be worked over a star-shaped foundation of stitches.

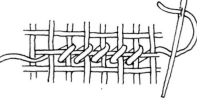

TENT

Tent stitch is the smallest of the stitches rendered on needlepoint  canvas. It should be worked on single-thread canvas with meshes small enough to permit the tent stitches to cover the ground. In times past, tent stitch also was worked as a threadcounted stitch into loosely woven linen. This stitch is worked from left to right. When worked on canvas, tent stitch crosses the intersection of a warp and a weft from upper right to lower left. Bring the needle to the surface at the upper right side of the first warp-weft crossing, and take it to the back again on the lower left side. This process completes the first stitch. Bring the needle up again on the upper right of the second intersection and down again on the left side. Proceed horizontally across the work. If the stitches alone do not seem to fill the canvas adequately, a thread may be laid across the length of the row and tent stitches worked across it. As back stitch does, tent stitch puts more thread on the back than on the front of the work.

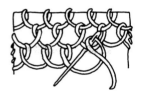

1

TULLE

Tulle stitch is made in the same way as detached buttonhole stitch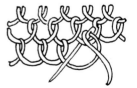

2

(see page 206); however, the stitches are not worked closely together but are placed a little distance from one another at regular intervals. If tulle stitch is worked across an opening in the ground fabric, the working thread should be brought into position for the next row, as shown in Diagram 1. If tulle stitch is worked on the surface of the ground fabric (Diagram 2), the needle and thread are taken to the back at the end of one row and brought to the surface again in correct position to begin the next row; no overcasting stitches should be made.

VAN DYKE

Van Dyke stitch makes a decorative line or band and requires two guidelines. Work progresses from top to bottom and begins on the left. Bring the needle to the surface of the work on the left guideline, and insert it midway between the guidelines and above the starting point, making a diagonal stitch. From the back bring the needle to the surface again a short distance to the left of where you inserted the needle at the top, and insert it on the right guideline slightly below the central rib, which is now beginning to form. Then, make a stitch across the back to the left guideline, and bring the needle up, carrying it to the central rib, passing the needle from right to left through the crossing of the stitches that are above it, and insert it on the right guideline just below the stitch above. Repeat this stitch for the length of the line or area to be filled. The spacing of the stitches and the angles at which they are made is a matter of choice. The threads should be kept fairly loose. In some instances the central rib can be kept under control more easily if a thread of the ground fabric is picked up as the needle passes through the crossings of the previous stitches.

stitches

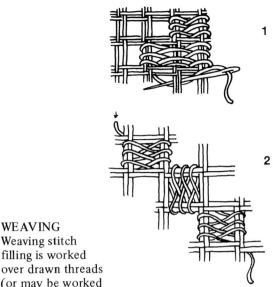

WEAVING
Weaving stitch filling is worked over drawn threads (or may be worked over foundation threads inserted in the ground). After some of the warp and weft threads have been removed from the ground, the remaining groups of warps or wefts are woven in patterns with a tapestry needle. (Diagram 1 is an example of weaving stitch as it is most often used; Diagram 2 is an unusual example of weaving stitch as it is used in the Russian border on page 179).

WHEAT EAR
Wheat ear stitch makes a decorative border or line that is a variation of chain stitch (see page 207). Work progresses from top to bottom. Begin by making two angled stitches. Then return to the surface of the ground fabric on the guideline one stitch length from the point where the first two angled stitches meet on the line. Pass the needle from right to left under the two angled stitches, and insert it again into the ground at the point from which it emerged. Bring the needle to the surface again in position at the left of the guideline and opposite the loop at about midpoint. Now the needle is in position to begin the first of the angled stitches in repetition of the stitches just finished.

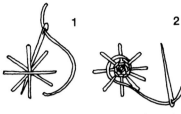

WHEELS, WOVEN
To embroider woven wheels, begin by making several long, straight stitches that cross one another in a wheel or star-shaped pattern. An uneven number of spokes is necessary to work the stitch. Try to arrange the stitches so that one interval between the spokes of the wheel is a little larger than the others to provide space to make the extra spoke that will give you an uneven number. To make this last stitch, bring the needle, preferably a tapestry needle, to the surface at the outer edge of the wheel between the stitches on each side of the large interval. Pass the needle under a stitch on the opposite side of the figure you are making, but do not catch the ground fabric. Now weave, using the same thread and needle over and under the spokes of the wheel. Because you have made an uneven number of spokes, when you continue around the wheel for the second passage, the thread will pass under spokes that it passed over on the first journey. If you have not caught the last spoke in the ground fabric and if threads are crowded into the spokes, the little wheel will begin to puff and round as more and more thread is crowded into it. Woven wheels are excellent additions to relief embroideries. They can be made in all sorts of thread, from metal to woolens.

Bibliography

Alford, Lady Marion. *Needlework as Art.* London: Sampson, Low, Martson, Searle & Rivington, 1886.

Arneberg, Halfdan. *Norwegian Peasant Art.* Oslo: Fabritius & Sooner, 1949.

Artamonov, M. I. "Frozen Tombs of the Scyths." *Scientific American,* May 1965.

Band-Bovy, Daniel. "Peasant Art in Switzerland." *The Studio Ltd.* (London), 1924.

Bart, Sir William Lawrence. *An Exhibition of Old Embroideries of the Greek Islands and Turkey.* London: Burlington Fine Arts Club, 1914.

Beer, Alice Baldwin. "Why Textiles?" *Chronicle of the Museum for the Arts of Decoration of the Cooper Union.* Vol. 2, no. 7 (June 1955).

Bennett, Wendell C. *Ancient Arts of the Andes.* New York: Simon & Schuster for the Museum of Modern Art, 1954.

Berry, Burton Yost. "Old Turkish Towels." *Bulletin of the College Art Association* 14 (December 1932).

——. "Old Turkish Towels II." *Bulletin of the College Art Association* 20 (September 1938).

Bilachevsky, N. "Little Russia (the Ukraine)." In "Peasant Art in Russia," edited by Charles Holmes. *The Studio Ltd.* (London), n.d.

Bird, Junius, and Bellinger, Louisa. "Paracas Fabrics and Nazca Needlework." *The Textile Museum Catalogue Raisonne.* Washington, D.C.: National Publishing Co., 1954.

Born, W. "The Development of European Footwear from the Fall of Rome to the Renaissance." *Ciba Review* (Basel), no. 34 (June 1940).

Caulfeild, S. F. A., and Saward, Blanche C. *Dictionary of Needlework.* 2nd ed. London: L. Upcott Gill, 1885.

Cavallo, Adolph. *Tapestries of Europe and of Colonial Peru in the Museum of Fine Arts, Boston.* Boston: Museum of Fine Arts, 1967.

Cennini, Cennino d'Andrea. *The Craftsman's Handbook "Il Libro dell' Arte."* Translated by Daniel V. Thompson, Jr. New Haven: Yale University Press, 1933.

Christie, Archibald H. *Pattern Design.* New York: Dover Publications, 1969. First edition, Oxford, 1910.

Christie, Mrs. A. H. *English Medieval Embroidery.* Oxford: Clarendon Press, 1938.

——. *Samplers and Stitches.* London: Batsford Ltd., 1920.

Clouzot, Henri, and Morris, Frances. *Painted and Printed Fabrics.* New York: The Metropolitan Museum of Art, 1927.

Cobban, Alfred, ed. *The Eighteenth Century.* New York: McGraw-Hill Book Co., Inc., 1967.

Cole, Alan. *Ornament in European Silks.* London: Debenham & Freebody, 1899.

Crawford, M. D. C. *Heritage of Cotton.* New York: Grosset & Dunlap, 1924.

Cunnington, C. Willet, and Cunnington, Phillis. *Handbook of English Costume in the Seventeenth Century.* London: Faber & Faber Ltd., 1953.

Daniels, Margaret Harrington. *Early Pattern Books for Lace and Embroidery.* Needle and Bobbin Club Bulletin no. 17. New York, 1933.

——. *Embroidery and Botany.* Needle and Bobbin Club Bulletin no. 19. New York, 1935.

Davison, Mildred. *An Altarpiece from Burgo de Osma.* Museum Studies no. 3. Chicago: Art Institute of Chicago, 1969.

——. "Handwoven Coverlets in the Art Institute of Chicago." *Antiques,* May 1970.

——. *Shoes of Our Ancestors.* Chicago Art Institute Bulletin no. 28. Chicago, December 1934.

De Dillmont, Therese. *Encyclopedia of Needlework.* Mulhouse, France: D.M.C. Library, n.d.

De Farcy, Louis. *La Broderie du XIᵉ Siècle Jusqu'à Nos Jours.* Angers: Belhomme, 1890.

Digby, George Wingfield. *Elizabethan Embroidery.* New York: Thomas Yoseloff, 1964.

Dolby, Anastasia. *Church Embroidery.* London: Chapman & Hall, 1867.

Edwards, Ralph, and Ramsey, L. G. G. *The Connoisseur's Complete Guides.* New York: Bonanza, 1968.

Fastnedge, Ralph. *English Furniture Styles 1500-1830.* London: Whitefriar's Press Ltd., 1955.

Freeman, Margaret B. *The St. Martin Embroideries.* New York: Metropolitan Museum of Art, 1968.

Geddes, Elizabeth, and McNeill, Moyra. *Blackwork Embroidery.* London: Mills & Boon, 1965.

Gentles, Margaret. *Turkish and Greek Island Embroideries.* Chicago: The Art Institute of Chicago, 1964.

Gloag, John. *Georgian Grace.* London: A & C Block Ltd., 1956.

Groves, Sylvia. *A History of Needlework Tools and Accessories.* London: Country Life, 1966.

Hackenbroch, Yvonne. *English and Other Needlework Textiles and Tapestries in the Irwin Untermeyer Collection.* Cambridge: Harvard University Press for the Metropolitan Museum of Art, 1951.

Hansen, H. J., ed. *European Folk Art.* New York: McGraw-Hill Book Co., Inc., 1967.

Harbeson, Georgianna Brown. *American Needlework.* New York: Bonanza. First edition, Coward McCann, 1938.

Hautecoleur, Louis. "Le Travail du Bois." *L'Art Decoratif* 28 (July-December 1912).

Harcourt, Raoul. *Textiles of Ancient Peru and Their Techniques.* Seattle: University of Washington Press, 1962.

Hauglid, Roar. *The Native Arts of Norway.* Oslo: Mittet & Co., 1953.

Hauser, Arnold. *The Social History of Art.* Vol. 2. New York: Vintage Press, 1960.

Huish, Marcus. *Samplers and Tapestry Embroideries.* London: Longmans, Green & Co., 1913.

Holme, Charles. "Peasant Art in Italy." *The Studio Ltd.* (London), n.d.

Ionides, H. E. "Bebilla." *Embroidery,* June 1936.

Irwin, John, and Brett, Katherine B. *Origins of Chintz.* London: Her Majesty's Stationery Office, 1970.

Johnstone, Pauline. *Byzantine Tradition in Church Embroidery.* London: Alec Tiranti, 1961.

——. *Greek Island Embroidery.* London: Alec Tiranti, 1961.

Jourdain, M. *English Secular Embroidery.* London: Kegan, Paul, French, Trubner & Co. Ltd., 1910.

Kendrick, A. F. *Catalogue of Textiles from the Burying Grounds in Egypt.* Vol. 1. London: Victoria and Albert Museum, 1920.

——. *English Embroidery.* London: B. T. Batsford, 1904.

——. "A Book of Old Embroidery." *The Studio Ltd.* (London), 1921.

Lambert, A. "East European Textile Design." *Ciba Review* (Basel) 66 (April 1948).

Lefébure. *Embroidery and Lace.* London: H. Grevel & Co., 1888.

Leix, Alfred. "Late Classical and Early Christian Textiles of Egypt." *Ciba Review* (Basel) 43 (May 1942).

Little, Frances. *Early American Textiles.* New York and London: Century, 1931.

Mailey, Jean, and Hathaway, Calvin. "A Bonnet and a Pair of Mitts from Ch'ang Sha." *Chronicle of the Museum for the Arts of Decoration of the Cooper Union* (New York), December 1958.

Marshall, Frances, and Marshall, Hugh. *Old English Embroidery: Its Technique and Symbolism.* London: Horace Cox, Windsor House, 1894.

Mayer, Christa C. *Masterpieces of Western Textiles.* Chicago: The Art Institute of Chicago, 1969.

Morris, Barbara. *Victorian Embroidery.* New York: Thomas Yoseloff, 1963.

Myer, Prudence R. "A Reinterpretation of the Noin-Ula Embroidered Shoe Sole." *Artibus Asiae,* no. 10 (1957).

Nevinson, John L. *A Catalogue of English Domestic Embroidery.* London: Victoria and Albert Museum, 1938.

Oprescu, George. *"Peasant Art in Roumania."* London: *The Studio Ltd.,* 1929.

Pesel, Louisa F. *Stitches from Eastern Embroideries.* London: Percy Lund, Hamphries & Co. Ltd., 1912.

——. *Stitches for Old English Embroideries.* London: Percy Lund, Hamphries & Co. Ltd., 1912.

——. *Stitches from Western Embroideries.* London: Percy Lund, Hamphries & Co. Ltd., 1912.

Priest, Alan, and Simmons, Pauline. *Chinese Textiles.* New York: Metropolitan Museum of Art, 1931.

Rae, Olive Milne. "Needlework Pictures." *Connoisseur,* April 1905.

Ricci, Elisa. "Italian Pattern Books of the Sixteenth Century." *The Collector,* September 1930.

——. *Old Italian Lace.* Vol. 1. London: William Heinemann, 1913.

——. "Woman's Crafts." In *Peasant Art in Italy,* edited by Charles Holme. London, n.d.

Rice, David Talbot. *Islamic Art.* New York: Frederick A. Praeger, 1965.

Rice, Tamara Talbot. *Ancient Arts of Central Asia.* New York: Frederick A. Praeger, 1965.

Sidamon-Eristoff, Princess Alexandre, and De Chabelskoy, Mlle N. "Peasant Art of Great Russia." In "Peasant Art in Russia," edited by Charles Holme. *The Studio Ltd.* (London), n.d.

Schuette, Marie, and Muller-Christensen, Sigrid. *The Art of Embroidery.* London: Thames & Hudson, 1964.

Schwab, David E. *Story of Lace and Embroidery.* New York: Fairchild Publications, 1951.

Seligman, G. Saville, and Hughes, Talbot. *Domestic Needlework.* London: Country Life, 1926.

Slomann, Wilhelmi. *Bizarre Designs in Silks.* Copenhagen: E. Munksgaard, 1953.

Stafford, Cora E. *Paracas Embroideries.* New York: J. J. Augustin, 1941.

Stapley, Mildred. *Popular Weaving and Embroidery in Spain.* New York: William Helburn, Inc., 1924.

Stearns, Martha Genung. *Homespun and Blue.* New York: Charles Scribner's Sons, 1963.

Stephani, Ludolf. *Some Ancient Greek Textiles Found in South Russia.* Translated by Eugenie Talmachoff. Needle and Bobbin Club Bulletin 26, no. 2 (1941).

Symonds, Mary (Mrs. Guy Antrobus), and Preece, Louisa. *Needlework through the Ages.* London: Hodder & Stoughton Ltd., 1928.

Thornton, Peter. *Baroque and Rococo Silks.* New York: Faber & Faber, 1965.

Varju-Ember, Maria. *Hungarian Domestic Embroidery.* Budapest: Anthenaeum Printing House, 1963.

Volbach, W. Fritz. *Il Tessuto nell' Arte Antica.* Milan: Fratelli Fabbri Editori, 1966.

Wace, A. J. B. *Mediterranean and Near Eastern Embroideries,* London: Holton & Co. Ltd., 1935.

Wace, A. J. B., and Dawkins, R. M. "Greek Embroideries I and II." *Burlington Magazine* (London), November-December 1914.

Wheeler, Candace. *Development of Embroidery in America.* New York: Harper & Bros., 1921.

Williams, Leonard. *The Old Arts and Crafts of Spain.* Vol. 3. Chicago: A. C. McClurg, 1908.

Index

Alexandria, Hellenistic, x
Altai region embroideries, viii
Altar frontal, 8, 19, 25, 28
American textiles, 148
Animal motifs, 53
Applied motifs, 48
Appliqué
    reverse, 184, 187
    on velvet, 28
Assisi work, 65
Auriphrygium, 15
Awl, 18

Back stitch, 204
Baroque style, 124
Basket stitch, 205
Bayeux Tapestry, viii
Beading, 48
    coral, 124
Bebilla, 159, 162
Bergomensis, supplementum
    chronicarum, 59
Berry, Burton Yost, 156
Bessarabian tapestries, 175
Bizarre embroideries, 77, 162
Blackwork, 33, 170
Bokhara couching, 208
Botanical motifs, 5
Braid stitch, 43, 216
Brun, C. F., 15
Bullion stitch, 206
Burgo de Osma altar frontal, 19, 25
Burgundian embroidery, x
Burial chambers, viii
Buttonholed couching, 208
Buttonhole stitch, 206
Byzantine period, x, 162, 179

Calthorpe purse, 73
Catalogus plantarum, 43
Catherine of Aragon, 33
Catherine of Braganza, 54
Ceylon stitch, 206
Chain stitch, 115, 207
Chanakkale, 152
Changing scale, 198
Charles I, 38, 43, 53
Charles II, 54, 76
Chenille embroidery, 140
Chevré, 156
Chopine, 140
Cochineal dye, 5
Color schemes, 166, 187
Compartiments de broiderie, 127
Copernicus, 59
Copes, x, 8
Copying, philosophy of, vii
Coral stitch, 207

Coronation Mantle of the Holy
    Roman Empire, viii
Couching, 19, 207
Counterpane, 115
Cracowes, 140
Cretan stitch, 209
Crewel embroidery, 76, 82, 93
Crossed back stitch, 205
Cross stitch, 209
Cuna Indians, 184
Cutwork embroidery, 43

Damask gold, 43
Darning stitch, 152, 210
da Vinci, Leonardo, 69
Design
    sources, vii
    transferring, 199
Detached buttonhole stitch, 206
Domestic embroidery, x
Double darning stitch, 166, 210
Double faggot stitch, 211
Double running stitch, 162, 218
Drawnwork, colored, 179
Drizzling, 140
Dürer, Albrecht, 69
Dyes, 1, 5, 82
    in America, 149

East India Company, 76, 97
Ecclesiastical embroidery, x, 29, 33,
    53, 124
Egyptian murals, vii
El Greco, 15
Elizabeth I, 38
England, 33, 38, 43, 48, 53, 59, 73,
    76, 82, 93, 97, 115, 120, 140

Fabrics, 194
Faggot stitch, 211
Faïence, 152
Feather stitch, 212
Filling stitches 206, 208, 210, 212,
    214, 215, 219, 221
Fishbone stitch, 212
Floral motifs, vii, 33, 38, 43, 115,
    124, 162, 175
Florentine embroidery, x
Framework, 50, 196
France, 131, 135, 144
French knot, 214
Fretwork, 170
Frisé, 57
Frontispiece, vii, 8, 19, 25, 28

Gardens, influence on embroidery, 124
Georgian period, 115
Germany, 8, 15
Glaze embroidery, 28

Gobelin embroidery ateliers, 135
Gold embroidery, 8, 124
    in backgrounds, 19
    purl, 28
    threads, 43, 127
Gothic period, 124
Greece, 152
    vase paintings, vii
Ground fabrics, 194
Ground stitch, squared, 219
Grünwald, Mathis, 15

Henrietta Marie, 53
Herbals, 43
Hermitage (Leningrad), 65
Herringbone stitch, 213
Historia animalium, 53
History of embroidery, vi
Holbein stitch, 72, 213
Horror vacui, 53
Human figures, depiction of, 170
Hungarian stitch, 213

Indigo dye, 5
Interlocking stitch, 214
Islamic forms, 170
Isnik, 152
Italian cross stitch, two-sided, 210
Italy, 65, 69, 124

James I, 53

Knot, French, 214
Kuhmaul, 140
Kütahya, 152

Ladder stitch, 215
    in gold, 38
Laidwork, 18, 19, 214
Lasurstickerei, 28
Latticework, 50
Levant, the, 43
Line stitch, 215
Link powdering, 215
Long and short stitch, 131, 215
Long-armed cross stitch, 65, 69, 209
Louis XIV, 124
Lozenge design, overlapping, vii

Machine-made embroidery, x
Madame de Pompadour, 124, 140
Madame du Barry, 124
Mandinga Niranjo, 187
Mannerism, 124
Mantles, x
Manuscript painting, Persian school, 170
Marot, Daniel, 93

Martyrdom of St. Mauritius' Legion, The, 15
Mary, Queen of Scots, 53
Materials and techniques, 192-203
Metal embroidery, 8
Monochromatic embroidery, 65
Moroccan embroidery, 166
Moscovite needlework, 175, 179
Motifs
    American, 149
    animal, 53
    applied, 48
    botanical, 5
    Cuna Indian, 184
    floral, vii. 33, 38, 43, 115, 124, 162, 175
    Greek islands, 152
    history of, vii
    human figures, 170
    Russian, 179
    Salamancan, 170
    sources, 43, 53, 59, 120, 124, 166, 170
    stumpwork, 53
    Turkish, 159, 162
Mounting an embroidery, 196

Needlepainting, x, 140
Needlepoint, 97
Needles, 192
Niji-Novgorod, 166
Noin Ula, 140

Oltenian tapestries, 175
Openwork embroidery, 43
Opus anglicanum, x, 8, 53, 64
Opus teutonicum, 8
Oriental embroideries, 19, 179
Or nué, 28
Orphrey, 15
Outline stitch, 216
Overcast stitch, 216

Padded couching, 208
Padded satin stitch, 218
Palampores, 76
Palermo Mantle, viii
Panama, 184, 187
Paracas Necropolis peninsula, 1, 4
Passing thread, 15, 127
Pastiches, 57
Patchwork embroidery, 148
Pattern darning stitch, 210
Pazyrk mounds, viii
Persia, Sassanid, x
Peru, 1, 4
Peshkir, 156

Peter the Great, 179
Phrygians, 15
Pierpont Morgan Library, 59
Pinckney, Mrs. Eliza, 149
Pintadoes, 76
Plaisted, Rebecca Stonier, 53
Plaited braid stitch, 216
    in gold, 43
Plate thread, 127
Pontormo, 15
Popularity of embroidery, vi
Punto in aria, 144
Punto tagliato, 144
Punto tirato, 144
Purl, 28, 73

Queen Anne period, 97
Quilting, 115

Raised satin stitch, 218
Raised stem stitch, 219
Raised work in purl, 73
Reformation period, 33, 59, 124
Restoration period, 76
Reticello, 144
Reverse appliqué, 184, 187
Reversible embroidery, 156, 166
Rhombus design, vii
Robert Barker Bible, vii, 59
Robin brothers' garden, 124
Rococo stitch, 217
Rococo style, 97, 124
Rope stitch, 217
Roumanian couching, 208
Roumanian stitch, 175, 217
Royal Scottish Museum (Edinburgh). 33
Running stitch, 217,218
Rural embroidery, Spanish, 170
Russia, 175, 179
Russian overcast filling, 212

Sablé, 48
St. Petersburg, 179
Salamancan motifs, 170
San Blas Islands, 184
Saracenic textile industry, viii
Satin stitch, 135, 218
Scale, changing, 198
Scissors, 196
Seo de Urgel Cathedral, 28, 144
Sicily, viii
Silk embroidery, 8, 120
    and gold, 15, 25
    and metal, 59
Single faggot stitch, 211
Skyros embroidery, 144, 152
Slanted satin stitch, 218
Soumak, 1

Spain, 19, 25, 28, 170
    influence on Peruvian embroidery, 5
Speckling, 33, 43, 93, 218
Split stitch, 19, 219
Square chain stitch, 207
Squared ground stitch, 219
Startups, 140
Stem stitch, 1, 4, 219
Stiletto, 18
Stitch directory, 204-221
Stroke stitch, 215
Stumpwork, 48, 53, 59
    casket, 53
    motifs, 53
Sumptuary law, 69
Suppliers of needlework materials, 203

Tapestry, 82
Tapestry weave, 1
Techniques, *see* Materials and techniques; Stitch directory
Tent stitch, 220
Tests of embroidery, 1
Tetuan embroidery, 166
Textile arts, history of, vii
Textile Museum (Washington, D.C.), 1
Thimbles, 196
Threadcounted embroidery, 8, 201
Threads, 43, 127, 192
Tied herringbone stitch, 213
Transferring a design, 199
Tulle stitch, 220
Turkey, 156, 162, 166

Ukraine, 175

Vallet, Pierre, 127
Van Dyke stitch, 220
Verdure tapestries, 82
Victoria and Albert Museum, 73, 82
Visual aids, 196

Wall ornaments, 120
Weaving
    integration with embroidery, 1
    Islamic-originated designs, 69
Weaving stitch filling, 221
Wheat ear stitch, 221
Wheels, woven, 221
Whitework, 8, 69, 97, 140, 144
William and Mary period, 93

Yaroslavl, 179